D1551788

GHOSTWORKERS AND GREENS

GHOSTWORKERS AND GREENS

*The Cooperative Campaigns of
Farmworkers and Environmentalists
for Pesticide Reform*

ADAM TOMPKINS

ILR PRESS
AN IMPRINT OF
CORNELL UNIVERSITY PRESS
ITHACA AND LONDON

Copyright © 2016 by Cornell University

All rights reserved. Except for brief quotations in a review, this book, or parts thereof, must not be reproduced in any form without permission in writing from the publisher. For information, address Cornell University Press, Sage House, 512 East State Street, Ithaca, New York 14850.

First published 2016 by Cornell University Press
First printing, Cornell Paperbacks, 2016
Printed in the United States of America

Library of Congress Cataloging-in-Publication Data

Names: Tompkins, Adam, author.
Title: Ghostworkers and greens : the cooperative campaigns of
    farmworkers and environmentalists for pesticide reform / Adam
    Tompkins.
Description: Ithaca : ILR Press, an imprint of Cornell University Press,
    2016. | Includes bibliographical references and index.
Identifiers: LCCN 2015042511 | ISBN 9780801456688 (cloth : alk. paper) |
    ISBN 9781501704482 (pbk. : alk. paper)
Subjects: LCSH: Pesticides—Environmental aspects—United States—
    History. | Pesticides—Health aspects—United States—History. |
    Environmental health—United States—Citizen participation—
    History. | Agricultural laborers—Political activity—United
    States—History. | Environmentalists—Political activity—United
    States—History. | Coalitions—United States—History.
Classification: LCC TD196.P38 T66 2016 | DDC 363.738/4980973—dc23
LC record available at http://lccn.loc.gov/2015042511

Cornell University Press strives to use environmentally responsible suppliers and materials to the fullest extent possible in the publishing of its books. Such materials include vegetable-based, low-VOC inks and acid-free papers that are recycled, totally chlorine-free, or partly composed of nonwood fibers. For further information, visit our website at www.cornellpress.cornell.edu.

Cloth printing   10 9 8 7 6 5 4 3 2 1
Paperback printing   10 9 8 7 6 5 4 3 2 1

In Memory of
Frances Mary Brooks

For
Arianna Halona

Contents

ACKNOWLEDGMENTS

The genesis of this book began with an unexpected cancer diagnosis. What started as a trying time in my life catalyzed into something very positive, in part because of an offhand suggestion by Philip Jenkins that I not remain idle during my recovery. It was in between rounds of chemotherapy that I first found mention of pesticides in an old edition of *El Malcriado* in the Chicano/a Collection at Arizona State University. The archivist, Christine Marín, enthusiastically introduced me to the university's holdings on the farmworkers' movement. My interest piqued as I delved deeper and learned of a cancer cluster in California's Central Valley that some people attributed to an overuse of pesticides. As the project evolved and progressed, I continued to benefit from the guidance, support, and feedback of numerous individuals at every stage.

I will always feel a deep connection to Happy Valley and Penn State University because the Department of History so embodied the spirit of community. Adam Rome and Dan Letwin proved to be excellent mentors who helped me weave together environmental and labor historiographies and spent numerous hours in discussion with me about my research. Nan Woodruff offered similarly sound advice and encouragement. I especially owe thanks to Carol Reardon, Wilson Moses, Bill Pencak, and Matthew Restall. Lynne Falwell, Tyler Flynn, Matt Isham, Dan Kasper, Michael Lumish, Tim Orr, Dave Siry, and Michael Smith offered camaraderie and ready ears as I worked through ideas and arguments.

I made my home at Arizona State University for many years thereafter, and the breadth of my research expanded significantly during this period. I again had the good fortune of working with engaged and caring faculty. Above all, I wish to acknowledge my mentor and friend Paul Hirt, who encouraged me to think more broadly about pesticide reform, which ultimately made for more compelling and rewarding research. I cannot imagine having a better advocate, confidant, and critical eye to work with than Paul. The perspective, memories, and insights of Arturo Rosales led to expanding my investigation of farmworker organizations beyond Cesar Chavez and the United Farm Workers. Recalling Profe's infectious laugh and good nature in our discussions still brings a smile to my face. Christine Marín welcomed me to explore the Special Collections at ASU, provided contextual understanding and personal recollections of activism in Arizona, and introduced me to a phenomenal body of material in the then unprocessed M-COP Collection. Joni Adamson introduced me to literature in Critical Environmental Justice Studies and continued to be wonderfully supportive throughout this process. Adam Rome continued to provide sound feedback from afar.

Other members of the Arizona State University community during that period deserve acknowledgment as well. I was extremely fortunate to work with Linda Sargent Wood, who always had an open door, encouraging words, and sage advice. Maria Cruz-Torres, Rachel Fuchs, Brian Gratton, Gayle Gullett, Sharon Harlan, and Dirk Hoerder supported my endeavors or offered critical feedback on my research. Karla Alonzo, Dana Bennett, Patricia Biggs, Cody Ferguson, Elyssa Ford, Matthew Garrett, Royce Gildersleeve, Blake Jones, Cody Marshall, Karl Snyder, Jean Marie Stevens, Pete Van Cleave, and Scott Walker commented on parts of the manuscript or offered input in conversation. The committee members who provided research and writing support in the form of awards also deserve to be recognized: the Emma Goldman History Travel Grant in Memory of Professor Christiane Harzig, a Graduate College Dissertation

Fellowship, the History Doctoral Summer Research Fellowship, and the Max Millett Family Fund eased the expense of travel to numerous archives around the country.

The assistance that I received at several archives facilitated the process of finding useful material. I spent weeks at the Walter P. Reuther Library's Archives of Labor and Urban Affairs in Detroit, where William LeFevre and other archivists graciously brought out scores of boxes from the United Farm Workers Collection and provided suggestions for where I might turn next. I am especially grateful for the invaluable help of Kathleen Schmeling, the UFW archivist, who provided me access to unprocessed material that yielded a lot of evidence and answers. Elizabeth Clemens expeditiously assisted me with my image request. Katherine Krzys and archivists at the Arizona State University Special Collections and the Arizona Historical Foundation, and Melanie Sturgeon and the staff at the Arizona State Library, Archives, and Public Records spent an equal or greater amount of time helping me access material. The archivists at the California State Archives made Sacramento feel like a very warm and welcoming place. Theresa Salazar at The Bancroft Library helped me call up records from the Sierra Club Collection. Short trips to the State Archives of Florida in Tallahassee, the University of Florida Special Collections in Gainesville, and the Special Collections and University Archives at Stony Brook University all went well, in large part because the archivists helped me pinpoint the records that would be most useful.

Much of the material for chapter 7 came from the private holdings of the Farmworker Association of Florida. My deepest gratitude to Jeannie Economos and Tirso Moreno for allowing me to visit their headquarters in Apopka and sift through files relating to the Sustainable Tomatoes/Safer Communities campaign. Though Jeannie had an incredibly busy schedule, she always made me feel welcome. It was a truly rewarding experience and I am glad that I had the opportunity to visit.

Numerous other individuals confirmed my conclusions, clarified my understanding, noted gaps, offered alternative perspectives, provided suggestions, helped me acquire needed material, or otherwise offered support. My special thanks to Jeff Crane, Michael Egan, Carl Gabrielson, Roger Grabowski, Gustavo Gutierrez, John Hausdoerffer, Charles Laurier, Gena Maldonado, Michael McCloskey, Joel Plagenz, David Roe, Adam Sowards, Charles Wurster, and Erik Wurster. Audiences and fellow panelists at American Society for Environmental History conferences, a North American Labor History Conference, and the Asian Conference on Sustainability, Energy, and the Environment also provided welcome comments. Arizona State University, Lakeland College Japan, and NIC International College in Japan provided conference funding.

It has been a pleasure working with Cornell University Press. Thank you especially to Frances Benson, the editorial director of ILR Press, for supporting the book and securing reviewers; to Susan Barnett, Mahinder Kingra, Gavin Lewis, Kitty Liu, Emily Powers, and Susan Specter. I also appreciate the time and comments of two anonymous readers whose suggestions did much to strengthen my work. I, of course, bear full responsibility for any possible shortcomings that may remain.

Portions of chapter 5 previously appeared in an article, "A Different Kind of Border War: Conflicts over Pesticides in Arizona's Agricultural/ Urban Interface, 1977–1986," and are published under permission of *Journal of the West*/ABC-CLIO Winter 2011. Portions of chapter 6 previously appeared in an essay, "Cancer Valley, California: Pesticides, Politics, and Childhood Disease in the Central Valley," in *Natural Protest: Essays on the History of American Environmentalism*, edited by Michael Egan and Jeff Crane (New York: Routledge, 2008), and are reproduced by permission of Taylor and Francis Group, LLC, a division of Informa plc.

The support of friends and family members helped me through this process from start to completion. While space is too limited to name everybody, I would like to express my gratitude to Bonnie and Mark Kline, Frances Mary Brooks, Daniel Tompkins, Richard and Catherine Pierce, Amberley Kline, Jeannette Kline, Karen Halona, William Riddle, Katherine Halona, Leighton Peterson, Anthony Germinaro, Adam Jacobi, Ernie Carr, Midori Sasaoka, Seth DePasqual, Deon James, and Roshawn Bitsuie. Tachikawa Lumine Starbucks became like a second home to me during the final month of writing, so I must pay my respects to all of the baristas who made me feel welcome and, of course, alert. I would especially like to thank my wife, Starrla, who graciously lived through this experience with me, uprooted herself, and at times dealt with my absence. Finally, thank you to my daughter, Arianna, for bringing immeasurable joy to my life.

ABBREVIATIONS

ACSH	American Council on Science and Health
ACWA	Arizona Clean Water Advocates
ADHS	Arizona Department of Health Services
AFBF	American Farm Bureau Federation
AFL	American Federation of Labor
AFW	Arizona Farm Workers
AFWCP	Arizona Farm Workers Committee on Pesticides
ALRA	Agricultural Labor Relations Act
ALRB	Agricultural Labor Relations Board
AWOC	Agricultural Workers Organizing Committee
BPC	Board of Pesticide Control
CDFA	California Department of Food and Agriculture
CDPR	California Department of Pesticide Regulation
CFCs	chlorofluorocarbons
COEHHA	California Office of Environmental Health Hazard Assessment
CRLA	California Rural Legal Assistance
CSO	Community Service Organization

CSWRCB   California State Water Resources Control Board
DBCP   dibromochloropropane
EDB   ethylene dibromide
EDF   Environmental Defense Fund
EPA   Environmental Protection Agency
ETS   Emergency Temporary Standard
EWG   Environmental Working Group
FDA   Food and Drug Administration
FDACS   Florida Department of Agriculture and Consumer Services
FIFRA   Federal Insecticide, Fungicide, and Rodenticide Act
FoE   Friends of the Earth
FSA   Farm Security Administration
FWAF   Farmworker Association of Florida
GWFC   Grape Workers and Farmers Coalition
IWW   Industrial Workers of the World
M-COP   Maricopa County Organizing Project
MLAP   Migrant Legal Action Program
NFWA   National Farm Worker Association
NIMBY   not in my backyard
NRDC   Natural Resources Defense Council
OCAW   Oil, Chemical, and Atomic Workers Union
OSHA   Occupational Safety and Health Administration
PEOPLE   People's Environmental Organization for Pesticide Legislation
           and Enforcement
ppb   parts per billion
PRD   Pesticide Regulation Division
RG   Record Group (archive cite)
S   Series (archive cite)
SG   Series Group (archive cite)
SRPMIC   Salt River Pima Maricopa Indian Community
SS   Subseries (archive cite)
TCE   trichloroethylene
UAW   United Auto Workers
UFW   United Farm Workers of America, AFL-CIO
UFWOC   United Farm Workers Organizing Committee
UNEP   United Nations Environment Programme
USDA   United States Department of Agriculture
UV-B   shortwave ultraviolet radiation

GHOSTWORKERS AND GREENS

CONFRONTING THE CONSEQUENCES
OF THE PESTICIDE PARADIGM

A chemical euphoria overtook American agriculture in the twentieth century. Dabbling with botanical control agents and soap-based emulsions to control insect threats, which had begun in the nineteenth century, soon gave way to experimentation with arsenical compounds that carried a greater kick. As growers became more enmeshed in the world of agricultural chemicals, their poison-free "friends" of the past, biological and cultural forms of pest control, seemed less appealing and less suited for the times. The United States Department of Agriculture (USDA), pesticide manufacturers, land grant colleges, and entomologists acted as facilitators that encouraged the use of a cornucopia of chemicals. DDT proved to be the gateway substance that led to the use of exponentially greater volumes of more powerful chemical combinations in agricultural production. Growers denied the existence of problems as evidence began to appear, choosing instead to trust more heavily in a variety of economic poisons until in the post–World War II period they became almost wholly dependent upon pesticides for crop protection.

The suggestion of addiction in the preceding paragraph is deliberate. "Chemical dependence" is a phrase most often employed in the discussion of persons who habitually use drugs or alcohol, yet it is an equally fitting descriptor of growers' increasing reliance on pesticides in their operations and is a helpful frame of reference for understanding their strong resistance to reform efforts from 1962 onward. Agricultural chemicals came to greater use with the accession of Leland Howard, an entomologist who touted their supremacy over other methods of pest control, to the head of the USDA's Bureau of Entomology. The volume of pesticides applied to fields grew markedly in the first half of the twentieth century before skyrocketing in the post–World War II era with the introduction of DDT to commercial markets. In what political scientist Christopher Bosso characterizes as the "golden age of pesticides," with little debate about risks and minimal regulation, production of the compound tripled from 100 to 300 million pounds in the five years after the war's end and doubled again in the decade following.[1] DDT and other new brands of synthetic chemicals promised fast action, greater efficiency, and universal applicability. Growers, captivated by the promise of total control and possible eradication of pests, applied pesticides in ever-increasing volumes. Insect pests, however, showed a remarkably proclivity for developing resistance to the chemicals designed to kill them. Still, researchers, pesticide manufacturers, and growers continued to invest heavily in chemical controls even as pests developed immunities to some of them. Growers saturated their fields with voluminous concentrations of more powerful chemical combinations, holding to the faith that pesticides would best prevent crop damage and financial loss. The remarkable ability of insects to continually develop new resistance to potent pesticides actually helped entrench chemical controls further in the modern industrial agriculture production system.

The chemical dependency in agriculture bears comparison to path dependency in other technological systems. Historians David Nye and Thomas Hughes introduce the concept of path dependency into their discussions of energy systems. They contend that when a system is in the process of being developed, decision makers have a wide range of options and flexibility in its design and function. As the system matures, however, it becomes path dependent: earlier choices narrow the range of options available for changing it.[2] This model applies just as aptly to the system of pest control used by growers in the United States. As chemical controls became entrenched in agricultural production, biological and cultural control methods seemed less viable. Historian James McWilliams recognizes a path dependency in agricultural pest management, asserting that the investment of growers, government, and manufacturers in chemical solutions "limited the way in which scientists and farmers framed the pest situation and contemplated their options."[3] The investment and the faith in chemicals made the switch to other forms of pest control an improbable prospect.

Some regulation existed during the "golden age of pesticides" but it was not intended to impose a burden on growers by limiting their pest control options. The Insecticide Act of 1910 required that agricultural chemicals carry accurate product labeling, while the Federal Insecticide, Fungicide, and Rodenticide Act of 1947 (FIFRA) made it necessary for manufacturers to attest to the efficacy of a pesticide and register it with the USDA before introducing it to the commercial marketplace. FIFRA also mandated that warning labels inform growers about potential risks to health, plants, or vertebrate animals. It did not, however, keep dangerous chemicals from being sold. Regulations to protect public health and the environment proved severely lacking and pesticide use rose unabated. Neither growers nor the USDA pushed for more stringent regulations to limit use of chemicals that posed a threat to human or environmental health. The parties with a vested interest in agricultural policymaking at this time all held to the "pesticide paradigm," that agricultural chemicals were an indispensable component of modern agricultural production.[4] Since the public remained uninterested in pesticide issues in the immediate postwar era, an iron triangle of interests developed; hence, policymaking, as Bosso demonstrates, was "clearly accommodative in tone," with government officials primarily concerned with the interests of their clients, the agricultural industry.[5]

Rachel Carson awoke the nation to the dangers of pesticides in 1962 with the publication of *Silent Spring*. She was one of a group of scientists who harbored concern about some of the unintended consequences arising from the proliferation of economic poisons. They believed that complex scientific data needed to be communicated to the public in an understandable, nonpartisan manner, democratizing the information so that people would be better able to make informed personal and political decisions about the use of a broad range of potentially hazardous chemicals and new technologies in society. According to historian Michael Egan, the science information movement, of which biologist Barry Commoner was at the forefront, believed that informed debate and dissent are fundamental to the maintenance of a functioning democracy and consciously worked to make the best available information accessible to the public.[6] Carson held to this philosophy as well and intended *Silent Spring* to be a call for citizen engagement in pesticide politics and regulation. She believed that citizens had a right to participate in decisions on how and to what extent pesticides would be used on farms, forests, and suburban neighborhoods. Historian Karl Brooks asserts that Carson tapped into a public concern about the environment that had been building prior to 1962, stating that "Americans' shared personal and civic experiences—what they had done, seen, and thought before 1963—laid a cultural powder trail that *Silent Spring*'s bright flame ignited."[7] Carson's communication of scientific information to the public empowered individuals and groups with knowledge, giving them a degree of expertise that could be used to influence public policy and private practices.

Civic Engagement, Science, and Environmental Health Reform

Numerous scholars recognize the fundamental importance of public engagement in issues related to industrial toxins, environment, and health. Robert Gottlieb locates the first campaigns for environmental reform in the Progressive Era, with citizens like Alice Hamilton initiating efforts to control pollution in the urban environment.[8] Examining the roots of environmental health science, Christopher Sellers contends that "an energized labor movement unsettled employers' assumptions about whether they were treating their workers fairly and catalyzed new legislative and judicial foundations for tending to worker health" between 1910 and 1930.[9] Alan Derickson argues that public health officials knew about the deleterious effects of coal dust for over fifty years, yet proved reluctant to address the issue of black lung until the "confrontational collective action" of a worker-based social movement necessitated change.[10] David Rosner and Gerald Markowitz assert that response to silicosis, an occupational lung disease, paralleled the rise of labor activism in the 1930s, while the

subsequent waning of government attention to the problem followed a decline in union influence.[11] In their next collaboration, *Deceit and Denial*,
Rosner and Markowitz show that the lead and vinyl industries hid information about occupational risks and used soft money and donations to political action committees to placate certain elected officials and forestall the
enactment of new regulations. The industries' actions, they state, became
known as a result of lawsuits brought by poisoned workers.[12] Cancer expert and doctor of environmental and occupational medicine Samuel
Epstein concludes that nearly every legislative regulation or reform to protect workers and consumers against cancer had its roots in a public interest
group or labor organization.[13]

Public engagement in pesticide issues similarly proved a necessary
predicate to reforming pest control practices in agriculture, since both
growers and the USDA, the primary regulatory agency prior to 1972, presumed that chemicals were the single best pest control option. In an attempt to make agricultural pest control less harmful to the environment
and human health, nongovernmental organizations employed a variety of
strategies to curb pesticide usage that ranged from focusing on a single
chemical to passing laws that reshaped the regulatory landscape. Growers'
associations and the USDA consistently opposed efforts to restrict the use
of agricultural chemicals or remove them from the marketplace. Similar
to the tactics employed by industrial manufacturers, they tried to delay
reform by downplaying risk, fostering doubt about existent scientific data,
calling for more scientific studies, and leaning on sympathetic politicians
and government officials for support. Pesticide reform advocates generated publicity and contested industry claims. Their efforts helped restrict
or ban several dangerous pesticides and have forced growers to adopt safer
pesticide use practices, though there are certainly still issues that remain to
be addressed.

Scientists concerned about the unintended consequences of technological innovations sometimes struggled over the degree to which they should
be visibly involved in political discourse. Certainly not all reach the same
decision as Barry Commoner, Rachel Carson, and others in the science information movement. Historians Naomi Oreskes and Erik Conway state
that "scientists consider their 'real' work to be the production of knowledge, not its dissemination, and they view these two activities as mutually exclusive," noting that scientists who try to bridge the gap between

academic and popular audiences risk being unfavorably labeled as "popularizers."[14] Hence, while *Silent Spring* reached millions of readers, subsequent scientific findings revealing the human health and environmental risks of pesticides did not get publicized in the same fashion. Some scientists also feared that political engagement would jeopardize the objectivity upon which scientific work is premised.[15] Environmental and health policy, however, grows from an amalgam of scientific knowledge, ethical premises, and public opinion. It is necessarily important, then, that scientific knowledge be effectively communicated to the public.[16]

Political scientist Karen Litfin argues that "knowledge brokers" serve as "intermediaries between the original researchers, or producers of knowledge, and the policy makers who consume that knowledge but lack the time and training necessary to absorb the original research."[17] These knowledge brokers play the same role in shaping public opinion. The information presented by them often bears the imprint of their values. Different knowledge brokers interpret scientific results in varying ways, choosing which results to emphasize and how to address the issue of scientific uncertainty. Consequently, Litfin holds that science alone will "not likely to save us from environmental ruin, persistent political action informed by carefully chosen discursive strategies might."[18]

Common Ground and Collaboration in Pesticide Reform

Indiscriminate use of pesticides concern environmentalists and farmworkers alike and their representative organizations have acted as important knowledge brokers advocating for pesticide reform. An interest in the preservation of environmental and human health committed a number of environmental organizations to campaigns for pesticide reform in the nearly fifty-year history of activism since the publication of *Silent Spring*. Organizations of farmworkers or groups representing them shared a similar desire to make agricultural pest control safer, since farmworkers risked injury to their personal and family health when exposed to pesticides in the fields. While both environmental organizations and farmworker groups acted as knowledge brokers and engaged in separate efforts to reform pesticide use practices, their common interest in protecting human health facilitated the development of episodic collaborative campaigns.

Farmworker groups, in particular, recognized the value of building bridges to outside organizations and groups. Farmworkers represent a marginal, often invisible, segment of the populace. These "ghostworkers," as they were called for a time in Arizona, wield less power than workers in other industries as a result of poverty, migratory work patterns, exemption from protective labor laws like the National Labor Relations Act, and sometimes undocumented immigrant status. Decades of effort at organizing farmworkers in the first half of the twentieth century failed to come anywhere close to the gains of unions in the industrial sector. Historian Jacquelyn Jones argues that agricultural migrants in the East were "systematically alienated from every level of the body politic" in the 1930s and 1940s.[19] Cindy Hahamovitch similarly characterizes migrant farmworkers as "stateless" persons lacking political power.[20] Years of frustrated organizing efforts made clear that farmworkers needed allies if they were to win gains from growers or government. This fits sociologist Melvin Hall's argument that people are the primary source of power in poor people's organizations and that forming relationships with outside groups may be used as a means of building strength in a campaign.[21] Sociologists Guy Burgess and Heidi Burgess similarly contend that one way for "low-power" groups to compensate for the absence of political and economic strength "is to enlist the help of external or more powerful groups."[22] Since farmworkers lacked political and economic capital, it behooved them to build bridges to other organizations and the public to enlarge their base of support.

Ghostworkers and Greens shows how farmworker groups often drew connections to the larger public in their pesticide reform efforts in order to increase the number of people supporting their campaigns and compensate for their lack of political and economic power. While several agricultural chemicals carried the risk of poisoning farmworkers, the United Farm Workers Organizing Committee (UFWOC) focused its initial campaign on DDT, the infamous persistent pesticide whose threat extended well beyond the bounds of the field. The launch of subsequent campaigns followed incidents of widespread poisoning of the public by pesticide residue. Cesar Chavez and other organizers argued that growers' misuse of pesticides threatened the public and farmworkers alike and that the problem could be resolved with a strong union presence in the fields. Other farmworker groups like the Maricopa County Organizing Project, Arizona Farm Workers, and the Farmworker Association of Florida focused their attempts to elicit public concern on issues of pesticide drift, ground-water quality, and ozone depletion. They similarly connected farmworker health issues to broader concerns. Additionally, these groups devoted re-sources to educational efforts among farmworkers, teaching workers and their families how to best protect their health around dangerous agricul-tural chemicals. The organizations used lawsuits to gain leverage as well. The public face of their campaigns, though, typically sought to establish a bond with people and groups having little direct connection to the fields.

This book also demonstrates that environmental organizations es-poused a similar rhetoric of cooperation, suggesting that environmentalists and workers should work together on issues when interests overlapped. Organizers of the first Earth Day stressed the value of building alliances with organizations associated with other causes, stating that the potential for cooperative campaigns was innumerable because pollution affected everyone regardless of race or social standing. Recently formed environ-mental organizations like the Environmental Defense Fund (EDF), the Natural Resources Defense Council (NRDC), and Friends of Earth (FoE) embraced the expanded vision of environmentalism readily. Of the older conservation groups, the Sierra Club showed the greatest enthusiasm for tackling new challenges. This is made clear in *Sierra Club Bulletin* editori-als from the early 1970s that spoke of the compatibility of environmental-ism and social justice. Environmental organizations knew that workers and environmentalists would not agree on everything, but recognized the value of finding common ground and cooperating on issues of mutual in-terest. Many environmental groups continued to voice support for partner-ships with labor organizations in the 1980s and beyond.

These attempts at outreach lack visibility in scholarly literature as divi-sions between the blue and green movements are often emphasized more than common ground. The "jobs versus environment" trope pervades popular and academic discussions on the topic. Historian Richard White contends that "environmentalists so often seem self-righteous, privileged, and arrogant because they so readily consent to identifying nature with play and make it by definition a place where leisured humans come only to visit and not to work, stay, or live," and reasons that this leads them to "frame environmental issues so that the choice seems to be between hu-mans and nature."[23] This is certainly true of the epic battles over the future of old-growth forests in the Pacific Northwest that White references in his essay. Yet this understanding can also be an oversimplification, a false dichotomy employed by opponents of regulation in a classic "divide and conquer" strategy.[24] Sociologist Brian Mayer acknowledges the class differences to which White refers, but suggests that "externalities such as environmental pollution and occupational health hazards disproportionately affect those at the lower end of the socioeconomic structure, the working class, which theoretically creates allies between environmentalists and organizations like unions that tend to represent working class individuals"[25] The efforts of labor and environmental organizations to address issues of seemingly mutual concern warrant closer scrutiny by scholars so that the nature of relations between the two movements can be better understood. This work contributes to that understanding with its investigation of the engagement of environmental organizations and farmworker groups in pesticide reform.

Previous comparative expositions of pesticide campaigns do not adequately address cooperation between the two groups. Historian Robert Gordon, who often explores the intersections of the labor and environmental movement, argues that "the battle to restrict the use of DDT is in many ways indicative of the gulf between the United Farm Workers (UFW) and the environmental mainstream," contending that the Sierra Club and other leading environmental groups cared about the effect of persistent pesticides on "natural wildlife, not on Latino farmworkers."[26] Qualitative social scientist Laura Pulido maintains that environmentalists chose to "focus on quality-of-life issues in which the social actors are fairly removed from the actual threat," incorrectly asserting that "once DDT was banned, mainstream environmental groups retreated from the issue of pesticides for a number of years, thinking the problem was solved."[27] In a subsequent co-authored article, Pulido and anthropologist Devon Peña hold that "mainstream environmentalists focused on protecting wilderness areas and consumers from pesticides, while ignoring the plight of farmworkers," and assert that environmentalists' "narrow articulation of the environment" rendered them "incapable of an oppositional politics that would allow them to make connections between agribusiness, the state, environmental degradation, and [the] highly exploited." They suggest that environmentalists' constrained view of pesticide problems was attributable to their "positionality" as college-educated white persons (often male), "privileged in their socioeconomic status," who lived far from the fields and had a "limited political consciousness."[28] A close examination of the rhetoric and actions of mainstream environmentalists shows that such sweeping generalizations are problematic. Here I illustrate that environmental organizations and farmworker groups recognized their common interests on multiple occasions and collaborated in a number of efforts both before and after the 1972 DDT ban.

The work histories of leaders and organizers introduced in the following case studies, in fact, sometimes overlapped the social justice and environmental movements. EDF co-founder Victor Yannacone represented the NAACP for nine years before shifting his attention to environmental issues. Chicano activist Arturo Sandoval also organized activities for the first Earth Day in the southwest. Earth Day organizer and Sierra Club lobbyist Linda Billings later translated her concern about farmworkers and pesticides into a new position as the director of pesticide farm safety staff at the Environmental Protection Agency. Al Meyerhoff began his career with California Rural Legal Assistance before becoming an NRDC attorney. David Roe authored California's Safe Drinking Water and Toxics Enforcement Act when he was an EDF senior attorney. He later transitioned into a senior council position at Human Rights First. Historian Adam Rome argues that "the rise of the environmental movement owed much to the events of the 1960s," and suggests that scholars should consider the underexplored connections between environmentalism and other social movements.[29] Undoubtedly, the examples of overlap in this study and those mentioned by Rome represent only a sample of persons who transitioned from an environmental group to an organization focused more specifically on social justice and vice versa.

Cooperative efforts between farmworker groups and environmentalists often depended upon the work of bridge-builders within one or more of the organizations. I argue in this book that bridge-builders transcended differences between organizations and ably negotiated the cultural terrain of diverse movements to foster working relationships.[30] Staff professionals played a critical role in farmworker organizations. Nurse practitioner and boycott coordinator Marion Moses, for example, initiated contacts with scientists and the Environmental Defense Fund on behalf of Cesar Chavez and UFWOC in the 1960s. Maricopa County Organizing Project attorney Nadine Wettstein similarly established working relationships with the local chapter of the Sierra Club and Arizona Common Cause to establish Arizona Clean Water Advocates. Farmworker Association of Florida Pesticide Safety and Environmental Health Project Coordinator Jeannie Economos and Administrator Sister Gail Grimes served as the primary contacts for FoE in the Sustainable Tomatoes/Safer Communities campaign. Sierra Club leaders—Raymond Sherwin, William Futrell, Will Siri, Michael McCloskey—issued invitations for partnerships with labor unions on issues of mutual interest, while some lobbyists like Linda Billings networked with different farmworker groups. NRDC attorney Al Meyerhoff undertook efforts to maintain a working relationship between his organization and the UFW in the wake of Cesar Chavez's passing. These individuals facilitated the growth of collaborative efforts between the farmworker movement and the environmental movement.

Sociologists Sherry Cable, Tamara Mix, and Donald Hastings suggest that the most effective working relationships between environmentalists and environmental justice activists occur when the environmental justice organization has a professional staffer who shares a common background (well-educated and middle-class) with environmentalists and functions as a bridge between the groups.[31] These case studies add support to that contention. Often the individuals within the farmworker organizations who communicated with environmental groups had not previously worked in the fields. Rather they were professionals committed to principles of social justice, and their level of education and professional background likely facilitated communication between the organizations.

Differences in strategy and timing limited cooperative opportunities to some extent. Though the collaborative efforts between movements often proved temporary, I contend that this does not weaken the significance. Political scientist David Meyer maintains that cooperative endeavors and coalitions lack permanence and that "the peak of mobilization is always limited." He argues that "changes in policy, political alignments, or even rhetoric alter the constellation of political opportunities for each organization."[32] Organizations do often drift apart at the conclusion of a trial or when efforts to enact new regulatory laws end in success or failure, but in the cases studied here, channels of communication remained open for future collaborations between farmworker groups and environmentalists that maintained a keen interest in pesticide issues for roughly fifty years since the release of *Silent Spring*. The different organizations, however, also addressed a host of different issues and shifted resources to address other concerns during that time as well. This book shows that the possibility of reestablishing cooperative arrangements arose when the different organizations returned their focus to pesticides at the same time and when strategies and goals aligned.

Overview

Chapters 1 and 2 briefly explain the development of chemically intensive, industrial-style agriculture in the United States. The first chapter shows how growers' early concerns about economic poisons gave way to an ardent belief that pesticides were an indispensable necessity in their ongoing war against insect predators. It simultaneously charts changes in government agencies and professions connected with agriculture and the evolution of clientele politics and pesticide regulation through the Federal, Insecticide, Fungicide, and Rodenticide Act of 1947. The chapter following focuses on another key change in the transformation of farms into what Carey McWilliams so poignantly characterized as "factories in the fields." It examines the growth of a large marginalized, often migratory, workforce that was systematically disempowered by growers and government. These hidden hands of the harvest fell out of view of the public eye and did not benefit from the protection of the growing body of labor laws in the mid-twentieth century. Consequently, it behooved the people most effected by the deleterious effects of pesticides to find allies outside of the agricultural industry in their reform campaigns because they had been rendered powerless in formal politics. Together these chapters set the foundation for the examination of cooperative efforts in pesticide reform that follow in subsequent chapters.

Chapter 3 begins with the publication of *Silent Spring* in 1962 and shows how concerned scientists disseminated information about the ill effects of pesticides directly and indirectly to UFWOC and environmental groups. The belief that an informed citizenry would be better able to debate and make decisions about innovations that had potentially adverse effects on people and the environment underlay this scientific information movement. Both environmentalists and farmworker groups showed increasing concern about pesticides, particularly DDT, as they understood more about the problem, but developed fairly different strategies in their attempts to make change. I argue that the variance in strategies limited but did not preclude opportunities for collaboration between the two movements. Cooperation happened most often in mounting legal challenges.

The next chapter tracks the pesticide reform efforts of UFW and mainstream environmental organizations in the years immediately following the DDT ban. Contrary to the predominant scholarly narrative, environmentalists remained invested in the issue. Environmental organizations, particularly the Sierra Club, showed interest in a broadened range of environmental issues and expanded their lobbying efforts to address many of these concerns. They consistently stressed the fundamental importance of securing the public's "right to know" about pesticides and better democratizing decision making on related issues. Opportunities for collaboration with the UFW proved fleeting though, because union battles with the Teamsters between 1972 and 1976 consumed so much of the organization's resources.

Chapter 5 narrows the focus to state-level pesticide politics in Arizona during the 1970s and 1980s. Both farmworkers and suburban families affected by pesticide drift tried to make the grower-dominated Board of Pesticide Control more responsive to the concerns of the public. However, these efforts rarely occurred concurrently, so collaborative campaigns did not develop between the groups for many years, in part because growers' associations recognized the potential power and threat of a cross-class coalition and strategized to keep one from developing. When the opportunity finally arose in 1984, farmworkers joined with suburbanites and environmentalists to overcome the power of the agricultural lobby and reshape pesticide governance in the state.

The next chapter also looks at state-level activism with an examination of responses to the deregulatory efforts of California Governor George Deukmejian in the 1980s. With the gains of the previous decade under assault, environmentalists and unions partnered to counter the governor's attacks. The labor-environmental coalition filed lawsuits to force enforcement of existent law and continued to support legislative measures that would help protect public health. California Rural Legal Assistance partnered with environmental organizations on multiple occasions during this period. Meanwhile Chavez and the UFW set their sights on eliminating five pesticides from use, hoping that a renewed nationwide boycott would bring enough economic pressure to bear on growers that they would negotiate new contracts. Environmentalists, by comparison, committed their energies to mobilizing California voters to pass a sweeping toxics initiative that fundamentally changed the state's regulatory landscape. Both efforts shared the common goal of better protecting the health of farmworkers and the public, but variant scopes and campaign strategies hampered collaboration. Still, cooperation between the UFW and environmentalists occurred on a limited basis in California during this period.

The final case study, in Chapter 7, encompasses pesticide politics from the local to the international level, centering on the long struggle to halt usage of methyl bromide. Signatory nations of the Montreal Protocol, an international treaty to curb ozone depletion, amended the agreement with a phase-out schedule for methyl bromide soon after its deleterious effects on the atmosphere were discovered. Growers associations put up a fierce resistance to the plan, using uncertainty in science to foster doubt about its necessity. Environmental groups and farmworker organizations functioned in part as a counterweight against growers' lobbying; in particular, the Farmworker Association of Florida partnered with FoE in a campaign against methyl bromide. Together they publicized that the fumigant posed a threat not only to atmospheric integrity, but to the health of farmworkers in the fields and people living in adjacent communities. This chapter also discusses joint efforts between farmworker groups and environmental organizations in California to advance the phase-out schedule. Though the fumigant continues to be used to a limited degree in the United States to this day, the collaborative efforts of regulatory proponents added information about the hazardousness of methyl bromide to bank of knowledge and hastened the switch to viable alternatives. Just as they have done consistently since the mid-1960s, environmental organizations and farmworker groups continue to compile pesticide data; analyze risks and educate the public; initiate reform campaigns in attempt to resolve pressing problems; and collaborate with each another when timing, strategies, and goals overlap.

1

Sowing the Seeds of
Chemical Dependency

The end of World War II heralded an era of agriculture in which many
growers unflaggingly put their faith in chemicals as their primary means
of pest control. Synthetic compounds offered growers a previously un-
obtainable mastery over nature. Pesticides had a long history of usage in
the United States prior to the introduction of synthetic chemicals, but
were never relied upon as completely as they were after 1945. The embrace of these powerful new poisons solidified a path dependency in
agriculture that made it ever more difficult for growers and entomologists to switch from chemical control technology to other systems of pest
management.[1]

Farmers employed folk remedies, botanicals, and soap-based emulsions as agricultural development spread westward across the nation.
Pyrethrum became the first botanical insecticide sold commercially, but
its high cost limited its appeal.[2] Soap solutions offered a more affordable pest control option beginning in the 1840s, making usage more feasible as monoculture became more common.[3] Changing vast stretches of

complex ecosystems into much simpler forms significantly heightened threats of insect damage to crops. California growers who imported non-native nursery stocks for cultivation in the burgeoning citrus industry accidentally imported a host of serious pests, like the San Jose Scale, as well.[4] Transcontinental rail lines further hastened the spread of pest infestations. The unwanted insects feasted in the new simplified environments and had few native predators to keep their numbers in check.[5] Growers increasingly considered insecticides as an option as they faced greater risks of crop damage.

Copper acetoarsenite, commercially sold as Paris Green, became the first widely used chemical poison in agricultural pest control in the early 1860s. Other compounds bearing names like London Purple, Paris Purple, and Scheele's Green soon competed for favor on the market, but Paris Green remained the arsenic-based poison of choice well into the late nineteenth century.[6] Arsenic, of course, kills more than target insects and negative stories periodically filtered through to the press. The poison likely killed thousands of fish in the Connecticut River in 1878 after heavy rains washed the chemical into the waterway from adjacent fields.[7] It also posed risks to careless farmers, and to consumers who purchased fruit with excessive residues.[8] Its extreme toxicity actually made it popular with individuals harboring suicidal intent or murderous thoughts.[9] Despite its potential for causing unintended harm, American farmers applied two thousand tons of Paris Green to crops annually by 1896.[10]

Pesticide applications increased with the development of a professional class of economic entomologists. Most farmers lacked the financial resources necessary to pay for independent consultations, yet a series of devastating locust outbreaks between 1873 and 1876 made clear the need for improved pest control. Missouri state entomologist Charles Valentine Riley argued for an increased federal role and helped convince Congress to allocate funds for the creation of a three-man Entomological Commission in 1876.[11] The passage of the Hatch Act in 1887 created opportunities for the growing class of professionals who soon found employment in a host of government agencies and public institutions, including the US Department of Agriculture (USDA), land grant universities, state agricultural experiment stations, and extension services.[12]

Still, neither farmers nor entomologists wholly put their faith in chemical control methods. Farmers continued to employ cultural methods of control that had worked for them in the past. These practices included the alteration of planting schedules, intercropping, hybridization, and the use of lure plants to draw predacious insects away from cash crops.[13] The majority of chemicals in this period carried unproven, often fraudulent claims about the effectiveness and safety of the products. The USDA reported that nineteen out of forty-five tested samples of Paris Green contained unallowable amounts of sodium sulfate. Other pesticides contained high levels of arsenic that would burn crop foliage. Nearly 20 percent of tested pyrethrum contained a "poisonous substance" that posed a threat to applicators.[14] No regulatory laws existed, though, to prevent companies from making dubious claims about adulterated pesticides. Consequently, many farmers remained wary and those that did not sometimes suffered financial loss.[15] The difficulties of preparing mixtures, the instability of some compounds, and the necessity of considering variables like weather slowed the process by which chemical controls were incorporated into agricultural production practices.[16]

Entomologists did not solely focus on chemical solutions either, choosing instead to experiment with a variety of techniques to protect crops from insects. Experimental farms tested biological, cultural, and chemical controls to determine the best combination of strategies.[17] The United States Entomological Commission, for instance, recommended that Great Plains farmers extinguish autumn prairie fires so that there would be fuel for controlled burning to combat locust infestations in the spring.[18] Respected entomologist Charles Riley recognized the utility of pesticides like Paris Green and London Purple in some circumstances, but thought it "unwise and unsafe to employ such poisons, or to recommend them" in other situations.[19] Riley continued to show favor for biological controls after becoming chief of the Bureau of Entomology in 1881, holding that every insect pest had a predator to keep its population in check.[20] Biological controls received an additional boost when the nonnative ladybug, a natural predator of the problematic fluted scale, saved the California citrus industry from devastation. Yet separate campaigns against the gypsy moth and the boll weevil that respectively employed biological and cultural controls proved embarrassing public failures for the Bureau of Entomology.[21]

The unsuccessful gypsy moth and boll weevil campaigns contributed to the Bureau of Entomology's shift toward more chemical solutions in agriculture. Leland Howard, who replaced Riley as chief, always harbored more interest in agricultural chemicals than his predecessor. Unlike earlier generations of entomologists who received their training on the farm and in the fields, Howard gained his knowledge in the classrooms and laboratories of Cornell University. The time spent at Cornell undoubtedly exposed him to the discourse of scientific colleagues who still characterized entomologists as amateurish bug-catchers, despite their clear attempts to define themselves as a professional class. The development of chemical solutions to solve pest problems held the possibility of granting entomologists access to the more prestigious ranks of scientists. Pesticides' promise of universal applicability, fast action, and predictable results fit the mood of an era that valued standardization, efficiency, and progress.[22] Howard increasingly treated agricultural chemicals as the best and most reliable form of pest control.[23]

If farmers were to rely more heavily on chemical controls, they had to trust more completely in the effectiveness of pesticides. New York in 1898 and California in 1901 passed legislation intended to curtail fraudulent claims from pesticide manufacturers.[24] Howard and other entomologists lobbied Congress for national legislation that would establish guidelines for the manufacture and sale of agricultural chemicals.[25] The National Grange, the American Apple Growers' Congress, the New York State Fruit Growers Association, and several state horticultural societies urged Congress to pass a bill regulating agricultural chemicals, believing it necessary to protect farmers' economic interests. Major pesticide manufacturers similarly supported the passage of the Insecticide Act of 1910, recognizing that profits would grow if trust in their product increased.[26]

The component parts of the Insecticide Act centered on protecting farmers from dubious claims about the efficacy of pesticides.[27] It required companies to accurately describe the effects of their products and list inert ingredients on labels. The act set purity and strength standards for the two most popular agricultural chemicals, Paris Green and lead arsenate.[28] It also charged the newly created Insecticide and Fungicide Board with the responsibility of making sure that manufacturers followed the new guidelines.[29] The board undertook scientific investigations to determine the effects of various pesticides on insects, fungi, and commercial crops; conducted hearings on alleged violations of the law; and engaged in educational outreach efforts to help bring pesticide manufacturers into compliance.[30] Concerns about human and environmental health did not factor into the passage of the law.[31]

Entomologists found opportunity to bolster their professional status and improve public perceptions of agricultural chemicals during World War I. Howard believed that the profession was poised to make an important contribution to the war effort by protecting critical foodstuffs and other agricultural commodities. He and others further concluded that the pressures of the global crisis necessitated that pest issues have solutions that were universally applicable, fast-acting, and effective. When boll worms infested fields of castor beans that were used to lubricate airplane engine cylinders, entomologists did not have the luxury of time to develop a biological or cultural response to the problem.[32] Farmers likewise valued solutions that delivered quick results and it was the bureau's charge to satisfy the demands of its primary customers. The Bureau of Entomology continued to consider biological and cultural controls, but turned increasingly to chemical solutions.[33]

American chemical companies, hoping to continue the expansion of their markets after the end of the European conflict, invested in research as never before and promoted the agricultural use of pesticides. Advertising attempted to sway consumers who still harbored a degree of distrust about the ability of chemicals to conquer pests without harming commercial crops. Manufacturers promised that their products would vanquish insect foes rather than simply control populations, casting pesticides as the best means to counter the insect hordes.[34] This tone matched the character of messages from the Bureau of Entomology and Leland Howard, who warned that "the great armies of insect pests . . . are our worst rivals and enemies."[35]

The rhetoric appealed to growers in an increasingly capital-intensive industry. Nearly all of the agricultural innovations of the twentieth century—machinery, pesticides, fertilizers, irrigation developments— raised the fixed cost of production. The technological developments promised increased yields with less labor, but required greater investments up front. The most commercially successful farmers adopted the new technologies despite the added cost. Those who chose not to adapt or could not afford to do so became less viable in the market-place and gradually disappeared. As a result, from the 1930s onward, farms became increasingly consolidated into the hands of persons with a higher level of education, wealth, and power. This group generally valued managerial skills and technological efficiency over hard physical labor.[36] Chemicals promising total control of pest populations proved attractive because they saved labor and seemed to offer the best protection of invested capital.[37] Environmental historian James McWilliams rightly contends: "Path dependency—in this case, the idea that agribusiness, the federal government, and the insecticide industry had chosen to fight insect infestations exclusively with chemicals—limited the way in which scientists and farmers framed the pest situation and contemplated their options."[38] Consequently the volume of insecticides applied to fields continued to climb as the twentieth century progressed and chemical controls became increasingly entrenched in agricultural pest management strategies.

Despite the growing chemical dependency in agriculture, scientists still knew little about the health effects of exposure to some of the most popular compounds. A consumer scare over arsenic on apples in 1925 prompted the Food and Drug Administration (FDA) to begin monitoring residues of lead arsenate. The agency had the approval of growers' associations anxious for a rebound in consumer confidence, though some growers demanded justification for the new policy and proof that the substance posed a health threat.[39] Assessing public risk in a widely varying populace of young, old, healthy, and infirm individuals proved a difficult task for the agency, particularly when attempting to find the chronic effects of low exposure to lead arsenate. The FDA opted to initiate animal-based experimentation, conducting lifetime feeding experiments on rats. It planned to make projections of risks to humans based on the findings.[40] Growers' associations opposed the research, fearing the results would lead to the establishment of low residue tolerance levels, and voiced their concerns to congressional allies.[41] Testing the chronic effects of a poison on humans, however, raised obvious moral problems and was not a feasible option. Still, Missouri Democratic Representative Clarence Cannon, who chaired the Agricultural Appropriations Subcommittee, responded by inserting a clause into the 1937 budget bill that read: "no part of the funds appropriated by this act shall be used for laboratory investigations to determine the possible harmful effects on human beings of spray insecticides on fruits and vegetables."[42]

The Public Health Service later undertook a study examining Washington orchard workers' exposure to lead arsenate. The study, though, examined data that would show acute rather than long-lasting or slow-developing effects. The difference in design made the agency less able to determine the associated risk of chronic health problems than the preceding FDA tests and yielded little useful information on the dangers of lead arsenate. Since the test results suggested that the chemical did not have severe health impacts, the Federal Security Administration raised residue tolerance levels for fruit. The action failed to generate a public response, because attention to the issue waned by the time that the Public Health Service completed its investigation. Little impetus existed to conduct additional tests, particularly when a well-organized agricultural lobby opposed further study.[43]

Attention soon shifted from lead arsenate to a new "miracle" chemical, DDT, during World War II. Its proven effectiveness seemingly provided a means by which farmers could exert total control over their insect enemies.[44] Some scientists tempered their optimism because of the uncertain effects of DDT on beneficial bugs. Eradication of some non-target insects had the possibility of increasing pest problems, and tests by pharmacologists also revealed that the compound accumulated in the fat cells of dogs. Prudence led some scientists to call for more testing before use became widespread. Nevertheless, glory stories of DDT decimating populations of mosquitoes and lice on the war front made the transition to civilian markets a near certainty, particularly because the lack of an appropriate regulatory framework made it nearly impossible for the government to keep any chemicals from being sold. The FDA had the power to set residue tolerance levels on foodstuffs and the USDA ensured that the poisons were correctly labeled, but neither could keep pesticides from being sold commercially if the labeling guidelines were followed.[45]

The manufacture and usage of DDT and other pesticides exploded after World War II. Production in the United States rose from 10 million pounds in 1945 to 100 million pounds in 1951.[46] Yet as the volume of use exponentially increased, indications suggested that DDT's reign as a chemical miracle worker would be short. The common housefly and two strains of mosquitoes had developed resistance to the chemical by 1949, even when the application was ten times stronger than in previous years.[47] New and powerful chemical combinations soon joined approximately twenty-five thousand other pesticide products registered for sale in 1947. The ever-changing and supersaturated nature of the pesticide marketplace made it extremely difficult for the government to monitor.[48]

Congress responded in 1947 with the passage of the Federal Insecticide, Fungicide, and Rodenticide Act (FIFRA), which required pesticides to be registered with the USDA before being sold commercially. Manufacturers had to attest to a product's safety and effectiveness by submitting a description of its chemical composition, results of residue tests, safety reports, analytical methodology, and the proposed label to the USDA's Pesticide Regulation Division. New labels needed to include a warning about potential harm to humans, vertebrate animals, and vegetation (excepting weeds). The act also necessitated that companies add a dye to agricultural chemicals sold in white powder form, in hopes that the discoloration would prevent individuals from mistaking the poisons for similar-looking products (sugar, flour, salt, baking powder) used in cooking.[49]

State-level legislation preceded and sparked the congressional action. Nine states passed laws to address a spate of injuries and deaths resulting from the accidental use of white powdered pesticides in food preparation. Fifty persons at a state hospital in Salem, Oregon died and 467 others became ill after eating food contaminated with the insecticide sodium fluoride. A Salvation Army community center in Pennsylvania mistook the same substance for flour and served food that killed twelve and sickened fifty-seven people. Similarly, a field cook in Texas unknowingly used an arsenic-based insecticide in the preparation of pancakes for farmworkers, resulting in the immediate death of a large number of men.[50] New York, Pennsylvania, Texas, Oregon, North Carolina, South Carolina, Louisiana, Tennessee, and New Hampshire responded with legislation designed to minimize accidental poisonings, though the legislative provisions varied from state to state.[51] The USDA, pesticide manufacturers, and distributors favored the passage of

FIFRA, because it would bring uniformity to pesticide regulation, vesting enforcement responsibilities with the Department of Agriculture. The American Farm Bureau Federation, the National Grange, and the National Council of Farmer Cooperatives voiced support because the registration and labeling requirements promised to better protect growers from ineffective or harmful products. No consumer, conservation, or labor organization testified at the congressional hearings on FIFRA prior to its passage.[52]

FIFRA proved to be a relatively loose regulatory law that did little to keep dangerous agricultural chemicals off the market. Political scientist Christopher Bosso asserts that the legislation, as originally passed, "displays all the dynamics of classic clientele politics . . . [because] the pesticides issue was not salient to any but those directly benefiting from pesticides, and the scope of the debate was severely limited to those most intimately involved."[53] If the USDA concluded that a pesticide did not comply with the tenets of the law, the agency could notify the company and provide opportunity for correction. The company, however, could refuse to follow the recommendations and register its product under protest.[54] To force its removal from commercial markets, USDA had to prove the hazardousness of the pesticide in court. The length and difficulty of this procedure helped assure that the agency would take a noninterventionist approach.[55] The Pesticide Registration Division consistently bowed to pressure when companies challenged a denied request.[56] The regulation was so toothless that environmental lawyer William Rodgers Jr. reported that the USDA had never "secured the cancellation of a registration in a contested case" in the twenty-three years following the law's passage.[57]

Farmers' growing chemical dependency remained unchecked and usage of pesticides grew exponentially through the 1950s. The powerful new synthetic chemicals of the postwar era brought problems as well as promise. The indiscriminate poisons killed target species and beneficial bugs alike. The killing of insect predators eliminated a natural control of minor agricultural pests, allowing their numbers to explode to the point that they represented a serious secondary threat to farmers. The problems of pest resistance, pest resurgence, and the growth of secondary pest populations did not cause farmers to turn back toward biological and cultural controls. Rather, they invested even more heavily in chemical solutions.[58] Pesticide companies funded entomological research in universities, government dollars financed field tests, and farmers struggled to stay a step ahead of their insect foes in order to meet the global demand for American agricultural products in the Cold War era.[59] Pesticides, including those that posed a threat to human and environmental health, saturated the United States as it entered the 1960s.

2

Hidden Hands of the Harvest

The modernization and professionalization of agriculture also reshaped many farm owners' thinking about labor and production. Prior to the growth of an industrialized agricultural system, families and local hired hands handled the bulk of farm chores outside of the plantation South. This changed in the twentieth century as multitudes of migrant laborers shouldered the burden of work on large farms. Labor relations in this context bore comparison to the relations between manager and employee in industrial settings, yet distinct differences between the field and the factory arguably made agricultural labor exceptional. While work increasingly followed an industrial logic, farm owners chose to stress the differences and argued that twentieth-century labor legislation should not apply to farmworkers. They regularly acted in concert with the government to deny farmworkers political power in order to maintain a cheap and plentiful supply of labor.

The industrial model of modern agriculture in the United States has roots in the slave South; its development in free society, however, can be traced to California in the late 1800s. The transference of virtually intact Spanish land grants to American owners and the railroads' acquisition of 16 percent of the state's public land influenced the development of the California countryside.[1] This pattern of property ownership did not facilitate the growth of small family-based farms; rather it was conducive to the development of expansive industrial-style agriculture dominated by a small elite group of land speculators. Insurance companies, bankers, lawyers, and investors came together to form land syndicates intent on turning big profits. Versed in the corporate model of management, the syndicates introduced new land use, cropping, and labor management trends to agriculture.[2]

California had distinct climatic advantages over other parts of the country, but growers in the state faced a unique set of challenges. Eastern farmers resided closer to major urban markets and had lower transportation costs. Additionally, while the nation largely covered the cost of western water projects, growers still bore some responsibility for irrigation fees.[3] Such overheads threatened the economic viability of large-scale commercial agriculture in the arid West.[4] The growers, consequently, tried to maximize profits by specializing in products that commanded high prices in the East. They planted thousands of acres with single crops, recognizing that monoculture carried greater risk of pest infestation than diversified fields, but also knowing that it had higher profit-making potential.[5] Chemicals promised quick and efficient protection, but pesticides also added to growers' fixed costs.[6]

Labor proved to be the most variable cost of production. Growers strived to hire the cheapest and most marginalized workers, employing them only for the duration of the season.[7] Beginning in the late 1800s and continuing through the first half of the twentieth century, growers employed the logic of biological determinism. They rationalized that Asians and Mexicans possessed hereditary traits that made them better suited for stoop labor than white Americans, contending that small physical stature suited the demands of field work. Growers maintained that Chinese and later Mexican and Filipino workers also had a high tolerance for hot weather, did not strive for the same goals as white Americans, and were content with poor working conditions and a migratory life. They concluded that these characteristics made these ethnic groups particularly suited for seasonal field labor.[8]

California growers showed an early preference for Chinese workers because the group lacked political power, influence, and opportunity. An 1854 California Supreme Court ruling upheld a statute prohibiting testimony from Chinese persons in cases that involved white parties, thereby rendering the Chinese more vulnerable to abuse. White workers meanwhile engaged in campaigns of intimidation to deny the immigrants access to certain employments. Growers, in contrast, welcomed the Chinese into the fields because they were exploitable. However, the Chinese Exclusion Act of 1882 and the Geary Act of 1892, which provided for the deportation of Chinese persons residing in the United States illegally, reduced the pool of labor.[9] The exclusionary legislation forced growers to rely more heavily on a heterogeneous mix of marginalized workers in the early twentieth century.[10]

Labor activism developed slowly in the fields and encountered violent suppression tactics. Following the logic of industrialists, growers fostered artificial divisions among workers by segregating ethnic groups and basing their pay on different wage scales.[11] The divide-and-conquer strategy combined with the migratory nature of farm labor made organizing difficult. The American Federation of Labor half-heartedly attempted to organize California fields between 1903 and 1916.[12] With an interest in advancing the condition of all workers, the Industrial Workers of the World (IWW), popularly referred to as the Wobblies, showed more commitment to farmworkers. Nevertheless, regular and violent conflicts with state authorities resulted in fleeting gains for the IWW and its members.[13]

The most explosive conflict occurred in Wheatland during the summer of 1913. The Durst brothers advertised for many more workers than they needed on their hops ranch in order to foster job competition and drive down wages. Respondents accepted the reduced pay, but then encountered abominable living conditions with an inadequate and unsanitary supply of water, as well as an absence of other promised amenities. Rather than accept substandard conditions as had often been the case in the past, fieldworkers organized a grievance committee with a contingent of Wobblies. Ralph Durst called on the police to disrupt the organizing. The Yuba County sheriff, two deputies, and the district attorney arrived to disperse the peaceably assembled crowd of two thousand men, women, and children by firing a shot into the air. The gunfire triggered fighting, however, that left four people dead. The Wheatland Riot ended the workers' agitation and foreshadowed later verbal and physical attacks on the IWW. By decade's end, farmworkers once again faced a future without a representative labor organization.[14]

California growers lobbied Congress to ease restrictions on migration from China during this period, hoping to somehow return to the halcyon days of old. They amplified their appeal in 1917, recognizing that war in Europe would shrink the labor pool. The Department of Labor responded, but not by making allowances for Chinese fieldworkers. The changes, instead, occurred on the United States' southern border. Mexican nationals could thenceforward enter the country without paying a head tax and without passing a literacy test. The agency stipulated that incoming Mexicans must remain gainfully employed in agriculture while in residence. Migrants could not vacate these positions for better-paying opportunities without risking arrest and deportation, which consequently enabled growers to set the terms of employment with little fear of protest. Farm managers could use the threat of deportation to counter farmworkers' demands for improved field conditions and wages. As with the Chinese, growers wielded extraordinary power over Mexican laborers.[15] The department explicitly stated that the policy on Mexican workers was a temporary resolution to the wartime labor shortage, yet growers convincingly argued that they would still need migrants at the war's end. Hence the importation of foreign laborers who lacked the power to improve their work conditions continued.[16]

Growers used carefully crafted campaigns to erase memories of unrest in the 1910s from the public mind, while simultaneously working to increase production efficiency and control over labor. Advertising masked the industrial style of production in the fields, characterizing fruits and vegetables as the creation of sun, water, and soil.[17] Human labor had no place in the marketing schema. If an advertisement featured a person, it typically showed a delicate white woman offering fruit from the vine. Environmental historian Douglas Sackman argues that these print illustrations positioned women as "mediators between nature and consumer" in apparent reference to "the woman-as-Mother-Earth icon."[18] The women in the advertisements bore little relation to workers in the field, which helped divert consumer attention away from labor exploitation in the industry.[19] Behind the carefully cultivated bucolic images, growers established cooperative bureaus that developed a common wage structure to eliminate competition between employers and keep labor costs at a minimum. The collective organization of growers inhibited the growth of a collective organization of farmworkers, because workers had to confront a unified industry rather than single farms or growers.[20] As a result, wages declined even as advertising campaigns raised sales and profits in the late 1920s.[21]

Migrants who worked for large growers often lived in seasonal labor camps, but the availability of this housing did little to improve living conditions or financial security. Housing generally consisted of one-room shacks that would be shared by itinerant workers migrant families and often lacked bedding, running water, and sanitary facilities. Sometimes a pit toilet would sit at the end of a row of houses for use by upward of a hundred people. John Steinbeck reported that that a camp of approximately four hundred persons in Kern County had a single shower. Smaller housing areas or squatter camps usually lacked even these rudimentary amenities.[22] While facilities proved minimal, grower surveillance did not. Armed private security forces sometimes patrolled living areas and monitored activities, quashing any attempt at organization. Steinbeck characterized the growers' attitude as one of "hatred and suspicion," stating that they maintained order with "the threat of . . . deputies' guns" and "herded [workers] about like animals," using every means possible to "make them feel inferior and insecure."[23]

Farmworker activism increased nevertheless, leading growers and local authorities to respond with a vigor reminiscent of Wheatland in 1913. A decade of unrest began in 1930 with two spontaneous strikes by Mexican and Filipino farmworkers in Imperial Valley. The Trade Union Unity League, created by the Communist Party in 1929 to serve as an alternative union to the more conservative American Federation of Labor, responded by dispatching organizers to channel workers' dissent into a new branch of the Agricultural Workers Industrial League, an organization with roots in the IWW.[24] Growers, newspapers, and local politicians quickly played up the specter of a communist threat and arrested strikers and agitators. Local authorities and federal immigration agents harassed, arrested, and deported activist Mexican nationals.[25] The police and deputized members of the American Legion regularly used a show of arms, tear gas, and violence to intimidate farmworkers; break up strike meetings and pickets; and evict unionists from labor camps.[26] The number of conflicts and the severity of repression increased as the decade progressed. Farmworkers staged 37 strikes in 1933 alone and 143 more by the end of the 1930s.[27]

The California Farm Bureau Federation and Chamber of Commerce in collaboration with representatives from other grower associations, Santa Fe and Pacific railroads, Standard Oil, California Packing Company, and Bank of America formed the Associated Farmers in 1934 to combat the growing threat of farm labor activism.[28] The AF compiled records on known Communists, primed the media with information to stoke Red fears, and published and distributed thousands of pamphlets bearing titles like "The Red Network" and "California's Embattled Farmers."[29] They worked with legislators to pass antipicketing ordinances, stop the flow of relief payments to striking farmworkers, and prosecute labor leaders under the Criminal Syndicalism Act which was supposed to fight organized crime.[30] The cooperative efforts of growers, government, and industrial interests successfully blocked the numerous attempts of farmworkers in the 1930s to improve working conditions, earn a living wage, and form a permanent representative union.

The 1930s marks a period of great gains for industrial unions, but the same did not hold true for agricultural worker organizations. Franklin Roosevelt responded more positively to workers than did previous presidents, yet his response was not uniform. New Deal policies benefited workers in industries where unions had strength or were building it, and reaffirmed the power of industry in areas where the labor movement was weak or nonexistent. Labor historian Melvyn Dubofsky maintains that "power sometimes appeared to be the sole reality" for the president.[31] New legislation set agricultural and industrial unionism on different trajectories by legitimizing claims that farm work was an exceptional form of labor.

The passage of the Wagner National Labor Relations Act in 1935 marked one of the most significant legislative gains for the labor movement, but it excepted domestics and farmworkers from its provisions. Southern Democrats intent on preserving the racial hierarchy and California agricultural interests both expressed opposition to a labor bill that included farmworkers in its protections. These two groups wielded considerable power; whereas farmworkers had little political influence. Consequently, the monumental legislation that guaranteed workers the right to form a union and established a tripartite relationship between workers, employers, and the state to resolve labor grievances did not apply to the fields.[32]

Congress also left agricultural workers out of the Social Security Act and the Fair Labor Standards Act. These legislative exceptions, labor historian Cletus Daniel argues, "effectively codified the traditional powerlessness of farm laborers" and adversely affected them for decades thereafter.[33]

Instead of farmworkers being empowered by inclusion in the provisions of protective labor legislation, the welfare of migrant farmworkers became the charge of the newly created Resettlement Administration, which later morphed into the USDA's Farm Security Administration. The FSA began the Migratory Camp Program, constructing housing and offering instruction for self-improvement that focused on behavioral change and not labor organizing.[34] The program provided some relief, but no real reform.[35] Growers, nevertheless, became concerned that the facilities would provide refuge for labor organizers, because growers could not evict troublesome workers from government-run camps.[36] The American Farm Bureau Federation and its allies argued that the FSA camp program needed to be abandoned.[37] Congress subsequently ended FSA oversight of the program in 1943 and implemented a measure that required farmworkers to receive approval from county authorities before taking work elsewhere.[38] Three years later, Congress dismantled the FSA altogether.[39]

Government policy continued to affect the experiences of farmworkers and industrial workers in very different ways during World War II. When the United States entered the war, the supply of industrial labor tightened. Faced with the prospect of shortages, employers proved willing to negotiate with unions.[40] Labor unions counted five million new members by the end of the conflict.[41] Though the Taft-Hartley Act of 1947 curbed the scope of union initiatives and limited union tactics to some degree, workers still believed that they had become equal participants with management in an industrial democracy.[42] Farmworkers, by contrast, remained unorganized during World War II. The Farm Bureau Federation and growers pleaded with Congress, the USDA, and the president to prevent a labor shortage that would threaten food production. The Roosevelt administration subsequently negotiated with Mexico for the importation of farmworkers, referred to as braceros, in 1942.[43] Growers convinced Congress to extend the program after the war, importing well over 700,000 braceros between 1952 and 1954. The selective enforcement of immigration laws by the Immigration and Naturalization Service helped ensure that farm labor remained available, cheap, and compliant.[44]

While industrial unionists made great gains in their standards of living, agricultural workers' financial and living conditions remained largely unchanged during and after World War II. Some braceros lived in converted cow barns that still bore the smell of manure, some shared bunkhouses with other farmworkers, some resided in shacks and tents set up in the middle of orchards, and others lived in more orderly labor camps. The Department of Labor had agreements with states to provide adequate sanitary housing to braceros, but a lack of inspections convinced some growers that housing violations would go unpunished.[45] The 1951 Migrant Labor Agreement with Mexico stipulated that braceros would be paid the prevailing wage for domestic workers, but growers regularly manipulated pay structures to compensate Mexican nationals less than their American counterparts. Program participants subject to unfair treatment could lodge a complaint with the Department of Labor, but most foreign workers did not know the name or address of the area representative.[46] Braceros had the right to elect representatives to speak with growers about work contracts, although neither workers nor growers could alter the agreements without first receiving permission from the United States and Mexico. Growers still reacted to the election of field representatives with hostility and countered with threats of deportation.[47]

Agricultural employment practices on the East Coast mirrored those in California and the West by the mid-twentieth century. Responding to eastern growers' fears of labor shortages, the United States reached agreement with the British West Indies and the Bahamas in 1943 to import agricultural workers on a nonpermanent basis. Eastern employers similarly failed to furnish the living and working conditions promised in the arrangement. Imported Caribbean workers, like braceros, could be sent back to their home countries at any time at the whim of employers.[48] Like their western counterparts, eastern growers pitted ethnic groups against each other to forestall organizing and prevent farmworkers from achieving gains.[49]

Trusted newscaster Edward R. Murrow brought attention to the marginalized and largely invisible migrants in a 1960 *CBS Reports* special entitled "Harvest of Shame." Murrow characterized migrant families as "forgotten people" in the age of affluence, chronicling their abject poverty and deplorable living and working conditions. He reported that migrants worked for wages that were too low to advance their condition and lived in unsanitary housing, lacking toilets and clean water. Secretary of Labor

James Mitchell referred to farmworkers as the "great mass . . . of excluded Americans . . . whose plight is a shame." Murrow concluded that the "migrants have no lobby" and suggested that "only an enlightened, aroused, and perhaps angered public opinion" could influence legislation to improve conditions.[50] The television documentary shocked many Americans; yet, in the years immediately following, no new federal laws significantly changed agricultural labor relations.[51]

Between the late nineteenth and the mid-twentieth centuries farming increasingly transformed into a corporate capitalist endeavor with an industrial logic at its core. While the family farm remained, large-scale industrialized agriculture set the trends in production and accounted for an increasingly large percentage of the produce yield in the United States. The rising fixed cost associated with this shift drove less financially secure farm owners off the land.[52] Farming changed from an occupation that was relatively accessible to families of moderate means into an enterprise dominated by wealthy growers, investors, and corporations commanding greater levels of wealth and power than the typical farmer of the nineteenth century.[53] These growers formed powerful associations to advance their interests, regularly winning the favor of government officials at the local, state, and national levels.

Growers and their representative organizations successfully argued that agricultural labor was exceptional and should not receive the same protections and rights granted industrial labor. They stressed a mutual interest between growers and government to maintain an affordable and reliable food production system and used their political clout to ensure that agricultural laborers remained tractable and cheap. A reliable and compliant workforce, they argued, remained as vitally important to industrial agriculture as pesticides. Government cooperation with growers on labor policy made it difficult for farmworkers to organize and improve their living and working conditions. When labor activism posed a threat in the 1910s and 1930s, growers used extralegal means with the support of local, and sometimes state, officials to quash the movement.

The plight of marginalized farmworkers escaped the attention of most Americans through the first half of the twentieth century. Just as pesticides acted as an invisible shield to protect agricultural products, farmworkers acted as the "invisible" hands that gathered the crop. Growers consciously masked the chemical and human inputs of agricultural production, characterizing their produce as spontaneous creations of nature. Occasionally a pesticide scare, labor unrest, or a news program would disrupt this carefully crafted image. The public rarely maintained concern about industrialized agriculture, however. This would change to some degree in the 1960s as farmworkers brought their grievances before the public and asked for their support. Pesticides numbered among the issues addressed by a new farmworker organization led by Cesar Chavez. The group joined a chorus of concerned scientists, environmentalists, and consumers who demanded reform.

The Budding Movement for Pesticide Reform, 1962–1972

Introducing the public to the adverse effects of pesticides in 1962, Rachel Carson's *Silent Spring* began with a "Fable for Tomorrow," calling on the reader to envision a place in which "a shadow of death" hung heavy. Unexplainable sicknesses and death plagued people and livestock living in the area, baffling experts who tried to identify the cause: "No witchcraft, no enemy action had silenced the rebirth of new life in this stricken world. The people had done it to themselves."[1] The depiction of mysterious maladies in this fictional town laid the foundation for the argument that Carson constructed in subsequent chapters. She asserted that human desires to exert absolute control over nature through the wanton use of agricultural chemicals posed severe risks to human and environmental health.

Carson synthesized available scientific data and converted it into language understandable to the lay public. Detailed accounts of declining bird populations and fish stocks supported her contention that powerful pesticides, particularly chlorinated hydrocarbons like DDT, indiscriminately killed both target and nontarget species.[2] These chemicals break down slowly, accumulating over time in the bodies of animals and humans, and consequently pass up the food chain from plants to herbivores to carnivores. Carson warned that the danger extended beyond the animal kingdom and raised the threat of chronic disease in humans.[3] She predicted that one in four persons might ultimately be afflicted with some form of cancer if the use of chlorinated hydrocarbons and other chemical carcinogens continued at current rates.[4] Evidence showing the threats that persistent pesticides posed to human health so alarmed Carson that she expanded her discussion from a single chapter, as originally planned, to four.[5]

Despite this expanded coverage, Carson bore some criticism in subsequent years for not sufficiently addressing human health concerns. Anthropologist Devon Peña asserts that the book has "curious silences," surmising that "Carson's white and privileged middle-class background" made her blind to the "plight of the largely Mexican-origin agricultural workforce" and their "emergent struggles against pesticide exposure and associated health problems."[6] Such criticism is misplaced, however, because little data existed on the health risks faced by that population at the time of publication. Historian Linda Nash states that farmworkers' migratory lifestyle made tracking work-related illnesses and diseases difficult for public health officials in the 1950s and 1960s, adding that the "ability, or perhaps inability . . . to produce dependable knowledge about pesticide poisoning was conditioned by political and intellectual factors" that made investigators reluctant to challenge the power of agricultural interests.[7] Despite the scarcity of scientific information, Carson noted that accumulations of DDT in agricultural workers' bodies were two to three times higher than the average amount for the rest of the population. *Silent Spring* also discussed the effects of less persistent, but more acutely toxic organophosphate chemicals on farmworkers.[8] Historian Frederick Davis similarly recognizes the breadth of concern behind the warning in *Silent Spring*: "Carson believed that the organophosphates posed an equivalent, if not greater, risk to wildlife and humans than chlorinated hydrocarbons" and, hence, that she advocated for greater reliance on safer biological forms of pest control.[9] Carson could not reference farmworker campaigns for pesticide reform, because her death in 1964 preceded those efforts.

The book addressed a wide range of problems related to pesticides, because Carson intended it to be a clarion call for citizens to engage the issue. She believed that the public had a right to help decide how and to what extent the chemicals were applied to farms, suburban neighborhoods, and public lands, because the effects of chlorinated hydrocarbons were so far-reaching and lasting. Making reference to a Robert Frost poem, Carson told readers that they had approached a branch in the road; one way was a deceptively easy path that promised progress but ended in disaster, the other was a less traveled route that if followed would reach a sustainable future. She charged the reader with the task of deciding how to proceed as a society.[10] Just as her contemporary Barry Commoner believed that scientists had an "involuntary responsibility" to convey relevant scientific information to the public in a comprehensible and nonpartisan manner, Carson wanted to better equip the public with the knowledge necessary to make informed choices about pesticides.[11] Members of this science information movement shared a deep concern for humanity and the world, though as historian Michael Egan states, "that activism was obscured by the mantle of objectivity, which produced a far more subtle and convincing line of rhetoric."[12] Their efforts to disseminate knowledge fostered public debate about political decisions that carried potentially serious consequences for humans and the environment. Some citizens proceeded to engage in efforts to change public policy, including participating in newly organized campaigns to end the use of DDT.[13] Beginning in the mid-1960s, both farmworker groups and environmental organizations initiated pesticide reform efforts that fused data made available by concerned scientists with personal observations and experiences. The developing movements shared a common concern about the effects of DDT on human health, but their approaches to the problem varied. Still, the groups found opportunities for collaboration, particularly when mounting legal challenges.

The National Farm Workers Association and Farmworker Health

Social justice activist Fred Ross walked the unpaved roads of San Jose's barrio Sal Si Puedes in June 1952 in hopes of recruiting locals into the Community Service Organization (CSO). Three weeks of effort yielded little reward. Then a referral to a young man named Cesar Chavez changed his fortune. The gamut of issues discussed by the two included environmental contamination, with some conversation about a nearby polluted creek causing sores to develop on neighborhood children when it overran its banks.[14] The meeting spurred Chavez to action. He soon began working for CSO, registering voters in the community before expanding his range outward to other towns and cities in northern California.[15] He stayed with the organization for ten years, eventually quitting in March 1962 with the goal of organizing California farmworkers.

Chavez recruited Gil Padilla and Dolores Huerta to assist him in launching the Farm Workers Association, which eventually evolved into the National Farm Worker Association (NFWA).[16] They adopted the strategies of the CSO and spent countless hours going door to door in town after town to enlist farmworkers' support.[17] A new farmworker newspaper, *El Malcriado* ("problem child" in English), began to chronicle and promote positive developments involving the organization, using a humorous cast of caricatures that included greedy growers, corrupt politicians, shady labor contractors, and simple but hard-working farmworkers.[18] NFWA counted twelve hundred members by August 1965 and *El Malcriado* had three thousand subscribers.[19] Despite the notable gains, Chavez felt the group still lacked the strength necessary to confront growers.[20] Events beyond his control, however, would soon draw the NFWA into a labor dispute.

Filipino workers associated with the American Federation of Labor (AFL)–affiliated Agricultural Workers Organizing Committee (AWOC) initiated a sit-down strike in September, demanding wage improvements in nine Delano labor camps. Chavez found himself in an uncomfortable position. His organization lacked a strike fund to support a prolonged action, but he knew that many members were anxious to join the effort and that the strike had a greater potential for failure if the NFWA did not participate.[21] Organization officers decided to put the issue before the members and the overwhelming majority voted to strike. The NFWA adopted AWOC demands and added one. They went on strike not just for wages, but for recognition as a union as well; recognition that farmworkers' organizations had long been denied. Sociologist and former NFWA organizer Marshall Ganz recalls that this was an important addendum because it cast the strike in a different light than other labor conflicts, reminding potential supporters that farmworkers had to fight for even the most basic protections.[22]

Though the strike developed as a joint effort, the two organizations employed different philosophies in its prosecution. The backing of the AFL enabled AWOC to carry out a traditional labor protest of stationary pickets.[23] The NFWA proved to be more innovative, in part because their scarce resources demanded it. Organizers marshaled public support by casting the story in the moral terms of an oppressed group seeking rights long denied.[24] An early editorial in *El Malcriado* made a direct comparison to Rosa Parks and the Montgomery bus boycott, implying that the Delano strike would act as a similar sort of catalyst in the Mexican American movement for justice and equality. It asserted that "the farm workers association is a 'movement' more than a 'union' . . . and it will not be over until the farm worker has the equality of a living wage and decent treatment."[25] The NFWA appealed to religious, student, and civil rights groups, inviting delegations to view the plight of farmworkers firsthand. Visitors carried the stories home and built support for *la causa*.[26]

Outside volunteers helped develop tactics, infusing the movement with new ideas and broadening its appeal. Chavez embraced the philosophy of nonviolence and called upon civil rights veterans from the Congress of Racial Equality and the Student Nonviolent Coordinating Committee to share their experiential knowledge with strikers.[27] These volunteers expanded networks of communication and influenced the decision to engage in a consumer boycott of growers' products, both of which proved invaluable to NFWA efforts.[28] Recognizing the value of this collaboration, Chavez said: "If we were nothing but farm workers in the Union now, just Mexican farm workers, we'd only have about 30 percent of all the ideas that we have. There would be no cross-fertilization, no growing. It's beautiful to work with other groups, other ideas, and other customs."[29] Marshall Ganz argues that this diversity proved key to the success of the NFWA (and the subsequent United Farm Workers), because "the links of the UFW leaders to the worlds of the farm workers, churches, students, unions and others gave them far more—and far quicker—access to salient knowledge" than any of the previous or contemporaneous organizing efforts in the fields.[30]

As the number and diversity of organizers grew, so did the issues addressed by the group. The NFWA deemed health and welfare issues important before the strike and continued to emphasize them even though its initial demands addressed only wages and recognition. Volunteer nurse

Peggy McGivern established a part-time medical clinic to provide free care to farmworkers who could not afford doctors' fees.[31] Chavez, who had previously expressed concern about contaminated water in Sal Si Puedes, wanted to address the poor sanitation in labor camps and in the fields.[32] The 1966 "Plan of Delano," a manifesto published by *El Malcriado* that outlined farmworkers' grievances, listed suffering from "sickness" and "subhuman living conditions" in the same context as "starvation wages."[33] Chavez charged that "disease-ridden camps, filthy housing, dangerous and inadequate transportation, inadequate or no medical facilities . . . and a host of other evils" were the products of a unjust farm labor system and of public policy that had denied farmworkers the same rights and protections as workers in other sectors of the economy, implying that the issues were all legitimate concerns to be addressed by the farmworkers' movement.[34] Issues relating to pesticides did not enter the discourse during this early period.[35] That would change in the years following as the adverse effects of agricultural chemicals on farmworker health became a central concern of the movement.

Farmworkers long associated some illnesses with exposure to pesticides in the fields; however, the extension of health concerns addressed by NFWA from issues of sanitation to risks posed by agricultural chemicals did not happen immediately. Farmworkers in the 1950s connected eye irritation, swelling around the mouth, and other health problems to the spraying of fields.[36] Nonetheless, the first mention of agricultural chemicals adversely affecting the health of farmworker families appeared in *El Malcriado* in January 1967. The article discussed a letter sent by the City of Delano to residents warning that fertilizer chemicals had made tap water unsafe for babies. Much of the article focused on the burdensome cost of buying bottled water to safeguard children's health.[37] No suggestion about reducing the use of agricultural chemicals appeared in the text.

Several notable developments occurred within the farmworker movement prior to the incorporation of pesticides into the campaign. Pressure from an economic boycott of Schenley Industries' products, coupled with the media buzz generated by a 240-mile mass march up the Central Valley to Sacramento, brought the first of the Delano growers to the bargaining table in 1966. This convinced the AFL that it would be wise to merge AWOC with Chavez's organization, thereby establishing the United Farm Workers Organizing Committee.[38] A less newsworthy but nonetheless significant event happened amidst these other important achievements: nurse practitioner Marion Moses began to work full time for UFWOC.[39]

Marion Moses' burgeoning interest in pesticide-related health threats helped move the issue to the forefront of union concerns. Starting in 1966, she became acutely aware of the multitude of health problems that farm-worker families encountered.[40] These observations stayed with her as she moved to the position of boycott organizer in New York City during the following year and began to conduct research on pesticides during her spare time. After she communicated her developing interest to Chavez and explained that it was a time-intensive endeavor, he assented to her research plan in the summer of 1968.[41]

Moses developed a network of contacts that helped her accumulate scientific information about the health risks associated with agricultural chemicals and consulted *Silent Spring* (as well as, later, *Since Silent Spring*, a book authored by Audubon Society's Frank Graham Jr. in 1970).[42] She contacted the Scientific Institute for Public Information, co-founded and presided over by Barry Commoner. Several of the scientists, includ-ing Commoner, had already taken an interest in the effects of nitrates on infant health.[43] They arranged for tests to be done on Delano's water supply and published a report on its contamination in the organization's magazine *Environment*, asserting that "much of California's population, and particularly its poorest members, will be exposed to a threat whose magnitude we do not yet know."[44] The institute referred Moses to Charles Wurster, a marine biologist at Stony Brook University and co-founder of Environmental Defense Fund.[45] Wurster had researched the effects of DDT on Long Island's bird populations during his postdoctoral research and had concluded that the costs of usage far outstripped the benefits. The concerned scientist evolved into an environmental activist committed to the fight against DDT.[46]

While Moses developed contacts and collected pesticide information, UFWOC attorney Jerry Cohen tried to ascertain the names of chemicals and volume used on Delano fields. Former farmworker and UFWOC worker Jessica Govea pressed the legal department to devote resources to identifying pesticide health risks after encountering three women in the Farm Worker Service Center whom she suspected of suffering from pesticide poisoning.[47] Cohen responded, submitting a request to the Kern County Agricultural Commissioner for spray application records. The office refused him the information and then reportedly contacted the company that applied the pesticides, suggesting that it obtain an injunction to prevent the release of records.[48] The Superior Court issued an injunction two days later that prohibited Cohen from accessing pesticide permits, applicator reports, and county officials' pest control reports.[49]

UFWOC attorney David Averbuck attempted a slightly different approach when he entered the Riverside County Agricultural Commissioner's office with Amalia Uribe, a nineteen-year-old grape worker who suffered blurred vision, itchy eyes, and nausea when working in the vineyards. Uribe and other afflicted farmworkers suspected that a chemical powder used by the grower caused the maladies. Previous complaints to the grower had gone unaddressed and no medical attention was provided to the distressed workers. Uribe filed a request for information, stating that the records were needed for her physician to perform a cholinesterase base line test that would determine if her health had been adversely affected by exposure to pesticides. Commissioner Robert Howie refused to release the information just as the Kern County Agricultural Commissioner had done.[50] Agricultural commissioners in Fresno and Tulare Counties also blocked access to pesticide data. The obstructions raised by the commissioners and court heightened the attorneys' curiosity about the content of the closed records.[51]

When UFWOC initiated legal action in attempt to overturn the injunctions, the agricultural commissioners and commercial pesticide applicators argued that the records should remain sealed because they contained trade secrets that had been provided to the county commissions in confidence that they would not be shared. UFWOC countered the claim with the testimony of Kyle Van Den Bosch, a University of California Berkeley scientist who investigated the effects of pesticides on people and the environment. He maintained that access to the information was essential to the study of integrated pest management and should be made public.[52] The Superior Court would not be swayed. Judge George A. Brown held that "requiring the disclosure of this information would seriously hamper the essential cooperation existing between all segments of the pesticide industry and the farmers on the one hand and with the commissioners on the other."[53] David Averbuck successfully appealed the Uribe decision to the California Appellate Court, but the judge did not render the verdict until 1971.[54] The records remained sealed from the public until that time, making the cooperation of concerned scientists even more valuable.

Growth and Change in the Green Movement

Reflecting back on the lawsuits, David Averbuck remembered that there was "a great deal of sharing going on by people who were involved in different cases" and that it "was very common at the time if we had a certain kind of problem" to seek assistance from other groups concerned about pesticides. He specifically mentioned attorney Victor Yannacone Jr. and the organization he co-founded in 1967, the Environmental Defense Fund.[55] The EDF made an easy ally for UFWOC in its pesticide-related lawsuits. Whereas more established and older conservation organizations, like the Sierra Club and the Audubon Society, favored efforts to influence the executive and legislative branches of government, EDF pursued an aggressive strategy in the courts.

The NAACP's Legal Defense Fund provided inspiration for the Environmental Defense Fund in both name and strategy.[56] Before co-founding the organization whose unofficial motto was "Sue the Bastards," Yannacone had represented the NAACP for nine years.[57] The civil rights movement had utilized the courts to great effect in cases like *Brown v. Board of Education* and the EDF envisioned lawsuits playing a similar role in forwarding environmental protection. Charles Wurster stated that the "one asset" they had in the early days was an idea: "EDF would marry science and law to defend the environment in the courts. . . . To influence the legislative or executive branches of government often requires large numbers of votes or dollars, and we had neither. The judiciary seemed less influenced by those traditional pressures. Perhaps the judges would more readily listen to a handful of scientists if their plea was valid."[58] From its beginning, EDF embodied a concern for both environmental and human health.

Yannacone made the transition to environmental issues when he initiated a class action lawsuit against the Suffolk County Mosquito Control Commission to stop the spraying of DDT on Long Island in 1966. He contacted Brookhaven Town Natural Resources Committee, a grassroots organization that had formed in 1965 to address the spoliation of the local environment, for help in the case. Yannacone hoped to draw upon the expertise of scientists from SUNY Stony Brook and Brookhaven National Laboratory who attended the group's monthly meetings.[59] The recruited scientists compiled scientific evidence, wrote affidavits, and prepared charts, graphs, and photos to illustrate arguments. Yannacone convinced the judge to issue a temporary injunction against spraying DDT; and the county legislature prohibited usage shortly thereafter.[60]

The decision marked the entrance of the EDF onto the national scene. Following the limited yet significant victory, requests for assistance from other groups interested in environmental litigation poured into the small law office. Yannacone and four members of the Brookhaven group decided to incorporate as the Environmental Defense Fund in 1967, committing themselves to a future of casework on national environmental issues.[61] Charles Wurster worked to secure promises from notable scientists to give testimony without a consultation fee as the EDF prepared to sue over the use of chlorinated hydrocarbons in other states. Three hundred scientists from a variety of different disciplines and specializations volunteered their expertise to the organization's Scientists Advisory Committee.[62] The group then launched cases against DDT in Michigan and Wisconsin. The presiding judge in Wisconsin effectively banned the compound, ruling that it was an uncontrollable pollutant that violated the state's water law.[63]

The EDF predicated the arguments in these cases on the unnecessary harm caused to the environment, but the range of scientific expertise on its advisory committee made it equally capable of bringing a suit based on DDT's adverse effects on human health. Charles Wurster and the EDF viewed environmental problems as "inherently interdisciplinary" and arranged to have different experts speak to the problems of DDT within the context of their specializations. Wurster likened the presentation of scientific testimony in a case to "building a wall, one brick at a time" so as to foster an understanding of "DDT proponents as limited, narrow specialists unable to grasp the total environmental picture."[64] Yannacone employed this strategy in Wisconsin, calling on sixteen respected scientists to testify in the case.[65] The flexibility and breadth of scope on the Scientists Advisory Committee enabled the EDF to bring suits or testify in cases either on environmental grounds or on the basis that DDT posed a significant threat to human health. The organization's strength in science and its dedication to using the courts as a vehicle of reform made it a useful ally of UFWOC in certain legal situations.

The mission, structure, and character of the EDF aligned fairly well with UFWOC's pesticide interests. Some older conservation organizations, in contrast, had missions and histories that made it more difficult for them to address emerging pollution and social justice concerns. Since the EDF was a young organization, it had the luxury of defining its mission in the context of post–World War II environmental and social justice issues. The founders expressed their intent to facilitate a "closer working tie between science, law, and government" to foster better decision making in public policy that affected human welfare.[66] This mission enabled the group to address concerns that affected the natural or urban environment without deviating from their stated purpose. Both the Sierra Club and National Audubon Society had narrower fields of interest centered on the preservation of flora and fauna in the natural environment. When the National Association of Audubon Societies for the Protection of Wild Birds and Animals was formed in 1905, for instance, it declared that "the object of this organization is to be a barrier between wild birds and animals and a very large unthinking class."[67] The traditional concentrated focus on the preservation of nature fostered an organizational inertia that inhibited these groups from taking on many urban, suburban, and agricultural issues that emerged in the post–World War II era.

Older conservation organizations also suffered from an identity crisis in the late 1960s as their size and character changed dramatically. The Sierra Club counted 16,000 members in 1960 and over 114,000 in 1970. The National Audubon Society climbed from 36,000 members in 1965 to 60,000 two years later.[68] This influx of new members created some tension within the groups. Frank Graham Jr. recalls that "like penitents flocking to a church in times of pestilence, the newcomers were welcome, but graybeards among the faithful realized the congregation would inevitably undergo drastic changes in leadership."[69] Most Audubon members in attendance at the 1967 convention supported the creation of an "environmental defense fund"; however, the board of directors delayed the action, in part because some of them were affiliated with chemical companies.[70] The Sierra Club suffered similar growing pains. As executive director David Brower became increasingly active in environmental protection campaigns, a strong contingent on the board of directors wished to reverse the group's growing prominence as a force in conservation politics and return to being an organization that focused more on wilderness outings and mountaineering than on politics.[71] These struggles made older conservation organizations slower to respond to modern environmental problems.

Signs of organizational change did appear as the Sierra Club persevered through the period that president Edgar Wayburn characterized as "the most turbulent years in our history."[72] Wayburn touted the importance of involving the club in the "critical fight for man's total environment" in 1968, although major projects still centered on the protection and enlargement of national parks and other natural areas.[73] Conservation director Michael McCloskey remarked in 1969 that as "new technological assaults spread across America, we keep learning how many more things we must defend."[74] The club soon adopted a policy regarding waste disposal and the *Sierra Club Bulletin* began publishing short articles about pollution and industrial waste.[75] These small changes signaled a growing willingness to tackle new challenges.

Yet, in critiquing the environmental movement, Laura Pulido intimates that the Sierra Club showed a disinterest in pesticides, stating that some members actively supported the continued use of DDT. Her primary source for this assertion is an article penned by chemical company engineer and one-time club member Thomas Jukes.[76] He opposed action on DDT, asserting that the chemical was the unfortunate victim of an unfounded public hysteria caused by "'environmentalist propaganda."[77] Jukes had previously founded the New York chapter of the Sierra Club and at one time carried a lifetime membership in the organization. However, his opinions on pesticides cannot be interpreted as representative of the group. In fact, he quit the organization and relinquished his lifetime membership because he so vehemently disagreed with Sierra Club's call for a DDT ban.[78] Jukes later brought a libel suit against the Audubon Society after it suggested that he was a "paid liar" for the pesticide industry.[79] His estrangement from the Sierra Club and his suit against the Audubon Society demonstrate that Jukes's opinions were not representative of mainstream environmental organizations' stance on DDT.

The opposition of the Sierra Club and the Audubon Society to DDT usage developed over a period of years. Despite the lag in devoting resources to address modern environmental problems, both organizations voiced concern about the indiscriminate use of DDT earlier in the decade. The Sierra Club objected to the use of chlorinated hydrocarbons on private and public lands in 1965 because of the damage done to flora and fauna, and the Audubon Society expressed support for a ban on DDT usage two years later.[80] Then as more scientific information became available about the chemical's environmental and human health effects, the two storied giants of the conservation movement joined with the West Michigan Environmental Action Council and the Environmental Defense Fund in bringing a suit to halt the use of DDT in the closing days of 1969.[81]

Eliminating the Use of DDT

The Sierra Club, the Audubon Society, and the EDF all supported a DDT ban by the time UFWOC chose to address the issue, but it was the EDF's grounding in science and its aggressive plan for legal action that presented the best opportunity for collaboration with the union. However, since UFWOC did not put much faith in the courts or the legislature as vehicles for reform, cooperative work between the groups remained relatively minimal. The fleeting nature of the cooperation does not diminish its significance, however. The EDF's relationship with local environmental groups often proved to be equally short. Its partnership with the Citizens Natural Resources Association in the Wisconsin DDT trial, for example, lasted only for the duration of the case.

UFWOC's distrust of local and state governments is reflected in an interview Cesar Chavez gave shortly after his legal team was denied access to the Delano County Agricultural Commissioner's records. He maintained: "[T]here isn't a judge within a hundred miles of here who will rule in our favor. Then you have the police, the school boards, the water district, all the way up. They try to choke you off. . . . The moment you raise your picket sign your rights as a citizen are no longer secure."[82] UFWOC, instead, pursued a union contract believing that it provided the best possible protection to farmworkers. Dolores Huerta maintained the "only way that you can be sure that the so called laws are administered . . . is when you have somebody right there on the ranch . . . somebody that has the protection of a union contract to make sure these things are carried out."[83] Efforts, therefore, concentrated on pressuring more growers to sign collective bargaining agreements replete with health and safety provisions.

When UFWOC decided to address pesticide-related issues, the focus had shifted from Schenley Industries and Perilli-Minetti, which produced wine grapes, to growers who produced table grapes. The shift occurred in August 1967 with a strike on Giumarra Vineyards.[84] Table grapes proved tougher to boycott than Schenley or Perilli-Minetti products. Customers could easily identify which wines to avoid, but they had difficulty finding out the origin of table grapes. UFWOC researchers tried to track shipments, but other growers let Giumarra use their labels to confound organizers' efforts. Economic boycotts had played a central role in the farmworkers' campaign and Chavez did not want to abandon the strategy. He believed it to be so critical to the success of the movement, in fact, that he planned to spend three-quarters of his time on related activities.[85] UFWOC resolved the problems of tracking, identification, and growers' trickery by expanding the boycott to all California table grapes. This made it easier for consumers to participate.[86]

A farmworker who joined UFWOC staffers at a strategizing session suggested addressing pesticides in the boycott effort.[87] Farmworkers had a growing awareness about the health hazards of exposure, in part because staffers shared with them the information gathered from concerned scientists. Flyers printed in Spanish and English warned about the toxicity of DDT, aldrin, dieldrin, parathion, sevin, TEPP, and thiodan, and outlined symptoms of pesticide poisoning. Printed material also advised finding out how recently a field had been sprayed before entering it, and instructed farmworkers never to permit a ground rig or crop duster to douse them with chemicals.[88] Crop dusters, nonetheless, regularly buzzed the vineyards and dropped their loads with little regard for the people below.[89] Farmworkers urged that the issue be addressed, so as not to become "guinea pigs" for growers who used DDT "in reckless disregard of its effects on human life and the environment."[90] Their concern about pesticides also resonated with the public.

UFWOC incorporated the issue of pesticides into the table grape boycott at an opportune time when diverse groups of people shared an interest in the environment, even if environmental issues were not their primary concern. Historian Adam Rome argues that "no single constituency drove the environmental movement," maintaining that many liberals, women, and students critical of the status quo developed concerns during the decade and contributed to the movement's rise.[91] UFWOC targeted the same demographics for support. The boycott, in particular, needed to appeal to women who made decisions about food and family consumption while shopping. Rome asserts that many of the women activists in the 1960s described themselves as housewives and viewed their interest in environmental issues as a natural extension of their efforts to protect their children and families.[92] UFWOC framed the pesticide issue in a way that resonated with this type of woman.

It introduced pesticide issues, particularly relating to DDT, into the table grape boycott, using arguments about the shared risk of exposure to persistent pesticides as a means to build a bridge to consumers and encourage participation. UFWOC instructed its associates in cities around the nation to read circulated pesticide literature packets, look for relevant scientific information on their own, and seriously consider reading *Silent Spring* to give them a solid background on the subject.[93] Marion Moses prepared an educational slide presentation for use by boycott coordinators that combined recent scientific findings with anecdotes of pesticide poisonings as it critiqued regulatory inaction and advocated for adoption of the precautionary principle which would better protect public health by lowering the threshold for a regulatory response.[94] Volunteers told shoppers that DDT could not be washed from produce, that scientists linked the chemical to cancer in test mice, and that accumulations of the compound in the breast milk of nursing mothers were so elevated that the milk would be unlawful to sell had it come from a cow.[95] The basic message communicated that government agencies responsible for protecting public health had failed to do so, putting both farmworkers and the public at risk; but a union contract would enable UFWOC to act as a watchdog, protecting farmworkers and consumers alike.[96]

The issue of pesticides quickly moved to the fore of UFWOC's campaign. Chavez wrote a letter to table grape growers and their representative organizations in January 1969 requesting that if the growers would not meet with the union to discuss a collective bargaining agreement that they at least meet to discuss the use and control of pesticides, an issue that he stated had become the union's primary concern. He wrote: "We will not tolerate the systematic poisoning of our people. Even if we cannot get together on other problems, we will be damned—and we should be—if we will permit human beings to sustain permanent damage to their health from economic poisons."[97] Growers initially ignored the request, but economic pressure from the boycott succeeded in bringing ten of them to the bargaining table in June.[98] They offered the union a contract in exchange for a pledge of silence on pesticide-related issues.[99] UFWOC, however, sought to foster an industrial democracy in the fields that gave farmworkers some control over the chemicals to which they would be exposed. Contracts renegotiated with Perelli-Minetti in September 1969, for instance, provided workers greater control over field conditions by establishing a health and safety committee composed of an equal number of company and field crew representatives.[100] The talks with the ten growers broke down over this issue and the boycott and the warnings to consumers about pesticides continued.

Grocery stores, growers, and some members of government decried the emphasis on pesticides and health as unfounded scare tactics designed to prop up a failing union effort; so UFWOC called on its staffers to run laboratory tests for pesticide residues on supermarket grapes.[101] Peggy McGivern bought a bunch that had DDT residue registered at .0003 and .004 parts per million.[102] Attorney Jerry Cohen caused a stir at the Subcommittee on Migratory Labor hearings when he introduced a lab report that showed aldrin on grapes at 180 times the legally permissible level.[103] The grower pledged that the pesticide had not been used on the crop, which prompted California Senator George Murphy to enter the fray. He contended that the union's interest in pesticides was disingenuous, charging that it wanted only to "harass the industry" and had engaged in a "vicious type of deceit" by tampering with the tested grapes.[104] In fact, UFWOC had not engaged in any unscrupulous behavior; rather, the laboratory tests were not sophisticated enough to differentiate between aldrin and sulfur. This revelation raised further questions about the adequacy and accuracy of government pesticide monitoring.[105] The legal department also drafted a sample consumer lawsuit so that it would be easy for consumers to sue grocery stores and growers for selling an adulterated food "made defective by the presence of pesticide, insecticide, and herbicide residue." UFWOC suggested that nursing mothers or mothers who wanted to nurse but feared passing DDT to their children would make the best plaintiffs in the citizen suits.[106]

California Rural Legal Assistance (CRLA) followed the UFWOC lead, partnered with the EDF to petition the FDA in 1969 to set a zero tolerance level for DDT on food. The organizations represented five parents of minor children and one expectant mother. All of the parents had low incomes and three of the mothers breastfed their children. The parents did not know the amount of DDT used in agricultural production; however, they knew that growers used the chemical on table grapes because of the ongoing boycott. The petition stated the parents "have a deep concern for the welfare of their children, whose welfare appears to be seriously threatened by the omnipresent health hazard posed by the continued contamination of the American food supply with DDT." It noted that poor persons' diet typically caused them to have greater accumulations of DDT within their bodies and that DDT concentrated in mother's breast milk. Consequently, the World Health Organization estimated that nursing babies' daily intake of DDT was more than twice the maximum recommended amount. Despite the probability that nursing would likely cause their children to consume unhealthful levels of DDT, the mothers shared a "very natural, deep and intense desire to breast-feed their children so as to establish the strong emotional bond and to provide the, otherwise, most nutritious food available to their infants."[107] The argument concluded that the pervasiveness and persistence of DDT made it impossible for mothers to protect their children from contaminated foodstuffs.

The EDF and CRLA referenced the 1959 Delaney Clause of the Food and Drug Act, which barred any food containing an additive found to be carcinogenic in animals from being sold. Scientific findings showed that DDT was an animal carcinogen and that it was very likely to pose the same threat to humans. From the premise that the pesticide was a food additive, the EDF and CRLA argued that the Delaney Clause prohibited any food with DDT residues from being sold to consumers. Since the compound could not easily be removed from raw or processed food, zero tolerance would effectively ban use of the chemical in agriculture.[108]

The EDF also joined the Sierra Club, the Audubon Society, and the West Michigan Environmental Action Council to petition the secretary of agriculture to cancel the registration of DDT as a pesticide, thereby banning its use in agriculture. UFWOC, United Auto Workers, and the Izaak Walton League of America filed statements of support. A press conference announced the joint action with Charles Wurster fielding technical questions while flanked by representatives from the supporting organizations.[109] The groups presented evidence that DDT damaged the environment and caused cancer in test animals, and reported that human cancer victims had more than twice the accumulation of DDT in their bodies than victims of accidental death.[110] By year's end, the USDA pledged to end the use of DDT in residential areas, while the Department of Health, Education, and Welfare set a two-year phase-out goal for use on food crops. The petitioners did not find either response satisfying and looked to the courts for a full ban.[111]

The lawsuits solely targeted DDT and focused most heavily on the detrimental effects to the environment for practical reasons. Charles Wurster reasoned that DDT should be targeted first because it was the most widely used pesticide and its harmfulness was well substantiated. He maintained that it would be difficult to seek a broader ban on chlorinated hydrocarbons when the bulk of scientific evidence was concentrated on one compound; however, if successful, the precedent set would make halting the use of other dangerous pesticides easier. Wurster also asserted that it would be wiser to emphasize the threat to the environment rather than the harm caused to humans when making the case: the evidence of damage done to vertebrate and useful invertebrate animals was very strong, whereas evidence for adverse effects of DDT on humans was suggestive but weaker.[112] Later critics of the environmental movement have used this case to suggest that organizations like the EDF care more about wildlife than human welfare. Really it was an interest in constructing the strongest argument for a ban that underlay the emphasis on threats to nonhuman species in the case.

As the legal action continued, growers buckled to the pressure of the boycott. On July 29, 1970, twenty-six grape growers gathered at UFWOC's Forty Acres headquarters near Delano to sign contracts with the union containing health and safety provisions.[113] The content was premised on the organization's "Consumer and Worker Protection Clause," the preamble of which interwove concerns about human health and environment. It read:

> The Company and the Union recognize the need to supply consumers with healthy grapes picked and handled under the most clean, sanitary and healthful conditions possible. Furthermore, the Company and the Union recognize the need to conserve our natural resources and protect all forms

of life from the serious dangers and damages caused by the improvident use of economic poison. In the hope of taking progressive steps to protect the health of the farm workers and consumers throughout the world and conserving for all of mankind the benefits of our natural resources and surroundings, the Company and the Union agree as follows.[114]

The new agreements prohibited contracted growers from using the chlorinated hydrocarbons: DDT, aldrin, dieldrin, and endrin. The organophosphates parathion and TEPP could not be applied to the fields either. Additionally, the contracts provided farmworkers a means to restrict the usage of other harmful pesticides in the future. Each grower agreed to the establishment of a Health and Safety Committee that would have access to pesticide records and would help formulate rules and practices to minimize risk to workers. The committees would also establish safe reentry times for recently sprayed fields.[115] For the duration of the contracts, an industrial democracy existed to some extent in the fields, which thereby enabled UFWOC to act in its desired role of watchdog for both farmworkers and the public.

The environmental groups' efforts to win a national ban on DDT continued after UFWOC had barred its usage on contracted fields. In October 1970, Congress created the Environmental Protection Agency (EPA) and entrusted it with the responsibility of registering and regulating pesticides, duties previously performed by the USDA. Despite the change, the EPA initially proved nearly as reluctant to ban the compound, and the EDF brought suit again. The Consolidated DDT Hearing that followed had 125 expert witnesses and lasted eighty days. Finally, in June 1972, EPA Administrator William Ruckelshaus issued an order to ban nearly all uses of DDT in the six months following.[116]

Public perception of DDT changed markedly in the short span of ten years. The chemical that emerged from World War II as a celebrated miracle worker entered the 1970s under attack from individuals and groups spanning the social and political spectrum. Rachel Carson catalyzed the shift in public opinion with the publication of *Silent Spring,* which consolidated diffuse and complex scientific information into a concise compendium that was accessible to the public. The book's message resonated with diverse groups of people since the problems posed by persistent pesticides touched everyone's lives: from birdwatchers to farmworkers to nursing mothers to everyday consumers. Carson, like other concerned scientists of her day, feared the unintended consequences of technological development and wanted not just to democratize access to information, but to democratize decision making by encouraging citizen involvement in issues that potentially threatened their health and welfare.

Silent Spring appeared on shelves at the dawn of a decade defined by dynamic progressive social movements. Rights-based struggles for equality, justice, access to information, free speech, consumer protection, and a healthful environment grew in size and influence through the 1960s. Though these movements had a wide range of interests, activists within one cause sometimes drew inspiration and resources from organizations in another. Concerns about conservation, human health, and social justice overlapped. This presented an opportunity for farmworkers, consumers, and environmentalists to collaborate to solve interconnected problems posed by pesticides.

Environmental organizations and UFWOC used the information garnered from concerned scientists to complement their own observations of the deleterious effects of pesticides, using scientific expertise to strengthen arguments for a ban on DDT. Entomologist Kyle Van Den Bosch described the satisfaction felt when citizens and nongovernmental organizations answered Carson's call for engagement in decision making about pesticides, stating: "in happy union, we crashed into each other's arms . . . environmentalists needed an entomologist to help them in the pesticide controversy, and I, an entomologist, needed their resources, know-how, and political clout to support my entomo-radicalism."[117] But some organizations were better positioned to act than others. Traditional conservation groups transitioned somewhat slowly to the host of new environmental issues relating to human health and urban, industrial, and agricultural environments. New groups like the EDF embraced pollution, human health, and social justice concerns much faster. As a result the EDF proved most fit to collaborate with disparate interests, developing strategic alliances with scientists, lawyers, community organizations, and UFWOC in the late 1960s to prosecute the case against DDT in the courts.

The courts proved to be the venue where the greatest collaboration between UFWOC and environmental organizations occurred in the fight against DDT, in part because the different movements envisioned different solutions. Environmental groups committed substantial resources to working through the system toward a ban on the persistent pesticide. In contrast, based on a long history of negative experiences with government officials and agencies, farmworkers believed that the answer lay outside the traditional centers of power. UFWOC sought to democratize agricultural operations, making production procedures more transparent and giving farmworkers greater control over decisions that had the potential to affect human health. Occasionally the paths of environmentalists and farmworker advocates crossed when legal action was being taken, and the groups cooperated often in those situations.

The banning of DDT, first in UFWOC-contracted fields and then nationally, constituted a major achievement for the involved farmworker and environmental organizations, but it did not eliminate all of the pesticide threats. Dangerous persistent pesticides remained in use, as did a multitude of acutely toxic organophosphates. Concerned organizations continued to push for pesticide reform in the 1970s after the general use of DDT ceased. Some older conservation groups, like the Sierra Club, overcame their organizational inertia in this period and became more vocal proponents of pesticide reform.

4

Movements in Transition

Environmentalists, Farmworkers, and the Regulatory State, 1970–1976

Americans in towns and cities across the nation took part in the first Earth Day on April 22, 1970. They engaged in demonstrations, parades, teach-ins, cleanup activities, guerilla theater, and civil disobedience to alternately express their disapproval of practices that polluted the environment, call for a reduction in people's ecological footprint, and address problems with corrective action.[1] Proposed by Wisconsin Democratic Senator Gaylord Nelson and coordinated by student activist Denis Hayes and the new organization Environmental Action, events aimed to increase awareness about a range of environmental problems and serve notice that concern for the issues ranked high in the minds of many Americans.[2] Some critics suggested that "many activities were less real than symbolic, less ground breaking than jamboree," and wondered about the degree of backsliding that would occur as the actions wound down.[3] Nevertheless, the nearly twenty million participants in the day's activities demonstrated that the environmental movement was a growing force in American politics.[4]

Poor and minority communities responded to Earth Day with mixed emotions. Many people within these demographics harbored concern about urban environmental issues. The Chicago Freedom Movement maintained that African Americans were "tired of living in rat-infested slums" of the "cement reservation" and demanded in 1966 that the city clean streets in these neighborhoods and improve garbage collection services.[5] The Young Lords, a Puerto Rican organization in New York City modeled after the Black Panthers, launched a "garbage offensive" in 1969 that eventually forced the mayor to address sanitation service problems in Harlem.[6] Chicano activist and Earth Day organizer Arturo Sandoval led activists and news crews on a march through the streets of Albuquerque on Earth Day, believing that the day's events had the power "to make people understand that the kind of things that cause air pollution and water pollution are the same kind of things that cause poverty, that cause hunger in this country."[7] Yet not everyone rallied to the cause like Sandoval. A young Chicago black woman interviewed by an NBC newscaster stated that "the main reason that there weren't many blacks in the pollution marches today is the simple reason that we have too many problems. We got the problems with our homes. We don't have enough food. We can't get good jobs. The air, that's irrelevant to what we have to do."[8] Other people harbored fears that Earth Day was a conspiracy plotted by the "established order in this country to divert attention from the pressing problems of black people."[9] *El Malcriado* failed to mention Earth Day, although the UFWOC continued to picket against pesticides as it had done in the preceding weeks and months.[10]

Despite the skepticism that some individuals within poor and minority groups showed about the event, Sandoval and other event organizers employed a rhetoric intended to build bridges to other special interests and make the movement appealing to diverse groups of people. At a speaking engagement in Denver, Senator Nelson asserted that the environmentalism encompassed far more than the older form of conservationism. He maintained that the environment is "the rats in the ghetto. It is a hungry child in a land of affluence. It is 'public housing' that isn't worthy of the name. It is a problem whose existence is perpetuated by the expenditure of $25 billion a year on the war in Vietnam, instead of on our decaying, crowded, congested, polluted urban areas."[11] Environmental Action coordinators urged people and organizations within the movement to establish links with other groups by identifying common grievances, stating that the "alliances possible by organizing around environmental concerns stagger the mind" because pollution posed a threat to all people irrespective of economic standing or racial background.[12] Many environmentalists accepted these contentions and entered the 1970s thinking about a wide range of issues outside the traditional realm of conservation.

The Sierra Club addressed a wider range of subjects as it capitalized on the wellspring of public interest that was tapped by Earth Day. Club leaders felt the swell of enthusiasm for environmental causes in the months preceding. The club had shied away from demonstrations in the past, but it did not want to be bypassed by an event of such magnitude. It compiled a collection of essays into a volume entitled *Ecotactics* and authorized local chapters to coordinate Earth Day activities.[13] It also published *The Sierra Club Survival Songbook* in 1971, containing what the editors deemed to be the "best environmental songs in America today." Many of the selections fell well outside the scope of traditional conservationism and addressed matters like air and water pollution in urban areas, industrial pollution, and lead paint poisoning. The book included Don McLean's "Orphans of Wealth," a song criticizing affluent American society for turning a blind eye to the poor. It also featured Malvina Reynolds's "DDT on My Brain," which included a line about farmworkers suffering from the effects of exposure.[14] The Sierra Club did not necessarily address all of the included concerns equally. Yet their presence in the publication shows recognition of each as a matter that ought to be addressed. The growth in the Sierra Club's scope of interests paralleled the organization's growing acceptance of its place at the fore of the environmental movement.[15]

The breadth of the Sierra Club's political engagement expanded more than that of Chavez's United Farm Workers (UFW) or the EDF between 1970 and 1976. As it became a lobbying force, the club exerted its influence on public policy relating to pesticides. The EDF maintained its focus on using the courts as a vehicle for environmental protection, while the UFW continued to pursue more contracts with growers, believing that unionization would provide the best protection to farmworkers. With the greater engagement of the Sierra Club in pesticide politics, collaboration between environmentalists and the UFW increased between 1970 and 1976, though the cooperation between the groups proved to be less visible and less lasting than the cooperation UFW received from some religious and student organizations.

From DDT to Dieldrin and Beyond

The Environmental Defense Fund undertook efforts to halt the usage of two other chlorinated hydrocarbons, aldrin and dieldrin, while still working to ban DDT. Rachel Carson warned about the dangers of both chemicals in *Silent Spring,* noting that dieldrin tested five times as toxic as DDT if swallowed and forty times more toxic when absorbed through the skin.[16] Tests conducted by manufacturer Shell in 1968 showed that the chemicals were carcinogenic. Shell reported the results to the FDA the following year, but the agency took no action and did not share the findings with the public or other agencies. Senior FDA scientist O. Garth Fitzhugh reportedly withheld important information from the Mrak Commission, appointed to discuss a DDT ban, quipping: "I don't know why you should be so concerned about the carcinogenicity of DDT, you should see what we have on dieldrin."[17] He then refused to elaborate further, claiming that this was confidential information. The commission later reached the conclusion that aldrin and dieldrin were carcinogenic and should be banned, but it was the persistence of the EDF that forced the issue.[18]

The EDF first attempted to get the EPA to cancel all uses of aldrin and dieldrin in 1970, but the results of a two-year review process left most uses of the chemicals unaffected. It then filed a lawsuit in 1972 that compelled the agency to detail the risks and benefits of usage. A year-long cancellation hearing followed.[19] Growers' associations claimed that their members would suffer devastating losses without the chemicals, arguing that available alternatives failed to adequately protect crops or were cost-prohibitive.[20] They warned that the resultant decline in agricultural production would not only lead to domestic and international food shortages, but would negatively affect the United States' international trade standing by reducing available exports.[21] The EDF, conversely, presented scientific evidence on the compounds' hazards and attempted to demonstrate that growers had overstated their necessity. It introduced testimony from a

Nebraska farm manager who never used the pesticides, yet still produced comparable yields to those of other area growers. Attorneys also called upon a United Farm Workers organizer to testify.[22]

EDF attorney William Butler initially contacted the Migrant Services Foundation in Miami, because he had heard that "some of the few farm worker unions in Florida" had contracts prohibiting the use of the contested chemicals. He wrote: "Your clients are our clients in this matter, and it is our firm conviction their health, and even their lives, may be at stake."[23] It is unclear whether the migrant organization directed him to the UFW or if the EDF utilized a preexisting contact, but the two groups partnered again shortly thereafter. The UFW could offer valuable support to the case because of the pesticide clauses in its contracts. The uses of aldrin and dieldrin that Shell deemed critical for high-yield agricultural production included applications to orange groves, and the EDF wanted to show that orange production did not demand use of the chemicals.[24] The UFW had recently signed contracts with Coca Cola, makers of Minute Maid, covering forty thousand acres of Florida citrus groves.[25] The agreements, like those signed with table grape growers in California, prohibited the use of the two compounds.[26] The EDF hoped to undercut opposing arguments by showing that the groves still produced good yields after the pesticide provisions took effect.[27] UFW organizer Dianna Lyons testified that Coca Cola had agreed to halt usage of the chemicals and had not suffered a decline in product volume.[28] Lyons's testimony joined a host of others as the EDF built its case for the cancellation.

After considering all the evidence, the judge sided with the EDF and submitted his decision to EPA administrator Russell Train, who confirmed the decision on October 1, 1974, suspending registration because the chemicals exposed the public to an "imminent hazard." Shell appealed, arguing that the EPA lacked conclusive data and that benefits of use outweighed the associated risks. The appellate court held, however, that "when the subject is risk of cancer, convenience may be relevant but it does not weigh heavy in the scales," and maintained that it was sufficient to demonstrate the probability of harm.[29] Shell announced that it would stop manufacturing the chemicals in the United States in April 1975.[30] After years of effort, the EDF had successfully halted all use of aldrin and dieldrin in the United States.

Figure 4.1. Environmental Defense Fund co-founders Art Cooley, Charles Wurster, and Dennis Puleston stand outside the Riverside, Long Island courthouse in 1987. The confrontational "Sue the Bastard" strategy was first employed here in 1966. Photo by T. Charles Erickson. Courtesy of the Environmental Defense Fund.

The legal strategy worked, but it proved to be a slow approach. Cases took years to reach closure and only addressed one, or in this case two chemicals, at a time.[31] The increasing usage of the courts to limit the application of some agricultural chemicals coupled with heightened public concern about pesticides helped convince Congress in 1971 to consider new legislation to improve the regulatory framework.[32] Bills in the House and Senate sought to strengthen the inadequate 1947 Federal Insecticide, Fungicide, and Rodenticide Act, which functioned primarily as a labeling law to protect growers from dubious claims by pesticide manufacturers.[33] FIFRA did entrust the USDA with the responsibility of protecting the public from harm by agricultural chemicals. The USDA summarily ignored this component of the law though, refusing to cancel hazardous chemicals and registering some pesticides over protests from the Department of Health, Education, and Welfare. As Congress debated amending the law, the Senate Agriculture Committee tried to stall efforts.[34] When growers, industry, and their congressional allies came to the realization that changes to FIFRA would pass, the focus shifted from trying to stall the bills to trying to weaken them. They asserted that public fears about pesticides had little basis in fact, and warned that too stringent regulation would unnecessarily burden growers.[35]

Environmental organizations weighed in on the discussion, attempting to preserve strong environmental and human health protections in the new law. The Sierra Club's William Futrell lobbied for a citizen suit provision, contending that individuals deserved a hearing for their grievances when they felt that pesticides threatened their health and environment. He cited as evidence the role of the courts in banning DDT, stating that "without environmental lawsuits, it is doubtful if the agencies involved would ever have undertaken the examination of the role of DDT" in causing harm to humans and nontarget species.[36] Historian Pete Daniel's assessment of the Pesticide Regulation Division (PRD) of the USDA's Agricultural Research Service lends support to Futrell's contention. Daniel holds that "despite its crucial public health mission, the PRD operated behind closed doors, where a chorus of eager corporate registrants drowned out concerns for public safety."[37] The congressional Fountain Committee investigated the agency and similarly concluded that it had failed to fulfill its prescribed duty.[38] The EDF's

William Butler echoed the call for a citizen suit provision and added that human safety needed to be better protected, stating that applicators, farmers, farmworkers, and other persons coming into contact with pesticides or pesticide residues should be safeguarded. In regard to farmworkers, he maintained: "There is value in this instance of making explicit what probably is already implicit . . . that hazard to farm workers from pesticides is a subject of major concern in classifying and registering a pesticide."[39] Friends of the Earth, the Environmental Policy Center, and Defenders of Wildlife also supported an amendment to protect farmworkers and farmers.[40]

The passage of the Federal Environmental Pesticides Control Act in 1972 amended FIFRA, shifting the intent of the law from ensuring accurate labeling to protecting public health and the environment. Describing the importance of the change, Christopher Bosso states: "the pesticides subgovernment that so long had dominated the direction of policy was forced to compromise with those who did not share full faith in the pesticides paradigm."[41] Manufacturers had to present sufficient evidence of a product's safety and effectiveness to EPA when registering a pesticide. The agency then determined if the chemical could be used without significant adverse effects on people and nontarget species. Registrations only stayed valid for five years, after which reregistration with updated information was required. The EPA had the right to cancel a pesticide if evidence of an "imminent hazard" surfaced.[42] Provisions recognized the public's right to know by requiring that pesticide data be available within thirty days of registration so that the validity of claims could be evaluated. The act also acknowledged the right of citizens to bring suit against violators of the law or the EPA, if the agency failed to fulfill its enforcement responsibilities. It included specific protections for farmworkers, as proposed by Senator Nelson and supported by environmental organizations.[43]

These organizations supported the passage of the Federal Environmental Pesticides Control Act; still, they expressed some dissatisfaction with the final product.[44] Instead of basing chemical assessments solely on risk factors, EPA would employ a cost-benefit analysis in its review of pesticides. In addition to requiring the agency to use the poorly defined criteria of cost, risk, and benefit in its evaluation, the law lacked some of the strong wording that environmentalists desired. The federal government had to reimburse manufacturers, applicators, and farmers for their stores of suspended or banned chemicals, which environmentalists feared would make the EPA reluctant to take strong action.[45] This made the citizen suit provision that environmentalists lobbied for all the more important as an essential safeguard against laxity in regulation.[46] Despite these shortcomings, the amendments strengthened the framework for regulating pesticides over what had been in place prior to 1972.

A Tale of Two Unions

While the EDF worked to ban dangerous chlorinated hydrocarbons in the courts and environmental organizations exerted their influence in Congress to pass a stronger regulatory law, Chavez's union continued to fight for contracts in the fields. The union's revenue generation increased to such an extent by 1972 that the AFL-CIO determined that it was no longer an organizing committee and it subsequently became the United Farm Workers of America, AFL-CIO.[47] Immediately, after signing the grape contracts in 1970, the union shifted focus to the Salinas Valley to begin a campaign anew. While the union planned to expand its reach into other fields, the swift shift in focus came more as a result of necessity than choice.

Lettuce growers witnessed the union gains in the vineyards, and decided to sign "sweetheart" deals with the Teamsters before Cesar Chavez made inroads into the Salinas Valley. The Teamsters signed five-year agreements with twenty-seven growers within a week of being contacted by the Grower-Shipper Vegetable Association of Central California.[48] The number of contracts grew to approximately 200 by 1972.[49] Farmworkers had no advance knowledge of the negotiations and did not consent to be represented. State law did not require that the farmworkers be notified of the labor agreement, so neither the Teamsters nor the lettuce growers sought their input.[50] Foremen in the fields urged farmworkers to sign up with the union after the fact, reportedly threatening job loss if they refused. Still the majority refused to become Teamsters, and many expressed a preference for UFWOC.[51] Chavez's union spent the next several years competing for contracts in the fields.

Teamsters agreements differed markedly from UFWOC contracts in terms of wages, safety provisions, and workers' ability to influence production processes. The "sweetheart" deal with growers did little to improve wages, which had stagnated five years prior. The new provision guaranteed workers a modest half-cent a box increase per year for five years, a fraction of what a UFWOC lettuce contract guaranteed.[52] Whereas the UFWOC stipulated that workers be provided protective gear and have a voice in decision making about pesticides, the Teamsters offered growers lax provisions, requiring only that they comply with state and federal pesticide laws.[53] This allowed growers to continue using pesticides as they had done in the past, denying farmworkers the degree of control over the workplace environment provided in the UFW agreements.

Two of the larger lettuce growers, Inter-Harvest and Fresh Pict, decided to sign contracts with Chavez as he prepared to boycott, but the others readied for a fight.[54] Thousands of lettuce workers went on strike seeking UFWOC representation. Growers readily obtained injunctions, arguing that Chavez had no right to picket with the Teamsters in the fields. They supplemented the legal decision with direct action intended to unnerve the *Chavistas*. Shotgun-wielding security guards patrolled field perimeters. The Teamsters added men of their own, many of whom armed themselves with baseball bats.[55] Intimidation soon gave way to acts of violence against UFWOC and its supporters.[56]

After a month of intermittent episodes of violence, Monterey County Superior Court Judge Anthony Brazil issued a permanent injunction, ruling that UFWOC had violated the Teamsters' jurisdictional authority with an illegal strike.[57] Chavez's union responded with an escalation of pressure on lettuce growers, turning to the tactic that had proved so effective during the grape strike. UFWOC called on consumers to boycott lettuce until it was recognized as the legitimate union in the fields, which resulted in Chavez's arrest. The presiding judge attempted to impose a ten-thousand-dollar fine before being reminded by the union attorney that the maximum penalty was five hundred dollars.[58] Chavez instructed the gathered crowd to "boycott the hell out of them" as he was escorted to his cell by deputies.[59]

UFWOC addressed pesticide threats to some degree after the start of the boycott, but the issue did not assume the central position that it had occupied in the table grape campaign from 1969 to 1970. Attorney Jerry Cohen charged that lettuce growers misused pesticides to a greater extent than other crop producers, causing workers to suffer rashes and respiratory distress.[60] *El Malcriado* reminded readers of the strong health and safety provisions in UFWOC contracts. Growers' "greatest interest was in the crops," an editorial claimed, "not the people."[61] The union also used one lettuce grower's connection to Dow Chemical to intimate that Salinas Valley growers had a general disregard for human welfare. *El Malcriado* asserted: "Dow's napalm game [in Vietnam] doesn't seem so far away when you consider that along with the pesticide manufacturers and growers like Antle, they contribute to the yearly pesticide poisoning of over 80,000 people. When tallying the profits, they never think of the deaths, rashes and burns of the people in the fields caused by these dangerous pesticides."[62] Some boycotters adopted a similarly themed slogan: "Dow Chemical, which brought you napalm, now brings you Antle lettuce."[63] The boycott campaign attempted to focus public attention on the linkage between the chemicals used in war and pesticides used in the field, suggesting that both were equally dangerous. Still, despite the growing unpopularity of the war in Vietnam, UFWOC did not make this connection or pesticide-related health issues the main focus.

Organizers employed two lines of reasoning when trying to build consumer support from 1970 to 1972. First and foremost, UFWOC maintained that growers denied farmworkers a union of their choosing, contending that the lettuce contracts were the illegitimate product of collusion between growers and the Teamsters.[64] The jurisdictional dispute storyline failed to draw people to the cause, because the complexity of the issue proved difficult to quickly explain to customers entering a supermarket.[65] UFWOC emphasized a secondary message that stressed the connection between growers and government, asserting that certain politicians and government institutions consciously worked to undermine the farmworker movement. Government actions after the start of the boycott provided ready examples for them to publicize.

The jailing of Cesar Chavez provided an opportunity to grow public support. At no time during the previous grape strike had the charismatic figure spent any time in jail. UFWOC flipped the ruling from one designed to break the union effort to one that rallied people to the cause. The court ordered that the Chavez remain imprisoned until the boycott ended; organizers responded by telling supporters: "The sooner we stop Antle, the sooner that Cesar will be freed."[66] The union set up an altar across from the jail and held constant vigil. Ethel Kennedy and Coretta Scott King then joined two thousand farmworkers at a mass to show support for the cause.[67] Public sympathy gravitated toward the union in the matter.[68] The California Supreme Court soon ordered Chavez released, ruling that the injunction constrained his free speech rights.[69]

The union then shifted its attention to other government actions that it characterized as attacks on the movement. It publicized the jump in the Department of Defense's lettuce purchases, emphasizing that the department's consumption of grapes had trended the same way at the peak of the table grape boycott in 1969 and 1970. Boycotters called upon investigative reporters and congresspersons to look into the Pentagon purchases, while supporters around the country staged demonstrations at a number of different military bases.[70] The UFW then targeted the Republican Party after Nixon appointees to the National Labor Relations Board ruled that the union could no longer lawfully conduct secondary boycotts, a decision later reversed.[71] Boycott volunteers distributed bumper stickers that read "Abajo con los republicanos" ("Down with the Republicans") and "Republicans Hate Farm Workers" in an attempt to draw support away from the party in an election year.[72] The castigation of Republicans won the boycott an endorsement from the Democratic Party, which increased the number of supporters.[73] Still growers refused to negotiate.

Even as other matters consumed the bulk of attention, UFW interest in pesticides did not disappear. Staffers stayed abreast of developments even when they were not central to the current campaign. Attorneys monitored pesticide-related bills in the state legislature, supporting legislation that would provide better protection to farmworkers, and opposing grower-backed bills to reduce field oversight.[74] Still, these efforts paled in comparison with the attention paid to pesticides in 1969 and 1970.

An emerging story about grower negligence, Teamster inattention, and a potential government conspiracy in late 1972 provided an opportunity to better engage the pesticide issue without deviating much from the campaign's two primary lines of argumentation. A ground rig operator in the Imperial Valley noticed that some of the lettuce sprayed with the recently approved organophosphate Monitor 4 appeared to be burned around the edges of the leaves. California Department of Food and Agriculture (CDFA) tests showed pesticide residue in excess of established tolerance levels.[75] The agency revoked permits for the usage of Monitor 4 on lettuce and seized ten thousand crates of contaminated produce, but thousands of other shipments made their way to markets across the United States and Canada.[76] Information leaked that not all of the seized lettuce was destroyed. Jerry Cohen cited reports that contaminated stocks in La Habra were "reconditioned and released" and that heads of lettuce in Oxnard were "reconditioned and made into salad."[77]

Growers knew that large amounts of lettuce had excessive residues, yet continued to harvest their crop. Chemagro and Chevron Chemical Company, manufacturers of Monitor 4, advised that the over-tolerance lettuce could be "reconditioned" by peeling off the outer leaves. Most of the residue remained on the exterior, so the removal of that part of the produce made it more likely for the head to test within an acceptable range. Hence, while some of the lettuce was destroyed, other heads were stripped of some leaves and sent to grocers.[78] The practice raised an issue of legality since FDA requirements for pesticide residue sampling stated that a crop "shall not be washed, brushed, stripped, or trimmed except to the extent that this is a standard commercial practice prior to shipment for that commodity."[79] The CDFA reportedly knew that Imperial Valley lettuce was being "reconditioned" in December 1972 and took no action.[80] Consumer advocate and environmental activist Ida Honoroff testified that Newell Lundy from the Downey Department of Agriculture confided that the agency knew outer lettuce leaves were being stripped to meet tolerance standards. None of the involved agencies informed the public about the contamination until Honoroff broke the story on her radio program in late January, alleging that the problem would have gone unreported if she had not brought it to light.[81]

UFW integrated the story into their ongoing campaign, arguing that it was another example of grower and government collusion to deceive the public by suppressing evidence of contamination.[82] The union charged that growers shipped poisoned lettuce, that the CDFA "committed a possible crime" by allowing "reconditioned" produce to be shipped and sold, and that grocery stores still stocked contaminated product on their shelves.[83] Chavez revealed the scandal in St. Louis, held a press conference in Chicago, and sent telegrams to grocery chains and public health agencies across North America.[84] Boycott volunteers raised the issue with the public, emphasizing that consumers bore the cost of the Teamsters "sweetheart" deal because it prevented the UFW from ensuring that growers used pesticides safely. The union's legal department urged boycotters to stress that "there is still a great deal of poisoned lettuce still unaccounted for, and that the American public as well as the farmworkers is [*sic*] being poisoned by pesticides like Monitor [and] only a union contract will offer protection against these poisons."[85]

Pressure from the UFW helped convince state legislators to conduct a fact-finding investigation of the incident and hold a hearing on the Monitor 4 contamination.[86] A commission ventured to the Imperial Valley on the day before the hearing and collected testimonials from a number of farmworkers, including one who wished to speak in private for fear of losing his job. He told how his employer sprayed lettuce with phosdrin and then sent workers into the field to "recondition" it before the two-day waiting period expired. The farmworker's fingernails had rotted away from chemical exposure. Hoping to expand the discussion beyond Monitor 4 to other organophosphates, Jerry Cohen contended that phosdrin had the same potential risks as Monitor 4 and noted that hundreds of crates of lettuce with excessive residues of the chemical had been seized in Massachusetts one week prior.[87] He stressed that growers shifted from one dangerous chemical to another and cautioned that "just because they ban Monitor on lettuce, does not mean that poisoned lettuce is not on the retail shelves now."[88]

Neither the hearing nor the UFW's focus on pesticides in 1973 produced lasting effects. The hearing failed to assign blame for the contamination episode and did not broaden its scope to address other organophosphates such as phosdrin.[89] Usage of Monitor 4 on lettuce ended with an EPA ban, but growers continued to use it on other crops.[90] The hearing did not address the threat to farmworker health in great detail, despite the efforts of the UFW and its political allies to introduce the topic into the discussion. Organizers tried to expand concern about grower negligence and harmful organophosphates, castigating the Teamsters for denying there was a problem.[91] Yet within two months of the hearings, other matters arose to once again displace pesticides as a central concern of the union. Grape growers' contracts with the UFW expired in April 1973, after which they promptly signed Teamster "sweetheart" deals. A period of violent unrest followed, during which the UFW suffered increased attacks from Teamsters, growers, and local police. Marshall Ganz presents some statistics on the increased violence, stating that "two strikers were murdered, while picketers endured 44 shootings, 400 beatings, and 3,000 arrests" by August 1973.[92] These developments placed the union's survival in jeopardy.[93]

The boycott expanded to include grapes and Gallo wine, but UFW did not gain enough ground to force growers to negotiate. Fortunes changed to some degree with the election of Democratic allies to the state legislature and of Jerry Brown to the governor's office. Even though the UFW had put little faith in legislative solutions in the past, it decided that the electoral turn presented an opportunity to employ a new strategy. The union pushed for a new California farm labor law that would mirror the federal National Labor Relations Act. Growers did not protest the Agricultural Labor Relations Act, in part because they did not think that the UFW would emerge victorious from the secret ballot elections.[94] The ALRA passed in May 1975 and union elections were held the following February. Growers' prognostications proved wrong. Chavez's union fared much better than its counterparts, leading to the Teamsters' abandonment of organizing efforts in the fields.[95]

An Invisible Ally

Cesar Chavez contacted several environmental groups, including the Sierra Club, shortly after the Monitor 4 hearings in 1973, hoping to enlist their support in the struggle against the Teamsters. He wrote after receiving a mailing from Environmental Action regarding the Oil, Chemical, and Atomic Workers (OCAW) strike against Shell.[96] The letter stated that Environmental Action and a number of other environmental groups supported OCAW because the union had gone on strike over health and safety issues in the workplace. It pledged to rally people to the cause and expressed hope that this would be a catalyst for "broadening the base of the environmental movement."[97] Chavez sought to foster the same sort of alliance, asserting that "the unity which the union movement can have with the environmentalists is crucial to our survival—both in a spirit of justice and in a literal sense."[98]

Sierra Club president Raymond Sherwin showed a similar desire to build bridges between the labor movement and the environmental movement. Shortly before Chavez reached out to environmental groups, Sherwin published an editorial in the *Sierra Club Bulletin* stating that "trade union objectives" related to health and safety in the workplace "merit the vocal support of the Sierra Club and allied organizations, for the very basic reason that an unhealthy micro-environment anywhere reduces the overall vitality of our natural world . . . the two are inseparable."[99] Yet he wrote somewhat defensively in response to some members who had written letters to the national office to express their disappointment with the club's expansive new vision, particularly its support of the OCAW strike. Sherwin countered arguments that the Sierra Club was getting involved in too many issues, contending that the organization's "strength and vitality" would be more threatened by "ignoring environmental threats to the human condition than from fighting them."[100] These internal disagreements about the appropriate scope of the club's interests may or may not have shaped the response to Chavez's request.

Despite grumblings by some members, Sierra Club leaders persisted in promoting an understanding of environmentalism that incorporated concerns for social justice, while working to develop amicable relations with the labor movement. Director William Futrell continued to suggest that members adopt a broad view of environmentalism. Asserting that "environmental rights and civil rights are closely intertwined," he declared: "Our stand should be: love for the land and justice for its people. The land ethic undergirds the social structure of which justice is the crown."[101] Leaders carried the message beyond their membership as well. Vice president Will Siri spoke before a meeting of the California Labor Federation, telling the attendees that the labor movement and the environmental movement were "engaging in an unnecessary war."[102]

The past support of the labor movement for environmental initiatives showed that not only was peace between the groups possible, but collaboration as well. A number of unions supported the major environmental legislation of the 1960s and early 1970s. The AFL-CIO voiced support for the Clean Air Act in 1963 and spoke in favor of legislation that would curb water pollution. The United Auto Workers (UAW), the United Steelworkers, the International Association of Machinists, and OCAW backed amendments to the Clean Air Act in 1970 and the Clean Water Act in 1972.[103] More progressive unions, like the UAW under the leadership of Walter Reuther, advocated for the creation of a National Trails System with recreation opportunities in both urban and rural areas. The UAW and OCAW also proved willing to defend pollution control measures that had the potential to compromise members' jobs but promised to improve public health in exchange.[104] Some unionists participated in Earth Day events and some labor leaders appeared as featured speakers supporting environmental protection.[105]

Nevertheless, the accord that Will Siri spoke of needed fostering because fragility still defined relations between the labor and environmental movements. Not all unions backed environmental legislation. Whereas the UAW showed some willingness to sacrifice for the sake of public health, the United Mine Workers often opposed more restrictive environmental regulation out of fear that it would threaten jobs.[106] Industrialists who had fractured union solidarity in the past by stoking interethnic animosities used the same strategy to divide workers and environmentalists with the "jobs versus environment" argument.[107] John F. Henning, the executive secretary treasurer of the California AFL-CIO, for instance, blamed environmentalists for reducing jobs with the "no-growth nonsense."[108] Other workers felt that environmental organizations failed to sufficiently back important labor legislation. OCAW public relations director Ray Davidson, for instance, referred to environmentalists as "intellectual snobs" and remained upset that environmentalist groups had only offered mild support for the Occupational Health and Safety Act of 1970.[109] These factors sometimes fostered animosity and distrust between the two groups.

Still, many environmentalists and union leaders saw promise in a blue-green coalition and worked to build the relationship. Environmental Action and the UAW hosted the Black Lake Conference after the first Earth Day, a meeting of environmentalists, union representatives, students, and community organizers to discuss strategy for the future.[110] The gathering included workshops on industrial pollution, workplace health and safety, researching pollution problems, the process for initiating legal action, and the environmental movement's relationship with the urban poor. Many attendees found informal conversations about past experiences, tactics, and technical information to be the most rewarding part of the conference.[111] When the disparate groups mobilized in support of each other, the effect could be powerful. The environmental organizations that supported OCAW's Shell strike, for instance, distributed thousands of pamphlets urging members to boycott Shell products. Their efforts contributed to a significant decline in Shell gasoline purchases between February and April 1973.[112]

The Sierra Club engaged in outreach efforts, hoping to strengthen its relations with labor organizations. William Futrell pledged that the club would back bills of mutual concern and work to develop an intra-organizational "labor advisory council."[113] Executive director Michael McCloskey voiced similar support for collaboration at the OCAW national convention in October 1973. After citing occupational disease statistics that included people injured by pesticides, McCloskey reasoned that environmentalists should cooperate with workers because "workers and people with limited incomes are the chief victims of environmental disorders."[114] The rhetoric and outreach of club leaders demonstrated a willingness to make common cause with other organizations on issues related to environment and health.

Cesar Chavez requested that environmental organizations publicize the UFW struggle in their newsletters, organize members to picket in support, or contact Senator Gaylord Nelson of the Senate Subcommittee on Migratory Labor to call a hearing addressing the harm inflicted on farmworkers and consumers by pesticides.[115] Several environmental groups responded favorably. The Center for Science in the Public Interest promised to inform its readers about the boycott.[116] The Environmental Policy Center declared its admiration for Chavez, adding that "the Teamsters turn up as the enemy in so many of the problems we work on that a lot of the people we work with should see the value of keeping the Teamsters from spreading their power to agribusiness."[117] It requested a meeting with a UFW representative to discuss how its resources could be employed to promote the boycott.[118] The National Parks and Conservation Association expressed the belief that UFW actions to "prevent the misuse of pesticides" were "designed to achieve goals which are shared by the environmental movement as a whole," suggesting that the union submit an article for publication in their magazine with a readership of fifty thousand.[119]

Chavez wrote the Sierra Club as well. Director of the Washington office Brock Evans expressed personal support for the UFW and forwarded the request for publicity to the Executive Committee in San Francisco with a strong recommendation for approval. Evans lacked the authority to officially endorse the lettuce boycott, but exuded confidence about the possibility for collaboration. The club, he said, had to make certain that any endorsements of labor unions' actions had "a sound and strong environmental basis," but felt that the union would have little trouble meeting the requirement with its "strong stand on pesticide control."[120] Nonetheless, no endorsement or write-up on the issue appeared in the *Sierra Club Bulletin* in 1973, and there is no evidence in Sierra Club records that the Executive Committee weighed the UFW request.[121]

While the Sierra Club did not publicly endorse the boycott, it communicated with the union and worked to strengthen pesticide regulations in an effort to protect farmworkers. Brock Evans forwarded Chavez's request to the club's Washington lobbyist Linda Billings, who in turn contacted the UFW's Washington representative, Father James Vizzard. Billings drafted a letter in consultation with Vizzard to be signed by a number of "national groups" and sent to Senator Nelson in hopes of gaining a hearing on the threat of pesticides to farmworkers and consumers. As she contacted different organizations, Billings learned of another lobbying effort underway by the Migrant Legal Action Program (MLAP) focused on protecting farmworkers from a suite of organophosphate pesticides.[122]

In anticipation of the DDT ban, MLAP had petitioned the Occupational Safety and Health Administration (OSHA) in September 1972 to issue an emergency temporary standard (ETS) on organophosphates, maintaining that exposure to these chemicals was farmworkers' most pressing health concern. If OSHA determined that a substance posed a "grave danger" to people in the workplace, the agency could skip formal rulemaking practices and issue an ETS that temporarily set standards to protect worker health.[123] MLAP filed suit in the US District Court after the agency failed

to issue any new standards. Within a month, OSHA responded by drafting an ETS that applied to twenty-one different organophosphates used in
treating seven different crops.[124] The new regulation mandated that workers wait a specified number of days before reentering fields after the application of one of the listed chemicals.[125]

Growers' organizations, including the Florida Peach Growers Association and the Florida Citrus Production Managers Association,
sought to stop the action.[126] Under pressure from these groups and
their congressional allies, OSHA significantly weakened the provisions,
dropping the number of chemicals covered from twenty-one to twelve
and shortening the field reentry times for each by two days or more.[127]
Growers' associations filed suit nonetheless and obtained a temporary
injunction to keep the regulations from going into effect. They also
lobbied congresspersons to shift responsibilities for safeguarding farmworkers' health and safety from OSHA to the USDA, an agency more
sympathetic to grower interests.[128] OSHA, in the meantime, proceeded
with efforts to set permanent regulations. It announced hearings in several cities to discuss reentry times for sprayed fields, warning notices
around field perimeters, field sanitation and accessible medical facilities
for farmworkers, and protective clothing to reduce the risk of pesticide
poisoning in the field.[129]

Linda Billings, representing the Sierra Club, entered the fray to counter grower attacks against OSHA and push for stronger regulatory standards. Sierra Club joined the AFL-CIO and the United Auto Workers
to oppose the legislation that would transfer power to USDA. Together
they succeeded in eliminating the "anti-OSHA farm worker provisions"
from the farm bill before it passed.[130] Billings also worked to rally environmentalists to counter opponents of regulation who had appeared
in force at the first two hearings in Phoenix and Boise. She drafted and
mailed an information sheet to approximately thirty groups and Sierra
Club leaders located near the OSHA hearing sites, urging her contacts
to attend or write letters in support of stringent regulations that would
better protect farmworkers from harm. Billings asserted that "since a
strong public outcry was in part responsible for phasing out the use of
persistent pesticides, it behooves [sic] us to insist that the shift to short-
lived pesticides not result in increased hazards to farm workers through
improper regulation of their use."[131] She suggested that attendees stress

that OSHA had a responsibility to protect farmworkers; that data from pesticide manufacturers needed to be interrogated to test its accuracy and protect human health; that better data-gathering efforts on pesticide-related illnesses were needed; and that growers' overuse of agricultural chemicals should be curbed.[132]

The presence of farmworker organizations and their environmental allies at the public hearings did not result in OSHA's adoption of a permanent set of pesticide regulations. The inaction ultimately had little to do with the testimony presented. Rather OSHA fell into a jurisdictional disagreement with the EPA over authority to regulate field reentry times. The EPA claimed responsibility under FIFRA and OSHA finally conceded regulatory powers because of a provision in the Occupational Safety and Health Act that prohibited duplication of regulation by different federal agencies.[133] Farmworker groups brought suit in attempt to keep regulatory authority with OSHA because of its more concentrated focus on the welfare of workers and its stronger enforcement capabilities than the EPA. The Court of Appeals, however, sided against them.[134]

After the court rendered its decision, both farmworker organizations and environmental groups worked to preserve FIFRA and the power of the EPA from being constrained by the USDA. When FIFRA passed in 1972, it carried a sunset clause that required it to be reauthorized after three years. Congress began holding hearings to discuss the effectiveness of the legislation in May 1975 to determine whether the law should be given new life. Growers, pesticide manufacturers, and the USDA approached the hearings intent on making changes that would ease EPA oversight and give the USDA greater influence over regulatory decisions.[135] Various environmental groups, the UFW, and the MLAP countered the efforts of those bent on weakening the law.

One proposed amendment would supplant pesticide applicators' written or oral certification programs with a "register-signing system" in which a purchaser of agricultural chemicals would sign a form stating that the rules on the label would be followed. The American Farm Bureau Federation held that a more rigorous certification program "ignores the good safety record farmers have developed in the handling and use of pesticides" and would "impose an unjustifiable burden on the nation's agriculture."[136] The UFW, in contrast, warned that the "only applicators to benefit from a self-certification system are the very ones who need the training the most," and joined the MLAP in calling into question the claims of an untarnished safety record.[137] Environmental groups agreed that a state certification program would help minimize injuries from improper use and was essential to a good regulatory system.[138]

Another amendment aimed to give the USDA veto power over EPA regulatory actions on pesticides. This also drew fire from farmworker organizations and environmental groups. When that proposal failed to get adequate congressional support, a similar but weaker amendment was offered in its place. It would require the EPA to complete a cost-benefit analysis on proposed pesticide suspensions without public involvement. The agency would also be required to submit any proposal to suspend the use of specific pesticides to the USDA for consultation sixty days prior to it being made available to the public.[139] Both farmworker representatives and environmentalists argued that the adoption of this policy was undemocratic and would unfairly favor agricultural interests over concerns for environment and health. The groups maintained that the formulation of an accurate and just cost-benefit analysis required broad public input, not closed-door concessions to an agency that had a history of regulatory inaction and opposition to pesticide restrictions.[140]

The regulatory proponents defended the EPA's record and urged Congress to reauthorize FIFRA, but they also put forth recommendations to better protect farmworkers and the public from suffering harm from pesticide poisoning. Father Vizzard stated that the EPA's reentry standards marked a good start, but said that "stronger, more comprehensive and more reliable standards with tough, effective enforcement mechanisms" were possible and preferable.[141] The MLAP similarly requested that more attention be paid to the welfare of farmworkers, urging the agency to initiate better data collection programs so that it could more accurately set reentry standards to prevent undue exposure to health hazards.[142] EDF personnel also spoke of the need for a sound accident reporting system from which data on pesticide poisonings and misuse could be compiled and used to craft policies that minimized exposure to unnecessary risks.[143]

Congress reauthorized FIFRA in 1975 with minor changes. Despite the recommendations of farmworker organizations and environmental groups, an amendment gave the USDA a greater role in regulatory affairs. The EPA subsequently had to provide advance notice to the agency when: planning to change regulatory policy, initiate a cancellation process, or alter a chemical's registration status. The EPA also had to do a cost-benefit analysis of regulatory action on agricultural production before proposing a change.[144] Though the reauthorized legislation did not represent an unqualified victory for environmentalists and farmworkers, their efforts helped convince Congress to extend FIFRA and leave regulatory responsibilities with the EPA. Administrator Russell Train recognized the role that the Sierra Club and "several respected voices" had played in staving off the efforts of a "serious movement to greatly reduce EPA's authority in pesticide regulation."[145]

The Sierra Club, which had been hampered by organizational inertia in the 1960s, entered the 1970s more ready to embrace a role at the fore of the environmental movement. Its leaders mirrored the spirit of Earth Day organizers as they worked to expand the range of issues addressed. They spoke of the relationship between the microenvironment of the workplace and the larger world, and of the intersection between environmental rights and civil rights. The club recognized the threats posed by certain pesticides to humans and the environment and actively engaged in efforts to reform practices to better protect worker, public, and environmental health. The club believed that strong regulatory laws that allowed public oversight and participation in the rulemaking process offered the best protection for public and environmental health when enforced by agencies not beholden to the agricultural industry.

The Sierra Club and other environmental groups lobbied Congress and testified at public hearings in support of better laws regulating the use of agricultural chemicals. Concerns extended beyond safeguarding wildlife to protecting the health of the public and farmworkers. The Sierra Club, in particular, collaborated with unions, encouraged its members to attend hearings on pesticide regulation, and testified to Congress on the importance of reauthorizing a strong FIFRA and keeping authority over pesticide regulation away from the USDA and in the hands of agencies like EPA and OSHA that were more attentive to farmworker health and safety. The role of environmentalists in passing federal pesticide legislation and defending it from attack disprove Laura Pulido's mistaken contention that mainstream environmentalists abandoned pesticide reform efforts after the DDT ban, thinking that the pesticide problem had been resolved.[146]

The EDF and the UFW generally pursued the same approaches to pesticide reform that they had employed prior to the DDT ban. The EDF, with its "Sue the Bastards" strategy, used the courts to ban aldrin and dieldrin. UFW still believed that union representation best protected farmworkers, and consequently consumers, from the ill effects of pesticides. The union worked to increase the number of labor contracts with pesticide provisions, but success was slow in coming because of Teamster incursions. The conflict with the Teamsters caused the UFW to spend less time on pesticides between 1970 and 1976 than it had between 1969 and 1970. It continued to care about pesticide-related issues, but at a lower level of priority. Though it monitored pesticide politics in this period, it only made the issue a central component in its boycott campaign for a few short months in 1973. During this period, mainstream environmental organizations and other farmworker advocacy groups, like the Migrant Legal Action Program, were most responsible for advancing pesticide reform.

Despite the UFW's lack of focus on agricultural chemicals between 1970 and 1976, some environmental groups corresponded and cooperated with the union on related issues. These relationships were strategically forged between the respective groups' leaders and lobbyists, and as a result they lacked public visibility and permanence. Labor organizations spoke to their members about labor issues while environmental groups spoke to their members about environmental issues. Environmental groups did not have a public presence in UFW campaigns and did little to publicize the lettuce boycott; likewise, unions did not participate in environmental campaigns except when workers' interests were directly affected. However, environmentalists and farmworker organizations took similar stances on pesticide legislation, so that they worked towards common ends when Congress considered bills and heard testimony. Cooperation occurred fleetingly around these times as the groups strove to counter the power of growers, pesticide manufacturers, and the USDA. Environmental groups and unions continued to defend FIFRA, OSHA, and other federal legislation relating to health and environment throughout the 1970s and into the 1980s.[147] As these groups attempted to influence national policy, a major state-level pesticide conflict in Arizona that pitted growers and the state's pesticide regulatory authority against farmworkers and suburbanites was coming to a head.

5

A Different Kind of Border War

Arizona, 1971–1986

An "insecticide fog" drifted west from the fields that growers leased on the Salt River Pima Maricopa Indian Community (SRPMIC) Reservation into the developing city of Scottsdale on October 11, 1971.[1] People living within a mile of the fields reported breathing problems, coughing, and burning eyes, throats, and noses.[2] The spread of suburban development into other agricultural areas of the Valley of the Sun heightened the number of complaints about pesticides. Residents of southeast Mesa, Avondale, and Peoria voiced grievances in 1970 and 1971 as well.[3] Scottsdale drew the most attention, though. The *Scottsdale Daily Progress* ran a series of articles about the problems, which in conjunction with three television editorials raised public awareness about a burgeoning conflict at the agricultural/urban interface. Arizona House Representative Hal Runyan responded to the bevy of complaints, suggesting that the Board of Pesticide Control (BPC) take voluntary measures to resolve the problem and stave off a more restrictive legislative response.[4] However, the strength of the agricultural lobby in the state legislature and the failure of University of Arizona tests to show evidence of pesticide intoxication in Scottsdale helped forestall changes in pesticide policy.[5]

Ten days after the drift incident, Gustavo Gutierrez ventured out to SRPMIC lands to collect data on pesticide use, specifically the names of chemicals used and the volume in which they were applied to the fields. Gutierrez did not work for BPC or any other state agency. Rather he was one among a handful of individuals compiling data on pesticide use in Arizona for the United Farm Workers Organizing Committee.[6] Gutierrez, a native Arizonan who grew up working in the fields, began organizing an independent UFWOC local in 1967 and soon became a central figure in the farmworkers' movement in Arizona.[7] His organization supported the efforts of California farmworkers and organized strikes against local growers.[8] The Arizona branch adopted the same health and safety concerns as its California counterpart, maintaining that "normal things that people take for granted nowadays" such as sanitation and "these pesticides that they spray all over you" were important issues for farmworkers.[9] The very first issue of *El Paisano*, the newspaper published by the United Farm Workers Organizing Committee of Arizona, carried an article proclaiming that farmworkers needed a safety law because they worked in the state's third most dangerous occupation.[10] Since they harbored these health concerns, Gutierrez and others monitored pesticide applications in the fields around the Phoenix metropolitan area.

Little evidence exists that Arizona farmworkers and Scottsdale suburbanites, turned NIMBY (not in my backyard) environmentalists on the urban/agricultural fringe, collaborated on pesticide-related issues in 1971, even though both groups focused attention on some of the same fields. Scottsdale residents' concern about drift does not appear to have influenced Gutierrez or the Arizona UFWOC, because the field monitoring began a month before the suburban complaints. Similarly, the concerns of farmworkers went unaddressed in the suburbanite discourse on drift. The only mention of UFWOC in the *Scottsdale Daily Progress*'s series of articles referred to the health and safety clause in the union's California contracts, but said nothing about the local chapter's activities.[11] For nearly thirteen years thereafter, in fact, the farmworkers and suburbanites failed to join forces in pesticide reform efforts in Arizona.

Part of the reason for the lack of cooperation between 1971 and 1984 had to do with timing. The groups' interest in the state's pesticide politics peaked at different times. Growers' efforts, in part, contributed to this phenomenon. The suburbanite protest reached fever pitch in 1978, a year in which the reinvigorated farmworker movement in Arizona was still getting up steam. By the time that the farmworker organizations immersed themselves in Arizona pesticide politics in the 1980s, Scottsdale residents' interest had waned. A drift incident, however, reengaged suburbanites and provided an opportunity for collaboration with farmworker organizations. Mutual concern about pesticides' adverse health effects provided a common ground for interaction. Successful collaboration, though, depended upon the bridge-building efforts of professionals within activist organizations.

The Ghosts Emerge from the Fields

The UFW found it very difficult to make significant gains in Arizona during the early 1970s. Agricultural interests responded to union inroads by shepherding the Agricultural Employment Relations Act through the state legislature.[12] The legislation made it unlawful for unions to recruit members in the fields, prohibited secondary boycotts, allowed the courts to issue ten-day restraining orders against work stoppages during the harvest, and required that workers vote to strike under the observance of a governor-appointed board. This antilabor law severely restricted farmworkers' options in labor disputes, making illegal some of the most effective tactics employed in the Delano strike. Growers also began importing increasing numbers of undocumented workers from Mexico, who sometimes interfered with organizing efforts and could be used to undermine a strike. In 1974, for example, growers used two hundred undocumented workers to break a UFW strike at Arrowhead Ranch in the West Valley outside of Phoenix.[13] Violence broke out in Yuma as UFW members formed a "wet line" and attacked undocumented strike breakers. The incident tainted the union's image and alienated the growing numbers of Mexican nationals. The Yuma strike ultimately cost the UFW $1.6 million and ended without a contract.[14] These troubles, in part, caused the UFW to all but abandon Arizona farmworkers by 1975.[15]

A contingent of the organizers disagreed with the union stance on undocumented workers and established a more inclusive civil rights organization to represent the interests of all farmworkers. As with the UFW, activists within the fledgling Maricopa County Organizing Project (M-COP) strove to advance the civil and human rights of farmworkers, but they made no distinctions over legal status.[16] Organizers maintained that any agreement that failed to include undocumented workers in the provisions would "drive a wedge between Chicano and Mexican workers by creating a second and third citizen status among the workers."[17] This, they believed, would adversely affect all farmworkers. Creating solidarity in the fragmented workforce made sense because undocumented migration had increased substantially after the 1965 Immigration and Nationality Act made it more difficult to enter the country lawfully.[18]

Conventional wisdom held that undocumented workers could not be effectively organized. Mexican nationals lack citizenship, so state and federal politicians often have had little reason to intervene on their behalf in labor disputes, especially since many of their political constituents believe that they constitute a significant threat to American jobs.[19] Furthermore, undocumented workers face the threat of deportation, a circumstance that employers may use advantageously to rid themselves of employees who voice discontent over wages or working conditions. M-COP, however, speculated that growers' dependence on foreign labor during the harvest would, to some extent, mitigate the factors that made organizing undocumented workers difficult.[20]

Recognizing that the "greatest obstacle in organizing undocumented workers was fear," M-COP organizers Lupe Sánchez and Jesús Romo devised an innovative strategy to build trust and strengthen the resolve of farmworkers.[21] The two observed that "growers had almost total reign in the fields . . . surveillance was strict, and any outsider caught inside the fields faced a severe beating."[22] Still, in 1976 they managed to evade security teams and enter the migrant camps.[23] Many farmworkers, they found, lived underneath the canopy of citrus trees, using only black plastic tarps or makeshift lean-tos of old crates to shield themselves from the elements. Lack of sanitary facilities forced them to live amidst their own waste, while an inadequate water supply limited bathing options to the chemical-laden canals that bordered the fields.[24] The dissatisfaction caused by these conditions and by poor wages provided a base of issues around which to organize, if the organizers could win undocumented workers' confidence. To prove its commitment, M-COP identified exploitative "coyotes" (guides who led migrants across the United States–Mexico border for sometimes exorbitant fees) and brought them before "workers' trials" in the fields where the accused "coyotes" were made to compensate the aggrieved migrants.[25] Organizers also informed farmworkers that they had certain legal rights that were unaffected by their lack of legal immigrant status.[26]

M-COP discovered that most of the workers came from the same towns within the Mexican states of Querétaro, Guanajuato, San Luis Potosí, Nayarit, Michoacán, and Guerrero. Organizers traveled to these various points of origin to coordinate twenty-six strike committees.[27] In contrast to the United States where farmworkers operated from a disadvantaged position, villagers and local authorities in Mexico viewed migrants with respect because they recognized that workers' sojourns north of the border were an economic survival strategy to support their families.[28] Organizing in Mexico, consequently, lessened some of the advantage that growers gained from the migrants' undocumented status in the United States and made it easier to plan for a strike.[29]

After two summers in Mexico, two hundred farmworkers went on strike at the three-thousand-acre Arrowhead Ranch during the 1977 fall harvest, demanding improvements in their wages and living and working conditions. Sánchez and Romo recognized that the public could respond negatively to the undocumented workers' action, so they called on the press to paint a sympathetic picture.[30] Romo stressed, "We are not interested in getting them to sign [union]cards, we want to improve the living conditions of these people."[31] As word of the strike spread through the media, some area locals began to refer to the farmworkers as "ghosts of the orchards" or "ghostworkers" because they had previously been a relatively invisible segment of the state's labor force.[32]

Immigration and Naturalization Service agents wasted little time in organizing a sweep to round up recalcitrant workers.[33] Maricopa County sheriff's office personnel surrounded the fields, preventing the remaining farmworkers from receiving visitors. M-COP, in response, sought and received protection from a federal district court. Judge Carl Muecke informed growers' attorneys that the farmworkers had constitutional and statutory rights, including the right to assembly, regardless of legal status.[34] The order still did not stop the use of force and intimidating tactics on the ranch, so M-COP decided to expand the strike to the nearby Fletcher Ranch. After an INS raid on Fletcher Ranch netted another 122 workers,

Lupe Sánchez charged that "Border Patrol enforcement is in some serious degree being selectively applied where labor disputes are happening . . . in sufficient force to disrupt organizing efforts and to intimidate the work force, but never as a total sweep sufficient to threaten the harvest."[35] The repeated sweeps weakened the strike to some degree, but failed to break it. The farmworkers' continued effort forced Goldmar, Inc., the owners of Arrowhead Ranch, and Fletcher Ranch to come to terms.[36]

Farmworkers convinced growers to agree to a mix of concessions in the contracts signed with the Arizona Farm Workers (AFW), a newly created offshoot of the Maricopa County Organizing Project.[37] Wages increased to rates that were close to the federal minimum wage, though not always above it.[38] A contractual clause also required growers to contribute ten cents for every hour worked to a redevelopment fund, the sum of which would be used to foster the growth of self-sustaining communities in the farmworkers' home villages in Mexico. Cooperative Sin Fronteras, the organization that M-COP and AFW created to manage funds, oversaw projects that ranged from improving water delivery services to constructing a tortilla factory to removing invasive species from local lakes for village fisherman.[39]

Contracts also addressed a number of issues relating to the migrants' quality of life and work conditions. Fletcher Ranch agreed to provide space for camping and blankets, refrigeration facilities for food, better sources of drinking water, showers, and toilets.[40] Goldmar Inc. stated that they would notify workers before irrigating and provide forty-eight hours' notice before spraying pesticides. This advance warning allowed workers time to move their belongings from underneath the trees and prevent them from being ruined. Goldmar also agreed to provide protective clothing to pesticide applicators and have physicians test them regularly to monitor the effects of pesticide exposure.[41]

The newly signed contracts, however, did not resolve farmworkers' problems with pesticides. The workers rarely received information on the risks of chemical exposure. Many pesticide applicators and growers failed to notify farmworkers of spray dates, despite the contract clause. Crop dusters still often sprayed fields with little regard for workers in the camps or fields below, sometimes dousing them with hazardous chemicals.[42] A 1979 investigation by the Arizona Department of Health Services (ADHS) revealed that more than twenty-eight wells in the greater Phoenix area and thirty-three in Yuma County were contaminated with the highly toxic pesticide dibromochloropropane (DBCP), a compound shown to cause sterility in men.[43] The ranches under contract with the Arizona Farm Workers did not escape the contamination.[44] Even though farmworkers lived in the fields and used the wells for drinking and bathing, the supply was not categorized as residential and not recognized as a public drinking source. The limited jurisdiction of ADHS prevented it from addressing ranch water contamination. Consequently farmworkers continued to use the tainted water.[45]

M-COP and AFW committed to learning more about pesticides after signing contracts and devoted greater resources to reform after 1980.[46] As with the UFW, union contracts contained pesticide provisions, but they utilized the courts somewhat differently. Beyond that, M-COP and AFW adopted innovative strategies to address pesticide problems, concentrating resources on improving the state's regulatory system.[47] The Arizona organizations also planned "to act as 'shadow gov't' monitoring the activities" of the Board of Pesticide Control and sometimes the Department of Health Services.[48]

Maricopa County Organizing Project significantly expanded its engagement in the issue in 1983 when it recruited Nadine Wettstein, a Tucson civil rights attorney, to lead the organization's pesticide reform efforts and obtained grant money to create the Arizona Farm Workers Committee on Pesticides (AFWCP) and the Pesticide Project.[49] Wettstein decided that a farmworker representative should seek a seat on the grower-dominated Board of Pesticide Control. M-COP also wanted to have decision-making power on the use and application of experimental pesticides. Karen Kincaid, an M-COP organizer and paralegal, recruited pesticide applicators and farmworkers to document usage of agricultural chemicals, creating a catalogue of information to inform future efforts.[50] Arizona Farm Workers also addressed the varied governmental response to DBCP contamination. The union complained to ADHS about the differentiation between residential and agricultural wells, asserting: "harvesters here, in actual fact, are required to live in unsheltered labor camps within the orchards after working hours, with virtually no facilities at their disposal . . . they drink, cook with, and wash in whatever water is available, often limited to irrigation well and ditch water."[51] It proposed that the ADHS should categorize wells that serviced labor camps of twenty-five or more farmworkers as residential.[52]

M-COP then requested that the Department of Health Services run additional tests for ethylene dibromide (EDB) contamination.[53] Growers switched to EDB, a chemical that caused cancer in laboratory animals, after the DBCP ban.[54] Public concern heightened as traces of EDB began to show in California and Florida groundwater, and both states suspended use of the compound in 1983.[55] The EPA followed suit in September, issuing an emergency ban on the use of EDB as a soil fumigant because of concerns about groundwater quality.[56] The Arizona Department of Health Services, however, said that it could not conduct water quality tests without knowing where the chemical had been applied in recent years.[57] M-COP responded by gathering data on the sale and usage of DBCP and EDB and the location of labor camps and turning the findings over to the ADHS.[58]

The persistence and data-gathering efforts of M-COP and AFW paid off, with health officials reclassifying some wells in 1984. The ADHS began treating agricultural water like that from residential wells, so long as it served labor camps of twenty-five or more persons for at least two months of the year. The agency also developed "action standards" for DBCP and EDB that allowed it to close contaminated wells.[59] Yet the department lacked the necessary resources to conduct extensive investigations. M-COP's Pesticide Project and the Centro Adelante Campesino subsequently negotiated a cooperative agreement with the Health Department in 1986, in which the farmworker groups conducted preliminary tests on water supplies. If the results showed chemicals above tolerance levels, then the agency sent its own personnel to the field to take an official sample for testing before closing the well concerned.[60]

The AFWCP also encouraged farmworkers to directly participate in policing growers' pesticide usage practices by initiating a watchdog program that awarded whistle-blowers twenty-five dollars for reporting major violations.[61] One such report led to the discovery of an illegal dump that had empty containers of carcinogenic and teratogenic pesticides lying about haphazardly in close proximity to food crops, irrigation ditches, and a labor camp.[62] Farmworker tips identified violations on the part of both pesticide applicators and chemical companies, which on occasion spurred the EPA to investigate and levy fines in excess of $150,000.[63] Considering budgetary and personnel constraints within government agencies, such extensive policing of the fields and wells would not have been possible without the volunteered assistance of M-COP, its affiliated organizations, and migrant farmworkers.

The efforts of farmworkers and professionals within the Pesticide Project and the Arizona Farm Workers Committee on Pesticides helped protect farmworkers in the field and, arguably, the public at large. The grower-controlled Board of Pesticide Control remained the primary regulatory authority for pesticide application and use, though. The BPC had increased its pesticide monitoring efforts in the years since 1971, but still remained ineffective as the regulatory agency charged with protecting public health. The farmworkers needed to find allies who were similarly concerned about regulatory inadequacies if they hoped to significantly reform or abolish the board. Instances of pesticide poisoning and environmental contamination in the early 1980s provided the necessary catalyst for coalition building from 1984 to 1986.[64]

Trouble in Suburbia

Arizona growers in the 1970s recognized that they might face threats beyond insect pests and organized farmworkers. The changing urban demographic, particularly in the growing metropolis of Phoenix in Maricopa County, had the potential to challenge the power of the agricultural industry in politics. A 1979 study commissioned by the Agri-Business Council of Arizona stated that while the number of residents harboring negative attitudes toward agriculture remained low, they represented a latent force that could "become very powerful and could easily translate into increased public tolerance for public policies detrimental to the industry."[65] Phoenix had originally developed as an agricultural city surrounded by large-scale farming operations. Since it was the capital, state agricultural associations headquartered in the city and exerted powerful influence on economic, political, and social affairs. In the post–World War II era, however, rapid urban and suburban growth, based on a less and less agriculturally based economy, encroached on arable lands. By 1977, residential growth in Maricopa County alone forced ten thousand acres a year out of production.[66] Growers feared that the urban newcomers, whom they identified as liberal, would alter the balance of power. They deferred action when possible, made minor concessions to disgruntled suburbanites when necessary, and continually stressed the importance of the agricultural industry to the state.[67]

The BPC believed that suburbanites' concerns about pesticide drift lacked substance and arose primarily because of associated unpleasant odors that the agency thought were otherwise harmless. With this assumption, it often did not undertake serious investigations; rather, the agency followed up on complaints "for public relations sake" and used each case as an opportunity to explain the position of growers and pesticide applicators.[68] It considered a follow-up to a complaint to be an "educational meeting" more than an investigation.[69] The grower-controlled body generally viewed the public with antipathy even though it was charged with protecting them. BPC administrator Bob Rayburn warned: "every segment of agriculture is going to be adversely effected by legislation that already has reared it's [*sic*] ugly head, and it doesn't take much imagination on anyones [*sic*] part to see what is going to take place if some of the unbridled efforts of those opposed to pesticides in any form are allowed to continue to discriminate against agriculture and this means discrimination against the human race."[70]

The BPC would sometimes take minor ameliorative steps to quiet suburban protest and keep discontent from spreading. For instance, when the 1971 Scottsdale drift incidents started to draw national attention, the board disallowed the use of the odoriferous liquid Di-Syston in hopes that suburbanites would not resume their "cease and desist chant" through the mouthpiece of the media and "begin all over their harassment of the farmers, the applicators and this Board."[71] Such actions forestalled the development of a grassroots NIMBY environmental campaign, but failed to resolve the conflict at the agricultural/urban interface.

The suburban protest over drift in the greater Phoenix metropolitan area swelled significantly in 1978. Over a thousand letters flooded state agencies with complaints ranging from the odor of the sprays and the noise of the crop dusters to the effects of exposure on human health. Once again people living in fringe communities along the urban/rural border expressed the greatest concern. As their grievances continued to go unaddressed, they grew increasingly antagonistic toward the BPC and attempted to appeal to a higher authority. The Sun City Town Meeting Association passed a motion that Governor Bruce Babbitt should force growers to reform their chemical use practices to better protect public health.[72] Residents of Ellsworth Mini-Farms subdivision, circulated a petition demanding that action be taken to eliminate the aerial application of pesticides, because the effects of drift "severely violated" their "right to live as free Americans."[73] People living adjacent to SRPMIC fields raised the most virulent protests about pesticide drift.

Other parts of the Phoenix metropolitan area had shifting geographies of pesticide complaints, that followed the path of suburban sprawl. Scottsdale residents living on the border of SRPMIC continued to be exposed to drift, however, because the reservation boundary kept development from moving further outward. Their complaints peaked three times over a fifteen-year period: 1971; 1978 and 1979; and 1984 through 1986. This repeated exposure to drift reduced Scottsdale residents' patience for the BPC's foot dragging and inadequate responses. In fact, the Pima Road corridor separating city from reservation came to be referred to as the "Gaza Strip of the pesticide war," because of both the persistence and the intensity of conflict along the divide between rural and urban settlement.[74]

Scottsdale residents living along the Pima Road corridor expressed a sense of helplessness during heavy spray seasons, because fear of the agricultural chemicals made them feel like prisoners in their own homes. Numerous letters to the governor detailed the maladies suffered during the 1978 summer: headaches, dizziness, breathing difficulties, diarrhea, stomach cramps, fatigue, and nosebleeds. Most of those who experienced health problems lived within a mile of the fields. Concerned citizens reported that their suffering lasted the entire spray season, sometimes as long as six weeks.[75] A particularly powerful letter to Babbitt from a Scottsdale woman vividly described a nightmarish scene: "You're working at your desk. You have the sniffles so you reach for your handkerchief. You use it and lo and behold it [*sic*] covered with blood. And the bleeding goes on and on and on. You find yourself repeating this scene five or six times a day for several days. What's happening? You come home to find your little girl in tears. She can't control her bowels and has soiled herself. And your son awakens terrified he's dying because his pillow is soaked in blood. Another nose bleed."[76] The woman closed the letter by informing the governor that such experiences were commonplace for many people in the area.

Public pressure from Scottsdale and other outlying areas in the Valley of the Sun forced the BPC to call two meetings to address citizen concerns in October and November 1978, though residents were less than satisfied with the results. A distressed Scottsdale woman wrote Babbitt after one of the meetings, complaining that the board had "jeered and hooted," "laughed at questions," and "ridiculed" citizens who spoke out.[77] Another Scottsdale woman protested that her voice was being drowned out by the chemical companies, pesticide applicators, farmers, and others with a vested interest in maintaining the status quo.[78] Growers and the BPC found the scientific results of pesticide studies inconclusive and maintained that the residents suffered less from the toxic effects of exposure than they did from an "emotional problem of odor."[79] The BPC proposed talking with suppliers about reducing the levels of mercaptans in DEF, Folex, and Bolstar in order to reduce the chemicals' offensive odors. They blamed these three substances for most of the suburban discontent and left larger issues of human health unaddressed.[80]

Suzanne Prosnier, a Scottsdale mother whose family had suffered through the spray seasons since moving within a mile of the reservation, remained unsatisfied with BPC's response and disbelieving of the contention that the pesticides were no more dangerous than table salt or aspirin. She belonged to the fledgling NIMBY organization People's Environmental Organization for Pesticide Legislation and Enforcement (PEOPLE). The organization represented over four hundred Scottsdale families, many of whom actively engaged in pesticide politics by collecting data, writing letters, generating publicity, and providing testimony at public hearings. Prosnier assumed the position of research director and traveled to Washington to testify before the Subcommittee on Oversight and Investigations of the House Interstate and Foreign Commerce Committee. She maintained that residents had sought protection from the ill effects of drift for years and had met with frustration every time because of the inadequate response from state agencies, particularly the Board of Pesticide Control.[81] The testimony drew the interest of the EPA, which recognized that the problems relating to pesticide drift in Arizona's agricultural/urban interface had national significance because aerial spraying was commonplace throughout the country.[82]

The EPA called a three-day public hearing in September 1979 to hear testimony from the conflicting interests in Arizona. Growers, citizens, scientists, and pesticide applicators testified, offering widely varying interpretations of problems relating to pesticide drift. Growers and those with connections to the pesticide industry outnumbered other attendees by approximately four to one. They used the lack of conclusive scientific evidence to argue that the aerially applied pesticides did not adversely affect health.[83] Arizona Farm Bureau Federation representative Ralph Baskett Jr. complained of the "hysteria about the effects of chemicals on the environment and upon health" and stated that the Farm Bureau "opposed legislation or regulation based upon emotional, nondocumented complaints."[84] Yet opponents of increased regulation failed to offer a good answer for the suffering in suburbia. Residents from affected areas countered the charge of irrational hysteria with evidence from a door-to-door survey that showed their illnesses coinciding with the aerial application of chemicals. The results also revealed that the maladies disappeared when the spraying stopped or afflicted individuals traveled out of the area.[85]

Arizona government officials offered their assessments as well. ADHS director Suzanne Dandoy acknowledged the lack of conclusive scientific evidence to which growers appealed, but maintained that very few studies had been done to confirm or deny the "unmistakable association in time and place between the application of agricultural pesticides and the reporting of symptoms and illnesses in nearby residents." Dandoy also testified that the BPC lacked the staff and experience necessary to sufficiently address the problem, while warning that "putting the maintenance of these regulatory programs in government agencies dominated by the industries they regulated" jeopardized the "ultimate goal" of protecting the public from illnesses caused by toxic exposure.[86] Babbitt also charged that it was dominated by agricultural interests and had proven "tame" and "ineffective," as made clear by its "history of no regulation."[87] A review of BPC action, in fact, revealed that the board had failed to investigate 156 of 180 randomly selected complaints.[88] BPC administrator Bill Blackledge tried to defend the agency, stating that it did not need more stringent regulations, because it had "enough trouble keeping up with what we've got."[89]

After weighing the merits of the varying testimony, the EPA released a draft of its advisory opinion on July 23, 1980. It recognized that regulatory agencies and scientists act differently in the face of uncertain evidence and considered this difference when drafting the report. Assistant Administrator for Pesticides and Toxic Substances Steven Jellinek stated that scientists act cautiously and avoid drawing conclusions when confronted with uncertainty; regulators, on the other hand, do not have the luxury of withholding decisions until concrete links are established, because they are charged with protecting the public from harm. He reasoned: "Given this circumstance, the regulator must step into a murky world of imprecision where scientists are loathe to tread."[90] The EPA stated that no pesticides should be applied aerially when wind speeds exceeded ten miles per hour or within three hundred feet of areas designated as "sensitive." Such areas included places in which "unprotected people" resided, substantial commercial business operations existed, schools or churches would convene within twenty-four hours, and public parks and highways. The advisory opinion additionally held that individuals located within sensitive areas should be notified about pesticide applications in advance so that they might take whatever precautionary measures they deemed necessary to avoid unintentional exposure.[91] The advisory opinion remained silent on whether or not the grower-controlled BPC had an inherent conflict of interest in its regulatory responsibilities.

Growers viewed the advisory opinion as a significant threat to their economic livelihood and marshaled their forces to stop its implementation. They quibbled over buffer zone distances and argued that the advance notification clause would create an undue burden for applicators.[92] Growers' associations contacted their congresspersons who in turn exerted pressure on the EPA, asserting that the agency had overreacted and had failed to balance the responsibility of protecting the public health against the necessity of preserving cost-effective agricultural production.[93] The pressure proved effective as the agency suspended its work. The EPA reasoned that the "emotional and polarized climate" would prevent the advisory opinion from functioning as an effective "mechanism for giving guidance to applicators." Still, it predicted the conflict would not diminish as long as suburban development continued to intrude on agricultural land.[94]

Growers also did not think that their defeat of the advisory opinion would end the conflict with suburbanites. A 1979 survey of urban Arizonans revealed that less than a quarter of respondents believed that state growers were "very careful" when using pesticides, while approximately half of all respondents viewed pesticides as a "potential hazard" to themselves and their children.[95] Agribusiness interests subsequently took a multipronged approach to addressing the issue. Growers along the Pima Road corridor reached a "gentlemen's agreement" with Scottsdale residents. In effort to avoid rigid state or federal regulation, the growers engaged in a program of voluntary self-monitoring. They restricted the use of odoriferous chemicals in sensitive areas and adopted many of the proposed tenets of the EPA's draft advisory opinion.[96] The BPC tried to quash a proposed public education program focused on environmental problems along the urban/rural boundary, because it believed that the workshops would foster problems.[97] The Arizona Cotton Growers Association employed a public relations firm to remind urbanites of the importance of agriculture to the state and to warn them that pesticide bans would result in lower crop yields and higher prices. It assured the public that it had little reason to fear pesticide drift, comparing the skill of applicators to legendary mule skinners "who could flick a fly off the ear of the lead mule in a 20-mule hitch with his whip, without even bothering the animal."[98] The multipronged approach proved effective until a careless chemical application in 1984 reignited suburban fears.

New Allies and Old Enmities

Peace along Pima Road came to an end on October 11, 1984. Between five and eight o'clock in the morning, licensed pesticide applicators Gila River Industries, Inc. used a helicopter to apply ethyl-methyl parathion, a chemical with high acute toxicity, to twenty-two hundred acres of fields bordering Pima Road and the Scottsdale Community College campus.[99] The spray drifted over the roadway, coating cars with chemicals, and onto the college campus where dozens of students and faculty fell ill. Reports of nausea, headaches, and other illnesses flooded state health and environmental offices.[100] The incident awakened an anger in Scottsdale that had remained latent for over two years. Mayor Herb Drinkwater charged that the applicator displayed an "arrogant disregard" for people's lives and pledged that the city would not tolerate any threat to the health of its residents.[101] The governor expressed a similar degree of frustration over the "long standing problem" and asserted that "citizens must not be expected to suffer illness or anxiety over health risks due to pesticide applications."[102] The BPC responded by placing the pilot and Gila River Industries on probation for one year.[103]

The weak disciplinary action in the case was emblematic of the BPC's inadequate response to most pesticide violations. While its responsiveness to complaints improved after the 1979 EPA hearings, it still took relatively few disciplinary actions.[104] Though thousands of investigations took place between May 1979 and March 1983, BPC held only thirty-three hearings on reported infractions and took disciplinary action only eleven times. The Arizona Office of the Auditor General reported that the "Board has been perceived as a weak enforcement agency" and that the "criticism comes from many sources, including the Federal government, the industry and to some extent Board members themselves."[105] Since threats from elected officials did little to spur the board to action, the public shouldered the responsibility of improving regulation.

Representatives from the AFW and the AFWCP began appearing at BPC meetings six months prior to the Gila River Industries drift incident. Press secretary Don Devereux, Lupe Sánchez, and Karen Kincaid urged the board to support farmworkers in their effort to gain a representative voice in the agency.[106] It rebuffed their request.[107] The AFWCP filed suit against the agency in 1985, alleging that the composition of the board denied farmworkers equal protection under the law because they were the only group deemed ineligible for a seat.[108] The BPC allocated ten of its fifteen seats to the various sectors of Arizona agribusiness, including cotton, produce, dairy, alfalfa and feed grains, citrus, cattle, agricultural chemical industry, entomologists, pesticide applicators, and the Arizona Commission of Agriculture and Horticulture. An occupational health specialist and a Department of Health Services representative claimed two other spaces.[109] Three members of the public filled out the ranks, but a clause in the law stated that participating citizens could have no direct or indirect connection to agriculture other than as consumers. This precluded a farmworker representative from occupying a position.[110]

The Arizona Farm Workers Committee on Pesticides also alleged that the BPC failed to fulfill its obligatory duties to protect public health and property. To strengthen its case, it enlisted a diverse contingent of secondary plaintiffs who had been adversely affected by pesticides. Plaintiff Eloisa Lopez's family became ill after a crop duster violated regulations and applied sprays within one hundred feet of her residence. Connie Selby, an owner and operator of a Montessori school, joined the suit because a crop duster had dropped its load within one hundred feet of her premises when it was not supposed to come within a quarter of a mile.[111] The other plaintiffs had all worked in the fields applying pesticides to crops. J. D. Moore and Manuel Gonzales could not read English. The men claimed that they had not been warned about the chemicals' hazardousness or been provided with protective clothing to reduce exposure. Both Moore and

Gonzales had experienced the cumulative debilitating effects of the sprays and could no longer work. A third farmworker, Rafael Fernandez, also stated that he had not received safety instructions or protective gear from his employer prior to spraying fields with pesticides. Because of the lack of training, protective equipment, and sanitation facilities in the fields, Fernandez had suffered severe injury when a hose on the pesticide holding tank broke.[112] All of plaintiffs had reported their incidents to the BPC, but it took no disciplinary action in any of the cases.[113]

Attorney Nadine Wettstein also tried to recruit a victim from the Scottsdale drift incident as a plaintiff. The AFWCP initially took exception to the degree of attention the community received, stating: "It is interesting and sad to discover that our Gov. thinks that pesticides can only injure white children in Scottsdale and not brown children in El Mirage and the outlying towns in [the] west [valley]."[114] The organization's annoyance at the disproportionate attention to the affluent suburb, however, did not stop it from working with individuals from the afflicted community. M-COP chairperson Gustavo Gutierrez recognized the potential strength of coalitions, including collaborative efforts between workers and environmentalists. He maintained that "the Rank and Filers are faced by the same adversaries that the Enviormentlist [*sic*] are facing in this state capital . . . the same adversaries who's [*sic*] only concern is big business and the profit system, with no consideration for human suffering." He concluded: "There is only one way that we can change the course in which we are going [*sic*] there has to be a strong alliance between the Environmentalist and the Labor movement of this state . . . we have to pull our forces together."[115]

AFWCP did not have the option of forming an alliance with the Scottsdale grassroots environmental organization PEOPLE, however. The growers' "gentlemen's agreement" to adjust pesticide application practices served its purpose in alleviating much of the drift problem along the Pima Road corridor. Consequently, PEOPLE disbanded before the October 1984 incident. Since the group no longer existed, AFWCP contacted individuals within the community.[116] Professor Pat Brock, who suffered headaches, a runny nose, and skin irritation when parathion seeped through the community college's ventilation system, represented Scottsdale victims in the lawsuit. Together, they pushed for the immediate reform of the BPC or its abolition if corrective action could not be taken.[117]

Judge Thomas O'Toole ruled in favor of the defendant, but that did not end efforts to reform or abolish the agency.[118] The AFWCP had concurrently strategized to introduce a pesticide reform bill in the state legislature. Coordinator Laurie Martinelli recognized that "with all the publicity on pesticides and the Governor's recent response over the Scottsdale spraying, it is time to introduce legislation."[119] If legislation failed to pass in 1985, the group planned to introduce an initiative in 1986.[120] For the initiative to be successful, the AFWCP would need to foster partnerships with other organizations, combining resources to build public support before the November elections. Widespread public concern about pesticides and groundwater quality made the task of identifying allies easier.[121]

Winton Dahlstrom, a retiree with a history of environmental activism, moved to Sun City from Michigan in 1982 and soon became concerned that Arizona's drinking water would become as fouled as that in the industrialized Rust Belt.[122] His concerns had merit. State health officials reported that over one hundred wells had suffered contamination from DBCP in 1979, a series of tests in 1984 revealed that eighteen out of forty-four sampled wells had high levels of the EDB, and the industrial solvent trichloroethylene (TCE) as present at dangerous levels in Tucson's water supply.[123] Dahlstrom also learned the extent to which agricultural and

Figure 5.1. M-COP co-founder Gustavo Gutierrez stayed active in social justice campaigns for most of his adult life. He recognized the potential for diverse coalitions to overcome the political strength of common adversaries. Photo courtesy of Christine Marín.

mining interests had successfully blocked environmental legislation.[124] He took the lead of Arizona Common Cause's water quality task force after sharing his fears of groundwater contamination with the board of directors. Organizer John Anderson, working closely with Dahlstrom, began to reach out to different organizations and members of the public in 1984 in hopes of coordinating a response.[125]

Anderson organized meetings in Tucson and Phoenix to discuss the possibility of circumventing the agricultural and mining industry lobbies by drafting an initiative that would bring the issue of groundwater protection directly before the voters. He spoke with the Sierra Club in Tucson and drafted an outline of the proposed initiative. Representatives of a highly diverse group of interests showed up to the Phoenix meeting, including members of the Sierra Club and the Audubon Society; Pamela Swift, the founder of the grassroots organization Toxic Waste Investigative Group; members of the League of Women Voters; and Don Devereux and Nadine Wettstein from the Arizona Farm Workers.[126] Meeting attendees agreed on several key components to be included in the initiative to better protect the public from industrial and agricultural toxins. First, the emphasis would be on the state's groundwater supply, because they figured that "safe drinking water" would be a "dynamite rallying cry." The initiative, they believed, should begin with a "very, very strong statement" of public policy so that the courts would have a clear indicator of intent. The legislation would ban unregulated dumping, reduce water contaminants, and establish a clear regulatory authority within an agency free of industry influence, and put the burden of cost on the regulated industries.[127] A "right to know" clause ensured the public would be made aware of "the full range of risks they face from exposure to hazardous substances" and be better able to "make reasoned decisions and take informed actions to protect their own health and safety."[128] The law would also make it easier for private citizens to bring suits against polluting industries for damages suffered.[129]

Nadine Wettstein and John Anderson collaborated with David Baron of the Center for Law in the Public Interest and Tucson Assistant City Attorney T. J. Harrison to draft the initiative over the course of the next year.[130] Wettstein linked the concerns of farmworkers and the AFWCP to those of the coalition during this stage of development. A March 1985 press release endorsed by Arizona Common Cause, the Maricopa Audubon

Society, the Palo Verde (Phoenix) Group of the Sierra Club, the Maricopa County Organizing Project, and other organizations complained that "because of legislative inaction this session, the Board of Pesticide Control will continue to operate as it has consistently operated in the past—i.e., with little or no regard for the health and safety of either the public at large or those farm workers whose health is, perhaps, most at risk."[131] The final draft of the initiative transferred the regulatory powers of the BPC to the ADHS, a change that the AFW and suburbanites had tried to initiate in the past.

The coalition held a press conference on September 17, 1985 to announce the formation of Arizona Clean Water Advocates (ACWA, pronounced "aqua") whose singular purpose was to collect 72,637 valid signatures, 10 percent of the votes cast in the gubernatorial election, before July 3, 1986 in order to get the Water Quality and Pesticide Control Initiative on the November ballot.[132] This ambitious task required strong commitments from all of the participating organizations. Common Cause, the Sierra Club, and the Arizona Farm Workers arguably made the greatest contribution to the project. Sierra Club representative Alma Williams and Nadine Wettstein split duties for the Phoenix press conference, leaving the planning of the Tucson event to John Anderson. Williams then accepted the position of chairperson, while Wettstein assumed the role of budget officer.[133] ACWA estimated that it would need $33,800 to fund the campaign. Common Cause planned to contribute $10,000 in donations, while the Sierra Club and Arizona Farm Workers pledged $4,000 and $2,000 respectively.[134] It truly represented a merging of diverse interests into an effective grassroots coalition.

ACWA discussed pesticide-related issues throughout the petition drive, using the inadequacies of the Board of Pesticide Control as a primary example of how current regulatory mechanisms failed to properly protect the public from the adverse effects of toxins. ACWA targeted Tucson, Litchfield Park, Sun City, and Scottsdale at the start of its campaign.[135] Tucson's problems centered on TCE contamination, and Litchfield Park had a large number of agricultural workers, whereas Sun City and Scottsdale residents suffered health ailments caused by drift. ACWA maintained that "the adverse effects [of pesticides] are no longer limited to farm workers, but now are spreading to the public at large through drift and, more importantly, ground water contamination."[136] This statement implied that the concerns of farmworkers and the public were intimately linked and that the maladies suffered by farmworkers were symptomatic of risks to the public at large. It also directly connected the farmworkers' and suburbanites' health concerns to the broader issue of safe drinking water. This expanded the support base for pesticide reform well beyond the labor camps in the fields and the suburban developments along the agricultural/urban interface.[137]

The governor appointed a committee of legislators and interested parties to engage in negotiations when the initiative effort began to gain momentum, in hopes that compromise would yield a mutually acceptable legislative bill. Legislators initially believed that agricultural chemicals were peripheral to concerns about groundwater quality and attempted to separate the issues.[138] Common Cause, however, insisted that pesticides be addressed in the bill, because pesticides and water quality issues were inseparable.[139] The legislators relented and kept the pesticide component in the draft measure, with both sides making compromises in the process. The bill contained strict pesticide regulation clauses and would abolish the Board of Pesticide Control, but it divided enforcement responsibility among several different agencies, including the Arizona Commission of Agriculture and Horticulture.[140] The ACWA found the final bill satisfactory and opted to discontinue work on the initiative in May 1986.[141]

Voters approved the bill by referendum in November, passing the Arizona Environmental Quality Act into law. The sweeping new legislation established the Department of Environmental Quality and abolished the industry-dominated Water Quality Control Council and Board of Pesticide Control. It distributed BPC responsibilities to three different agencies. The Arizona Commission of Agriculture and Horticulture took over the licensing of pesticide applicators, the Industrial Commission assumed responsibility for overseeing farmworker safety, and the new Department of Environmental Quality undertook the task of preventing water pollution.[142] The law addressed many of the concerns harbored by farmworkers and suburbanites. It expanded buffer zones and made pesticide drift into nontarget areas illegal even if the applicator was spraying the chemicals in a permitted location. It safeguarded whistle-blowers and provided farmworkers the same health and safety protections as workers in other industries. Additionally, the act required that growers and applicators keep records of pesticide use, and created avenues for public participation and education.[143] Initiating a citizen suit against a polluting industry and the state, if the state failed to fulfill its regulatory responsibility, also became easier.[144] The citizen oversight provision would theoretically minimize the government inaction that had been so endemic to pesticide regulation in the past. Lastly, the Environmental Quality Act directed the Commission of Agriculture and Horticulture to create an Integrated Pest Management program with the intent that such a program would reduce the use of agricultural chemicals in Arizona.[145]

The Arizona Environmental Quality Act marked the end of fifteen years of intermittent conflict over issues related to the application and use of poisonous agricultural chemicals. Its passage into law came as the result of a number of factors. First and foremost, it may be attributed to the hard work of individuals within the Arizona Clean Water Advocates and the cooperation of the diverse supporting organizations. Several grassroots organizations had attempted to alter the state's pesticide politics in the years between 1971 and 1986, but they had found little success on their own. The agricultural lobby within the state exerted strong pressure on legislators to protect growers against proposed changes to the state's regulatory structure and law. Pesticide reform proponents overcame the power of the agricultural lobby by identifying like-minded organizations and linking their concerns into larger issues of groundwater quality.[146]

The success of the coalition had much to do with the timing of its collaborative efforts. The influence of the agricultural lobby over state politics proved to be weaker in 1984 than it was in 1978 or 1971. During this time, the urban population had doubled.[147] Most of the growth came as a result of migration from other states, which helped diminish the political power of growers and their representative organizations.[148] Growers recognized the threat posed by this shift and tried to win public support with outreach campaigns. They also made minor concessions to quell suburban discontent, particularly in Scottsdale, but the 1984 drift incident reawakened anger over pesticides in suburbia. Prior to this time, the engagement of suburbanites and farmworkers in reform efforts had seldom overlapped. The 1984 incident presented the AFWCP with an opportunity to capitalize on the increased public and political interest in pesticides and establish new cooperative relationships with other groups that objected to BPC's lax regulation.[149]

Organizations depended upon the active work of bridge-builders who connected diverse groups of people to foster a successful coalition. The separate engagement of farmworkers and suburbanites in pesticide reform in 1971 demonstrates that cooperation did not occur naturally, despite the shared concern. Networks formed from the active outreach of organization members, who were often organizers or participating professionals. The work of bridge-builders like Nadine Wettstein linked the concerns of farmworkers, environmentalists, suburbanites, and other members of the public. These networks enlarged the base of support for a comprehensive environmental law, which resulted in the passage of the Arizona Environmental Quality Act in 1986.[150] Similar efforts to pass a comprehensive environmental law took place simultaneously in California and met with fierce resistance from recalcitrant growers and the state's industry-friendly Republican governor.

6

RESISTING ROLLBACKS

California, 1982–1990

As the cameras cut and lights dimmed at the Convention Center Music Hall in Cleveland on October 28, 1980, voters mulled the closing remarks made by Republican challenger Ronald Reagan in the presidential debate with Jimmy Carter. Reagan suggested that Americans ask themselves if they and the nation were better off than four years prior and make their decision at the polls based on that answer. He closed the evening with a promise to lead a "crusade . . . to take government off the backs of the great people of this country, and turn you loose" to make America great again.[1] The remarks resonated with the public and helped break open a race that had been close.[2] Voters turned out in low numbers on November 4, but the overwhelming majority of those who went to the polls cast their ballots for Ronald Reagan.[3]

Reagan campaigned, in part, on a promise to unfetter business from a tangle of federal regulations that he claimed hampered economic growth. He questioned the necessity of the Occupational Safety and Health Administration, for instance, claiming that it served only to harass employers and did little to actually reduce workplace injuries.[4] He also targeted the EPA. Confusing sulfur dioxide with carbon monoxide, Reagan claimed that Mount St. Helens had spewed more sulfur dioxide into the atmosphere in a single blast than ten years of exhaust from automobiles.[5] While his understanding of chemical compounds appeared fuddled, the message did not. His campaign rhetoric put proponents of protective environmental and labor law on notice that past gains might be rolled back if he assumed office.

Reagan proved that his calls for deregulation were not empty rhetoric upon assuming office. Within nine days of being sworn in, he ordered a sixty-day freeze on hiring and rulemaking by federal agencies.[6] Regulatory bodies subsequently had to perform cost-benefit analyses before implementing new standards.[7] Advocates of deregulation assumed lead positions within regulatory agencies. On a 100-point scale, the new EPA director Anne Gorsuch earned a 33 and an 8 in 1976 and 1977 in a Colorado Open Space Council analysis that ranked the environmental consciousness of state legislators.[8] Severe budget and staff cuts followed. OSHA, for example, cut 160 of its 2,786 positions in 1981 alone, which resulted in a 17 percent decline in workplace inspections.[9] The administration also targeted existing regulation for review and change in its efforts to create a more favorable business climate.[10]

The actions put environmentalists and unionists alike on the defensive. The two movements sometimes looked toward one another for support in their efforts to withstand the attack on past gains. Speaking before the Industrial Union Department of the AFL-CIO in Detroit, Sierra Club president Joe Fontaine sought to "set the record straight," stating: "Environmentalists often are characterized as elitists who care more about birds and animals than people. . . . Those labels have been pinned on us by our opponents out of frustration."[11] After chronicling some of the organization's past support for labor-related issues, Fontaine discussed a new blue-green coalition, the OSHA/Environmental Network, that produced a report in 1982 titled "Poisons on the Job: The Reagan Administration and American Workers."[12] The report charged that the administration was jeopardizing the health of millions by weakening protections for workers, refusing to set new standards or strengthen existing ones, and restricting public access to information.[13] Fontaine noted that the political candidates supported by his club were the same as those supported by unions in 90 percent of elections, asserting that "it is up to groups like ours to put humanity and compassion back into government."[14]

The conservative turn that confronted unions and environmental groups in American political life stretched beyond Ronald Reagan. Republicans picked up twelve Senate seats, claiming a majority for the first time in a quarter-century.[15] A significant number of seats in the House of Representatives went to Republicans as well, though Democrats managed to hold the numerical advantage.[16] Conservatives also rose to power in some state-level contests. In California in 1982, Republican gubernatorial candidate George Deukmejian defeated Democrat Tom Bradley with a campaign that reprised the rhetoric of Reagan on regulatory and economic issues.[17]

Governor Deukmejian committed himself to weakening California's regulatory structure and encountered similar opposition from unions and environmental organizations. The groups defended existing regulatory agencies and law from attack and supported new initiatives to better protect public health. They worked toward common ends, supported similar legislative initiatives, and showed support for each another's efforts. Environmentalists and the United Farm Workers, however, typically conducted separate campaigns, because their strategies to effect change and the focus of their efforts varied to some degree.

Fault Lines

George Deukmejian maintained that the state could not "build prosperity by shackling those who create it."[18] He promised to "start with a thorough housecleaning of state government" and pledged to eliminate regulations and governmental bodies judged to have costs that outweighed benefits.[19] In regard to agriculture and pesticide regulation, he said: "When you get right down to it, the biggest pests in agriculture today aren't the bugs that eat crops, but the bureaucrats who smother productivity beneath a blanket of cumbersome regulations."[20] Growers, hence, had reason to be hopeful that relaxed regulatory oversight would follow the 1982 gubernatorial election.

Growers thought that both candidates, Tom Bradley and George Deukmejian, would represent their interests better than outgoing governor Jerry Brown, but they favored Deukmejian. Brown had presided over the appointment of a prolabor majority to the Agricultural Labor Relations Board (ALRB), vetoed bills that would have restricted the tactics employed by farmworkers' unions, and passed more stringent pesticide legislation into law.[21] Bradley promised to make the ALRB fair and balanced.[22] Deukmejian showed favoritism more clearly. He stressed that growers would have a "friend in the Governor's office" and characterized Chavez and the UFW as agitators who "harassed and threatened" farmworkers into joining the union and "vandalized" farm property.[23] The pronouncement convinced agricultural associations to enrich his campaign coffers with contributions that totaled between $750,000 and $1,000,000.[24] This accounted for approximately 20 percent of his expenditures.[25]

Deukmejian kept his campaign promise when he assumed office by changing the character of the ALRB. He appointed David Stirling, who had supported a number of grower-backed bills as a legislator, as the general counsel. This position functioned as a gatekeeper, screening cases to bring before the board.[26] Accusations soon surfaced of Stirling trying to exert even greater control by forcing the alteration of case decisions.[27] Several board members complained of "being punished for our efforts to carry out the law since such efforts are seen as signs of 'philosophical differences,'" adding that they expected to face "punitive action for disloyalty" if they continued to perform their jobs in the way prescribed by the Agricultural Labor Relations Act (ALRA).[28] ALRB members attempted to curb Stirling's power, but backed down when Deukmejian threatened to eliminate the agency budget if the action went forward.[29] The board still suffered a 27 percent funding cut.[30] Deukmejian then awarded a position to John P. McCarthy, a former agribusiness executive, and named Jyrl Ann James-Massengale, an attorney who represented growers when she worked for one of largest American labor law firms, as the new chairwoman of the ALRB in July 1984.[31]

The governor's actions greatly reduced the speed with which grievances were heard, leading to an immense backlog of cases. The board lost fifty positions in 1983, which contributed to the number of uninvestigated cases rising from 496 in December 1982 to 1,091 in the following year.[32] The number of cases heard during the first six months of the 1983–84 fiscal year numbered half the total for the same period in the year before as average processing time increased from thirty-one to fifty-one days.[33] Several ALRB staff members concluded that the ALRA was "being chipped away by an insensitive administration that has proven its unwillingness to enforce the law."[34]

These actions posed challenges for the United Farm Workers, which emerged from the 1970s as a lesser organization than it had been in the previous decade. After the passage of the ALRA in 1975, the union went through an intense period of internal conflict that resulted in the departure of most of its veteran staffers. Increased responsibilities and unanticipated organizational problems followed the signing of new contracts in the mid-1970s. Chavez reasoned that a lack of structure was likely "the single most important reason for our frustrations and failures" as it became "harder and harder to choose priorities because everyone has their own bailiwick."[35] He saw the solution in a business model of management, and promised that the new organizational structure would not favor the "suppression of different and dissenting points of view" over open discussion, but that is precisely what happened.[36]

Chavez required staffers to play the Synanon "game," in which participants vented their personal frustrations in a supposedly neutral forum, as part of the change. Advocates maintained that the public airing of grievances ultimately improved group communication.[37] The exercise did not work well in practice. After the "game" was incorporated into union affairs, Marshall Ganz claims, "Chavez transformed UFW deliberations into a controlled, exclusive, and judgmental process in which one's loyalty was constantly on the line."[38] Chavez drove several staffers out of the organization, feeling that disagreement with his planning or his union practices equated to conspiracy against the organization. Other veteran organizers and attorneys quit of their own accord, disheartened with the turn that Chavez and the union had taken. Hence, the UFW entered the 1980s as a more autocratic organization, lacking many of the creative minds that had been critical to its early success.[39]

Though the character and structure of the union changed, Chavez still returned to the boycott strategy that had proven so successful in the past to confront Deukmejian's depredations against the ALRB. Since he could not call a consumer boycott on the agency, he targeted grapes, hoping that the symbolism of the first storied campaign would spark public participation.[40] The UFW framed the action as an effort to "guarantee free election and good faith bargaining."[41] Consumer participation in the campaign would put economic pressure on growers until they were forced to ask the governor to reverse course on the ALRB.[42]

The loss of so many veteran organizers likely contributed to Chavez's decision to use a different tactic to build support. Rather than rely on the footwork of organizers in cities across the United States and Canada, the union put its faith in the promise of direct marketing and a Sperry mainframe computer.[43] The technological gamble presumed that a computer would be more efficient at reaching target audiences than human canvassers.[44] The UFW targeted labor unions, religious organizations, African Americans, Hispanics, and progressives in its mail campaign. The umbrella term "progressive" included peace activists, gays and lesbians, students, welfare rights proponents, animal rights supporters, and environmentalists.[45] Different solicitations aimed to appeal to the divergent interests of the targeted groups.[46]

Public support, however, did not materialize as predicted.[47] Some critics characterized the effort as a political attack that would do little to help farmworkers in the field.[48] Others felt that the union had lost its sympathetic underdog character when the ALRA had put it on more equal footing with growers.[49] Former UFW attorney Jerry Cohen questioned Chavez's reliance on direct marketing, asserting that "junk mail does not organize people, people organize people."[50] Ex-organizer Marshall Ganz echoed Cohen's sentiments.[51] Whether for one of these reasons or from a combination of factors, the UFW lacked widespread support as the boycott entered its twelfth month.[52]

The boycott did not initially address pesticides, though Chavez figured that the union would need to do so again in the future. He kept abreast of developments and the reform efforts of other organizations.[53] When contemplating slogans in 1983, Chavez considered adopting "Our mission is safe food" and "Our mission is to be a watchdog for clean food and good working conditions" before opting for the simple generalized statement, "Our mission is food."[54] He also thought the union needed "a single issue political action committee on water [and] pesticides."[55] National Farm Worker Health Group medical director Marion Moses, formerly of the UFW, remained closely allied with the union and handled the task of organizing a pesticide advisory group for Chavez. Moses enlisted four experts, including the former chief of the California Department of Health Services' Epidemiology Studies Section, to advise the union.[56] Still Chavez did not address pesticides during the first year of the new boycott.[57] Reawakened public fears about pesticide risks in 1985 presented an opportunity for the union to reengage the issue, revive a boycott whose public support was flagging, and build bridges again to the environmental community.

Varied Responses to Common Concerns

People complaining of tremors, cramps, and intense vomiting checked into hospital emergency rooms across California, Oregon, and Washington on July 4, 1985. More than eleven hundred afflicted individuals in five states and parts of Canada sought treatment in the days following.[58] All had consumed California-grown watermelons. The California Department of Food and Agriculture seized and destroyed thousands of tons of product in response, making no distinction between contaminated and uncontaminated fruit.[59] An investigation identified forty growers who had willfully violated state law by using the restricted pesticide aldicarb.[60] In an attempt to control the incident and restore buyers' confidence, the agency required growers to test their fields for illegal pesticide residues before harvesting any more crop.[61] Consumer wariness remained, however.[62]

Concerns about the long-term health effects of pesticide exposure also grew. A 1982 study by the state health department showed increases of stomach cancer and leukemia in Fresno County communities with detectable amounts of DBCP in their water supply, though no follow-up studies were done to establish a causal relationship between the chemical and the cancers.[63] The California State Water Resources Control Board (CSWRCB) then reported on increased evidence of groundwater contamination from the direct discharge of pesticides, runoff from irrigation, overspraying, and drift.[64] A subsequent report released in 1985 by the California Assembly Office of Research showed that fifty-seven different pesticides contaminated nearly three thousand wells in twenty-eight counties within the state.[65] The CSWRCB closed more than a hundred wells in the Central Valley. A number of others remained open with the understanding that water would only be drawn from them on an emergency basis.[66]

CSWRCB report author David B. Cohen maintained that the ability of scientists "to detect and quantify a growing list of organic chemicals in groundwater outstrips our ability to interpret the toxicological significance of these findings," which prolonged scientific uncertainty about the long-term effects of contamination.[67] He asserted that the difficulty of establishing a causal link between pesticides and chronic diseases like cancer did not mean that no link existed.[68] Cohen's intimations that water contamination from pesticides might have unforeseen health consequences coincided with the discovery of an abnormally high incidence of childhood cancer in the agricultural town of McFarland. The unexplained rise in the number of pediatric cancers raised concerns among some people that pesticides were putting human health at risk.[69]

McFarland mother Connie Rosales thought something was terribly wrong when six neighborhood children, her son included, living within six blocks of each other contracted cancer within a relatively short time frame.[70] More cases followed. Doctors diagnosed eleven children with different forms of the disease in the town of sixty-four hundred between 1981 and 1984.[71] Statistically, communities that size average three childhood cancers per ten-year period; McFarland's cancer incidence rate nearly quadrupled the national average in a third of the time.[72] The small town also experienced a rise in miscarriages, fetal deaths, and infant deaths.[73] Parents spurred the Kern County Health Department to conduct an enquiry, but controversy swirled around the investigation. Critics charged that the studies were underfunded, understaffed, and negligent in their failure to explore potentially fruitful sources of information.[74] The department did not examine the water company records from the period of suspected contamination nor did it try to ascertain crop-dusting practices near the town or accumulate data from the vicinity of a chemical warehouse near several of the victims' homes.[75] County Health Officer Leon Hebertson divulged that "one of the things that is specious is to believe that local health jurisdictions can staff and organize and plan to do cancer cluster or outbreak epidemiology of this type."[76]

As these incidents sparked renewed public concern about pesticides and health, Deukmejian moved to limit the public's ability to affect pesticide policy and blocked attempts to strengthen the state's regulations. He worked with Republican and rural Democratic legislators to pass a grower-backed bill that limited the public's ability to use the courts to challenge pesticide use practices.[77] The legislation relieved the state of its responsibility for completing an environmental impact report prior to a pesticide spray campaign. It also precluded public health concerns from being considered by the courts if a lawsuit was filed to stop a state-sponsored spray program.[78] The governor vetoed legislation, backed by California Rural Legal Assistance, that promised to better protect farmworkers by requiring growers to post warning signs around fields within twenty-four hours of spraying Class 1 (the most toxic) pesticides or within forty-eight hours of using less hazardous substances.[79] He twice vetoed bills that would have expanded the collection of cancer incidence data. Instead, Deukmejian limited funding for cancer registries to such an extent that data could only be collected in the eighteen counties that together contained 70 percent of the population. Less populated agricultural counties lacked the resources necessary to establish cancer registries, which arguably would have proved valuable in the investigation of rural cancer clusters.[80]

Environmental organizations joined groups representing farmworkers to oppose attacks on pesticide regulations, push for better monitoring and enforcement of the law, and lobby for stiffer penalties on violations. The Sierra Club, the Natural Resources Defense Council, and California Rural Legal Assistance partnered with eight other organizations in 1983 to counter bills that "threatened to severely weaken existing pesticide protection standards for public health and environment."[81] These groups tried to defeat the bill that limited the public's ability to use the courts to halt a spray campaign.[82] Sierra Club officer and epidemiologist Cedric Garland criticized Deukmejian's vetoing of legislation that would have required growers to promptly place warning signs along field perimeters after pesticide applications. The governor's actions, he maintained, "tied the hands of epidemiologists" seeking to understand the effects of pesticides on human health because "you can't do studies unless you know what workers were exposed to and workers cannot know what they're exposed to unless there are signs."[83] The Sierra Club, the NRDC, the Environmental Defense Fund, Friends of the Earth, Citizens for a Better Environment, CRLA, the California Agrarian Action Project, and the Coalition for Occupational and Environmental Health Hazards also pushed Deukmejian to investigate the watermelon poisoning incident, impose stiffer penalties for the misuse of pesticides, and test groundwater and investigate the pesticide regulatory program in Kern County.[84]

Environmental groups, the California Labor Federation, and the Agricultural Workers Health Center also supported Democratic Assemblyman Lloyd Connelly's successful attempt to pass a bill addressing the contamination of groundwater by pesticides in California.[85] Connelly believed that the state needed to address data gaps on the ability of certain pesticides to move through soil, so that it could come up with a regulatory solution to protect groundwater reserves. He also took issue with the lack of available information on the health effects of many of the pesticides used by growers. The recently released California Assembly of Research report "The

Leaching Fields: A Nonpoint Threat to Groundwater" stated that only eight of the forty top priority pesticides identified by the Department of Health Services had a complete set of health and safety studies, and only two of those had the information necessary to calculate the compounds' ability to percolate into groundwater basins.[86] Connelly's bill, the Pesticide Contamination Prevention Act, required pesticide registrants to provide information on the environmental fate of chemicals and charged the Department of Food and Agriculture with the task of establishing a soil and groundwater monitoring program.[87] The NRDC lodged its support, stating that the bill would make the important shift to preventative action from response that is "remedial and reactive."[88] The Sierra Club, the EDF, the League of Conservation Voters, and Citizens for a Better Environment similarly urged passage of the bill.[89]

The UFW inserted pesticide-related demands into the ongoing grape boycott in 1985. At a news conference with Marion Moses in September 1985, Chavez suggested that the watermelon contamination was only "the tip of the iceberg," adding that no one knew the effects on human health after years of exposure. He held that five chemicals used on grapes—parathion, phosdrin, methyl bromide, dinoseb, and captan—were more dangerous than aldicarb and should be banned.[90] In an effort to draw a link to the ongoing campaign, Chavez reasoned that growers interpreted "the Deukmejian Administration's cavalier attitude toward the Agricultural Labor Relations Act as a signal to ignore other laws, particularly those governing the regulation of the thousands of pesticides sprayed each year on California fields."[91] He supported his contention with reference to a vineyard that unlawfully used orthene and had to be quarantined.[92]

Marches from the towns of Earlimart, McFarland, and Richgrove to Delano in September commemorated the twentieth anniversary of the launching of the farmworkers' movement, though the issue of pesticides challenged for center stage. Participants carried small black flags bearing a single skull, while the front of the procession carried a banner that bore three skulls with the bilingual slogan "La Desgracia de los Pesticidas/The Scourge of Pesticides."[93] Chavez referenced related injuries and illness suffered by farmworkers, chastising growers for the "decades of abuse and damage they have brought upon the land." He then returned to a theme that resonated with the public in 1969, stating that the union was committed to "protecting farm workers—and consumers—from systematic poisoning" by growers' "reckless use" of pesticides. He warned consumers that "corporate growers . . . glory in their complacency" and called on them to support the boycott, maintaining that "there is nothing more important that we share in common with the consumers of America than the safety of the nation's food supply which we both depend upon."[94] With that, UFW switched the boycott focus to pesticides, announcing a new campaign shortly thereafter to bring attention to the health hazards that pesticides and residues posed to consumers and farmworkers alike.

Making obvious reference to the Steinbeck classic, UFW introduced the "Wrath of Grapes" campaign in January 1986.[95] As he had in his September speech, Chavez attempted to connect the concerns of farmworkers to those of consumers. He said: "The Wrath of Grapes' symbolizes the killing, maiming and poisoning of thousands of farmworkers—and their children—through the reckless use of deadly poisons in agriculture . . . [and] also represents the threats posed to consumers by pesticide residues contained on fresh grapes and other produce."[96] The UFW reiterated that the boycott had the power to protect people from pesticides by forcing growers to curb usage and alter practices. It held that growers should begin by banning parathion, phosdrin, methyl bromide, dinoseb, and captan.[97] The union soon released a sixteen-minute video bearing the name of the larger campaign. It opened with ominous music, the silhouette of a helicopter dropping chemicals on the fields, and scenes of distraught mothers of children who suffered pesticide-related health problems. Chavez then announced: "We're declaring war, war on the pesticides that are poisoning and killing our people."[98] The film focused heavily on McFarland and the spate of cancers and birth defects that afflicted some of the town's children. Connie Rosales, whose son Randy suffered from lymphatic cancer, numbered among the McFarland mothers who spoke about the town's cancer cluster. She said: "I'm very angry. I'm angry that something like this could go on around you in your environment and when you think you're safe. What we're dealing with here is invisible. The only problem is that our children are our flags. They're dying and that is showing us that there is something wrong here." After introducing another cancer cluster in the nearby town of Fowler, Chavez offered summary judgment of the health crisis, declaring pesticides that were "once considered a miracle of science" had become a "chemical time bomb threatening to contaminate our food supply and environment."

The film connected the suffering of McFarland mothers to the dangers facing consumers, emphasizing that pesticide risks stretched beyond the bounds of the towns bordering agricultural fields. Ramona Franco, who had worked in the fields until the eighth month of her pregnancy and had given birth to a child with no arms and no legs, reported being exposed to captan, one of the pesticides targeted in the UFW boycott. She charged that growers "never tell you when they spray pesticides, because they don't care about people's health." The film also introduced viewers to Salvadore DeAnda, a young boy who was diagnosed with an inoperable cancer on his ninth birthday, and Amalia Larios who was missing a portion of her spine at birth. The mothers of both children had worked in the fields when pregnant. Marion Moses then made a powerful analogy, warning: "Workers are kind of canaries, if you will, for the consumer out there because the workers are being harmed. These are the same [pesticide] residues that are ending up on the food that is being bought in the market and being fed to people . . . some of the chemicals that we're concerned about that do end up as residues are these carcinogenic and teratogenic or birth defect–causing pesticides that we don't think should be in the American diet." The film concluded with the contention that there was a "danger hiding in our food" that the growers would only address after feeling the economic pinch of the boycott. Chavez promised that once UFW achieved results with grapes it would move on to address pesticide problems in other crops.[99] A 1987 marketing analysis estimated that 90 percent of individuals within targeted groups had pledged to support the boycott after watching the video.[100]

The release of the *Wrath of Grapes* coincided with a campaign supported in part by the Sierra Club, the NRDC, and the EDF to pass a sweeping toxics initiative within the state of California that promised to restrict the usage of certain pesticides. Senior EDF attorney David Roe teamed with Sierra Club political director Carl Pope, Assemblyman Connelly, Democratic Assemblyman Gray Davis, and Democratic Senator Art Torres, a former UFW and California Rural Legal Assistance lobbyist and current Chairman of the Senate Toxics Committee, to co-author the initiative that became Proposition 65, the Safe Drinking Water and Toxic Enforcement Act.[101] If passed, it would prohibit the release of cancer-causing chemicals into drinking water, require that employees and the public be warned if carcinogens were to be used in their vicinity, and subject violators to

Figure 6.1. David Roe authored Prop 65 which fundamentally reshaped California's regulatory landscape when it passed into law in 1986 as the Safe Drinking Water and Toxics Enforcement Act. Photo courtesy of the Environmental Defense Fund.

a possible three years in prison and $100,000 in fines.[102] The legislation would apply to both industrial toxins and hazardous agricultural chemicals. The Sierra Club invested nearly $125,000 in the effort to pass Prop 65, making it the second largest donor to a campaign that promised to better protect the health of workers and the public alike. The NRDC and EDF also ranked among the ten highest financial contributors.[103] The UFW did not contribute significantly to the undertaking.[104]

In drafting Prop 65, David Roe and Carl Pope reasoned that the regulatory framework had to be fundamentally altered to better protect workers and consumers from the adverse effects of toxic chemicals. Pope held that the "chemical industry does not accept the legitimacy of the public's desire for safer chemicals" and had a "very limited concept of responsibility toward public health and environment," as did industries that used the chemicals in their production practices.[105] The government only regulated a small fraction of chemicals and industries fiercely resisted greater regulatory constraints.[106] Pope likened the current regulatory approach to building a dam at the base of waterfall, stating: "we may pile the stones up endlessly, but the water simply flows over, around, or through the bar-rier."[107] Roe explained: "If enforcement cannot occur until after the 'how much is too much' [chemical exposure] decision is made, then those to whom the law applies have every incentive to extend the 'how much is too much' debate for as long as possible. The burden is on the regulatory bureaucracy to go forward. Meanwhile, public frustration about the inef-fectiveness of the laws is vented on government, not on industry."[108] Prop 65 put forth an innovative solution to the problem. If passed, it would shift the burden of proof from the public and government to industry.

Prop 65 held that all companies using a substance known to cause cancer or birth defects in the production process or as a product ingredient had to warn workers and consumers about the potential exposure risks. The gover-nor bore the responsibility of publishing a list of known carcinogens and re-productive toxins by March 1987 and updating it annually to include the most current scientific information. No set chemical threshold exempted compa-nies from compliance. If the company did not want to use a warning label, it could either alter production practices to remove the toxic substance or seek an exemption from the labeling requirement. If it opted for the latter, it had to prove that the listed chemical posed no "significant risk" in the volume used.[109] Companies, in other words, had to show that their commodity was safe; rather than burdening the consumer and government with the time- and labor-intensive task of proving that a product threatened public health.[110]

Roe and Pope aimed to make the cost of using toxics high, believing that the value companies put on low production costs and high profits would encourage self-policing. The right-to-know component of the law had the potential to raise costs and lower profits for those who refused to volun-tarily curtail the use of dangerous substances in production. Pope reasoned that workers informed about health risks in the workplace would be more likely to organize against their employers, using strikes or the threat of labor stoppages to force a change.[111] Similarly, they suspected that a label warn-ing consumers of a product's potential harm would immediately affect a company's profit margins, because buyers would likely opt for comparable goods that posed no health threat.[112] Prop 65 also had a citizen suit provi-sion that threatened to raise the costs of using toxic chemicals, because the shift in the burden of proof from consumer to business made it easier for the public to win lawsuits. Roe maintained that a "citizen plaintiff can win without having to mount a complex toxicological case . . . the defendant is also inclined not to pursue a numbing battle of experts, since confusion in the courtroom is not sufficient to guarantee success in establishing the 'no significant risk' defense." Prop 65 supporters concluded that these factors would convince companies "to police themselves in advance."[113]

Opinions on Prop 65 split along predictable lines in the build-up to the 1986 election. Environmentalists, labor unions, and Democrats supported its passage. The petrochemical industry, the California Farm Bureau, and Republicans opposed it.[114] Hundreds of growers marched in protest, complaining that the proposition would make it more difficult to use pesticides on crops. Growers and industry representatives forecast trouble with the citizen suit provision, arguing that "bounty hunter" legal actions would be detrimental to business because the alleged polluter would bear the unnecessary costs of proving a product's safety.[115] Deukmejian weighed in as well, predictably maintaining that the proposed legislation would put an "unbearable burden on farmers and small businesses" and would effectively drive jobs away from the state of California.[116] Two-thirds of California voters did not buy the opposition's argument and cast their ballots for the Safe Drinking Water and Toxic Enforcement Act. The legislation's promise did not take form immediately, though, in part because the Deukmejian administration fought to minimize its applicability.[117] In the years following, environmentalists and the UFW continued to struggle against the administration, growers, and some scientists to implement protective measures safeguarding farmworkers and the public.

Wrangling over Risk and Regulation

The ballot totals on Prop 65 showed that many Californians harbored concerns about the adverse effects of toxics and pesticides. Deukmejian, nevertheless, tried to stay the course on freeing business from the constraints of regulation. UFW persisted in its efforts to ban the five chemicals to which it had given priority in the Wrath of Grapes campaign, while environmentalists maintained focus on the state's regulatory framework. Though the strategies of the UFW and environmentalists varied significantly, the groups found opportunity to extend support to one another in the face of a heated battle with the governor, growers, and a handful of scientists over pesticides, health, and acceptable risk.

The Safe Drinking Water and Toxic Enforcement Act required Deuk-mejian to appoint a twelve-person scientific panel to determine which tox-ins should be included on the list of dangerous substances. He selected two of the scientists recommended by environmental organizations. However, his choice of Bruce Ames for the panel, an outspoken and controversial scientist in the biochemistry department at the University of California Berkeley, acted as counterweight.[118] Ames publicly opposed Prop 65, contending that "the simple scientific fact of the matter is that manmade carcinogens represent only a tiny fraction of the total carcinogens we are exposed to" in the course of a lifetime.[119] He often tried to shift public at-tention from the toxins of industrial polluters to ones that could be linked to poor personal choices, warning that people needed to be more concerned about the cancer-causing effects of sunlight, various foods, and cigarettes. The subtle change in focus emphasized instances in which cancer-stricken individuals could be blamed for the disease that they contracted. Even after being appointed to the governor's advisory panel, Ames continued to refer to the toxics legislation as a "thoroughly silly law."[120] This raised the ire of environmentalists, leading Prop-65 co-author Carl Pope to charac-terize the appointment of Ames as an act of "sabotage" by the governor.[121]

When the panel completed its study, Deukmejian announced that only twenty-six carcinogens and three reproductive toxins would be af-fected.[122] The governor and his advisers selected the toxins using the strict-est interpretation of scientific classifications. For carcinogens, for example, the EPA groups chemicals in one of five different categories: Group A chemicals (*known* human carcinogens) are those substances that have been subject to epidemiological tests done on humans yielding conclusive evi-dence proving them carcinogenic; Group B (*probable* human carcinogens) are those that strong evidence from animal-based studies and more lim-ited results from human-based studies indicate that they are carcinogens; Group C (*possible* human carcinogens) includes chemicals for which there is some positive evidence from animal-based studies though evidence from human-based tests is either lacking or has yet to be completed; Group D are those that lack sufficient data or tests to determine if they are carcino-genic; and Group E (noncarcinogens) shows no evidence of causing can-cer in any species.[123] The governor and his advisory panel reasoned that only those chemicals in Group A should be included on the danger list. They discounted animal-based studies, premising their decision to exclude

chemicals in Groups B and C on the fact that these had not been sufficiently tested on human subjects.[124] DDT and EDB numbered among the
pesticides that did not make the list, though the EPA had previously determined that the chemicals were probable carcinogens and had restricted
their use.[125] Food industry groups then convinced Deukmejian to exempt
food, drugs, and cosmetics from the provisions of Prop 65. Ignoring the
law's intent, the governor maintained that federal standards would be sufficient to protect the public.[126]

A coalition of environmentalists and labor unions argued that the advisory panel's selection criteria did not meet the requirements of the law
and called for nearly two hundred more chemicals to be added to the list.
Prop 65 mandated that the governor's list, at a minimum, include the
carcinogens and reproductive toxins identified in California Labor Code
Section 6382(b)(1) and 6382(d).[127] The sections included both human and
animal carcinogens as identified by the World Health Organization's International Agency for Research on Cancer. The Labor Code recognized
both Group A (known) and Group B (probable) human carcinogens as
threats. The State Department of Health Services also advised Deukmejian that "animal-derived data is scientifically and ethically required
to be included" in the determination of chemicals that posed a health
threat.[128] Nonetheless Deukmejian contended that the law only applied to
known human carcinogens with conclusive evidence from tests on human
subjects.[129]

The labor-environmental coalition consisting of the AFL-CIO, the
California Rural Legal Assistance, the EDF, the Sierra Club, and the
NRDC brought suit against the governor to resolve the issue. The court
held that the Labor Code to which Prop 65 made reference included animal-
based studies; which meant that the governor's list should include both
known and *probable* human carcinogens and reproductive toxins. To further justify the inclusion of animal-based testing in the consideration, the
judge cited the California Department of Health Services' *Guidelines for
Chemical Carcinogen Risk Assessments and Their Scientific Rationale*. The
Guidelines maintained that drawing conclusions from animal-based experiments was necessary because of the ethical problems of conducting tests
on human subjects and the long periods of latency between exposure to a
carcinogenic substance and development of cancer in humans.[130] Furthermore, it held that

Sufficient evidence presently exists for the carcinogenicity in animals of about 200 chemicals. . . . For most of the 200 animal carcinogens for which there is "sufficient evidence," it is unlikely that we will ever know with certainty whether they cause cancer in humans because of the difficulty in obtaining appropriate populations suitable for epidemiological studies. Since it is unlikely we will ever confirm or deny the apparent carcinogenic potential of these 200 chemicals, it appears prudent in the interim to control exposure to them as if they had demonstrated effects in humans.[131]

The court sided with the plaintiffs, mandating that nearly two hundred additional chemicals be included on the list of the toxins.[132] Continued pressure from environmental groups also succeeded in getting the exemptions for the food, drug, and cosmetic industries repealed, although it took several years to do so.[133]

While the governor stymied the implementation of Prop 65, scientists hit a standstill in the McFarland cancer cluster investigation. The Kern County Health Department ended its study with no conclusive findings in October 1986.[134] Under increasing citizen pressure, Deukmejian allocated $200,000 to the Department of Health Services in December 1987 to hire a contingent of university scientists to review previously collected data. Critics, including Senator Torres, complained that a sound investigation could not be completed with so little money.[135] In comparison, the EPA spent $5.3 million to collect and analyze air, water, and soil samples from Love Canal over six months in 1980.[136] Torres also characterized the new investigation as wrongheaded, since it would only review data from the incomplete and problematic initial investigation.[137] Still the plan went forward without adjustment. The second investigation found "no smoking gun," but noted that four chemicals—dimethoate, fenbutatin oxide, dinitrophenol, and dinoseb—warranted further study.[138]

The UFW continued to focus attention on the town and argue that pesticides had caused the spate of childhood disease. By 1988, six McFarland children had succumbed to cancer.[139] The discovery of other clusters in the nearby agricultural towns of Fowler and Earlimart further heightened public concern about the adverse health effects of pesticides.[140] The lack of resolution and the governor's seeming callousness toward the problem presented an opportunity for the UFW to develop a campaign against pesticides and articulate the need for reform better than it had at any time since the initial Delano grape strike.

The union recruited a diverse array of activists to serve on its Environmentalists Committee in support of the Wrath of Grapes campaign. Marion Moses naturally agreed to contribute to the group. The union also enlisted the services of Prop 65 co-author Carl Pope. Lawrie Mott, an NRDC staff scientist and co-author of *Pesticide Alert: A Guide to Pesticides in Fruits and Vegetables*, also served on the committee. In *Pesticide Alert*, Mott wrote "I believe consumers have the power to force change . . . we've used the power of the purse to change the way that American industries make and sell their products."[141] Such sentiment meshed well with the UFW strategy for pesticide reform. Greenpeace regional director David Chatfield and California League of Conservation Voters executive director Lucy Blake participated in the group, as did two activists from newer grassroots environmental organizations. Diane Takvorian had worked with the poor before founding the Environmental Health Coalition in 1980 to address issues of pollution in poor communities.[142] Penny Newman had co-founded Concerned Neighbors in Action after millions of gallons of toxic waste flooded a Riverside suburb in 1978.[143] Walter Hooke rounded out the committee. Hooke had roots in labor and social justice issues, working as an advocate for the National Association of Radiation Survivors after serving in World War II.[144] Following his father's support of the UFW, NRDC attorney Robert Kennedy Jr. also advised Chavez on pesticide issues. Kennedy, however, was not listed as part of the Environmentalists Committee in 1988.[145]

Environmental groups assumed a more visible presence in the union effort in 1987 when representatives from several of them appeared at a press conference to endorse the boycott. Represented groups included: the Center for Science in the Public Interest, the Clean Water Action Project, Environmental Action, the Farm Animal Reform Movement, Friends of the Earth, the National Campaign Against Toxic Hazards, and the National Coalition Against the Misuse of Pesticides.[146] The names of national environmental groups subsequently appeared in some UFW pamphlets to show the breadth of boycott support.[147] Environmentalists also joined union members, community activists, and religious leaders in some public rallies, such as a human billboard at the Baltimore Convention Center, to bring attention to the threats that pesticides posed to the health of farmworkers and consumers.[148] The NRDC funded a project called Mothers and Others Against Pesticides that was co-chaired by Meryl Streep and

Figure 6.2. A family in Indio, California shows support for the United Farm Workers' Wrath of Grapes campaign that sought to halt the usage of five hazardous pesticides. "Abajo con las pesticides" translates to "down with pesticides." United Farm Workers Photo ID 3649, Walter P. Reuther Library, Archives of Labor and Urban Affairs, Wayne State University.

worked closely with the UFW. The project intended to educate the public about pesticide risks and inspire consumer-based change and political action.[149]

Chavez drew increased attention to the boycott when he began a thirty-six-day, liquid-only fast on July 16, 1988. The "Fast for Life," he stated, was a "fervent prayer that, together, farmworkers and the public" would "confront and resist . . . the scourge of poisons that threatens our people and our land and our food." He said that his literature review, conversations with pesticide victims and their families, and discussions with experts convinced him that the pesticide problem "threatens to choke out the life of our people and also the life systems that support us all." Chavez warned that people could not rely on the political system to solve the problem; rather, he held that "our combined energy and influence in the market place" would be required to break the "cycle of poisons and destruction and death that threatens our people and our world."[150] When Chavez finally broke his fast at a liturgy attended by approximately eight thousand farmworkers and supporters, he could not speak or stand without assistance. He had risked kidney failure and shed thirty-three pounds, approximately 20 percent of his body weight.[151]

Chavez intended the "Fast for Life" to continue even as he gave it up to avoid permanent damage to his health. In a statement read by his son Fernando, Chavez asserted that the fast should be carried on in hundreds of different places and passed from one person to next every three days until "every poisoned grape is off supermarket shelves." He urged that the acts of self-sacrifice continue "until the fields are safe for the farm workers, the environment is preserved for future generations, and our food is once again a source of nourishment and life."[152] Jesse Jackson, who stood by Chavez's side, took up the fast first, passing it to Southern Christian Leadership Conference president Reverend Joseph Lowery three days later.[153] Sierra Club Executive Director Michael Fischer continued the "Fast for Life," receiving the "chain" from Cesar's son Fernando on September 19 and passing it on to Robert F. Kennedy's daughter Rory on September 23, 1988.[154] Other "chains" of fasts developed apart from the initial one that began with Chavez, enlarging the web of participants.[155] Grape sales to New York City fell 22 percent, while Philadelphia witnessed a 6 percent decline over five months. UFW figured that per capita consumption of California table grapes dropped 13 percent between the start of the boycott and the beginning of 1989.[156]

Growers reacted to the efforts of the UFW, environmentalists, and concerned consumers with a carefully crafted rebuttal intended to cast doubt on activists' contentions and weaken the boycott. The California Table Grape Commission initiated a print ad campaign that carried a picture of a group of people assumed to be fieldworkers who questioned who would protect them from boycotts. Text, purportedly expressing a farmworker's view, feigned shock at the UFW claim that grapes carried dangerous pesticide residues and reassured the reader that the produce was safe. It contended: "Grapes don't hurt anybody. But boycotts do."[157] Grape growers also hired the Dolphin Group, a right-wing public relations firm, to establish the Grape Workers and Farmers Coalition (GWFC). Dolphin Group account managers posed as members of GWFC in public and countered charges made by the union. Though the group purported to represent the interests of both growers and farmworkers, the Dolphin Group employees who managed GWFC affairs testified under oath that they could not identify any farmworkers who belonged to the organization and did not know of any member list that would provide such evidence. In fact, it is probable that GWFC existed only on paper. A Dolphin Group senior account executive testified that there were no GWFC members when he began working the account, though he would not confess that it was created by the public relations firm.[158] What appears near certain is that the organization's name purposely misrepresented its membership composition to mislead the public into believing that its statements represented the opinions of farmworkers as well as growers.

The California Table Grape Commission also widely distributed the video *Big Fears, Little Risks: A Report on Chemicals in the Environment* produced by the American Council on Science and Health, a group that consistently defended food producers and industries from charges that their products posed a public health threat. The ACSH paid Walter Cronkite, the newscaster often referred to as "the most trusted man in America," to narrate the film in which a handful of scientists, including Bruce Ames, assured the public that their fears about chemical carcinogens were overblown.[159] According to their logic, the presence and volume of chemicals in the environment remained nearly constant, while science and definitions of "safe" were in a state of constant flux. The video asserted that these miniscule amounts of chemicals posed no greater threat to the human body than the natural carcinogens found in foods such as peanut butter or mushrooms. It then maintained that the body had an amazing defense system that was "designed to live in a world of carcinogens."[160] Growers undoubtedly hoped that the conflicting assertions of industry-friendly scientists would temper consumer fears about pesticide threats and reduce support for the UFW boycott and for environmentalists' attempts to pass more stringent regulations.

Nevertheless public interest in a variety of environmental issues seemed to favor passage of environmental legislation. Carl Pope, NRDC senior attorney Al Meyerhoff, Assemblyman Tom Hayden, and California Attorney General John Van de Kamp partnered to draft the measure that became Proposition 128, the "Big Green" initiative.[161] The California League of Conservation Voters, the National Toxics Campaign, Citizens for a Better Environment, Greenpeace, Campaign California, the California Public Interest Research Group, the AFL-CIO, and the UFW supported passage.[162] The sweeping initiative addressed issues ranging from pesticides to pollutants in coastal waters to ozone depletion and global warming. It, in part, would set a five-to-eight-year cancellation period for pesticides that were carcinogens or reproductive toxins, specifically stating that those chemicals in both Group A and Group B would be targeted. The California Senate Committee on Toxics and Public Safety Management estimated that sixty-nine pesticides would be subject to increased regulation and possible cancellation.[163] Prop 128 would also have transferred the authority to establish and regulate pesticide-related health standards from the CDFA to the Department of Health Services. Additionally, it would have removed the agricultural exception from state right-to-know laws to better protect farmworkers.[164] Carl Pope held that the initiative's breadth could be credited in part to Deukmejian's continued hostility toward environmental regulation, stating: "George Deukmejian is more responsible for Big Green than anyone else. It has been his lack of leadership, his veto of good environmental legislation and his refusal to implement environmental laws that forced us to put Big Green on the ballot."[165]

The sweeping nature of the proposed legislation, however, also made it easier for growers, other industries, and Deukmejian to attack it. Growers forecasted that the measure would cripple the state's agricultural industry.[166] Deukmejian charged that environmental groups were engaged in a "big lie campaign" and warned that Prop 128 would cause "tornado-like changes" in the state economy.[167] Growers, the chemical industry, and other opponents spent an estimated $10 million to oppose the initiative.[168] They contended that "Big Green" was too complex to be administered effectively and would financially burden Californians by raising taxes, the price of food, and energy costs.[169]

Growers succeeded in getting a competing initiative, the Consumer Pesticide Enforcement Act, on the ballot. Supporters of "Big Green" referred to it as "Big Brown," because it placed fewer restrictions on pesticides than Prop 128.[170] It would invalidate the pesticide provisions of "Big Green" if both measures passed.[171] In at least one instance, "Big Brown" backers at a "Big Green" rally wrongfully told attendees that Prop 135 was the initiative supported by environmentalists. The campaign also used slogans like "Protect Children From Pesticides" in an effort to confuse the public and draw votes away from Prop 128.[172] An estimated six hundred growers campaigned door to door, bearing gifts of flowers and chocolate-covered raisins, in greater Los Angeles neighborhoods urging people to vote for Prop 135.[173] An October Field Institute poll revealed that the counterinitiative strategy had the potential to derail "Big Green." The poll showed voter support divided with the potential of both measures passing.[174]

Results proved to be far more lopsided than the poll suggested. The initiative that supporters thought was a sure winner garnered only 36 percent of the vote.[175] It failed despite having backing from environmentalists, the AFL-CIO, and the UFW. Opponents' arguments that "Big Green" was too complex and would be financially burdensome factored into the initiative's defeat. Supporters also blamed voter confusion with the competing "Big Brown" initiative.[176]

The loss at the polls strengthened Chavez's resolve that "electoral politics isn't the only medium of change." Opponents of progressive measures could influence votes with multimillion-dollar campaigns; but Chavez maintained that the same was not necessarily true of boycotts. He asserted that "money and clout are impotent in the face of such simple challenges as boycotts," because majority support was not necessary to achieve victory.[177] While the UFW supported the "Big Green" initiative, it maintained its focus on building support for the Wrath of Grapes campaign. Chavez claimed that time was an ally and remained optimistic that the effort begun in 1984 would ultimately be successful.[178] The Wrath of Grapes boycott, however, also failed to achieve its objective, despite support from some environmentalists, concerned consumers, union members, religious affiliates, and social justice advocates. UFW called off the boycott in 2000, though it was pretty much forgotten by that time.[179]

While the defeat of "Big Green" represented a significant and unexpected loss for proponents of regulation, cooperative efforts among environmentalists, labor unions, and farmworker advocates posed a challenge to supporters of deregulation earlier in the 1980s. Deukmejian took office in 1982 with a plan to undo years of labor and environmental reform. He worked to diminish the regulatory framework by underfunding agencies, limiting the public's input into pesticide programs, and vetoing stringent new laws. Yet these plans were resisted and sometimes defeated by a labor-environmental coalition that recognized a shared common ground. Together unions and environmentalists filed lawsuits to compel enforcement of existent law, pushed for legislative measures that would better protect the health of workers and the public, and tried to apply economic pressure to businesses in an attempt to effect voluntary change within the industry. Environmentalists and worker groups collaborated and showed support for each other's efforts on multiple occasions, yet differences in the strategies and tactics of environmentalists and the UFW also resulted in campaigns that were largely carried out separately.

Environmentalists generally preferred the legislative track to enact tougher standards and the courts to force adherence to the law. They grouped pesticides with other toxics in the 1980s, which in turn affected the scope of their reform efforts. Rather than try to restrict usage of one or two hazardous substances at a time, environmentalists in California tried to pass sweeping initiatives at the state level that would curtail the use of both agricultural and industrial chemicals. Prop 65, for example, looked to reshape the regulatory landscape by shifting the burden of proof from the public and government to business. The broad-based initiative faced vigorous challenges by the governor and industry groups after its passage but withstood them to affect approximately 470 toxic chemicals in 1990. The number grew after the repeal of the food, drug, and cosmetic industry exemption in 1993. Hence, the overall impact of such broad-based legislative efforts was greater than it would have been had the groups chosen to address one toxin at a time.[180]

The UFW remained skeptical of the utility of law-making as a strategy for effecting change. After passage of the best agricultural labor relations laws in the nation, it still had problems with enforcement, particularly after the election of Deukmejian. It returned its focus to the boycott as it had prior to the passage of the ALRA. The successful boycott, it believed, would result in union contracts that would be better than laws, because union representatives would play a direct role in pesticide decision making and monitoring of use practices. Unlike the environmentalists with their legislative efforts, the union chose to focus on a much smaller group of chemicals, promising to address others in the future. The geographical scope of the UFW effort also differed from the environmentalists' campaigns. Whereas environmentalists campaigned hard within the state of California to build voter support for Prop 65 and "Big Green," UFW looked outside the state to the national and international community to increase consumer participation in the boycott.

Despite the significant difference in campaign scope and strategy, the UFW and environmentalists still found opportunity for cooperation. A small contingent of environmental activists from mainstream and grassroots organizations advised the UFW on pesticides. Some environmental groups endorsed the boycott and participated in the Fast for Life and other public rallies. The UFW did not contribute significant resources to the effort to pass Prop 65 in 1986, but the initiative campaign occurred at the same time that the union was trying to revive a flagging boycott. The launch of the new Wrath of Grapes campaign undoubtedly consumed much of the union's resources. The UFW did, however, support "Big Green" in 1990. Continued collaboration between farmworker groups and environmentalists occurred in the 1990s and beyond as the organizations worked to keep the United States on its phase-out schedule for methyl bromide.

7

FROM THE GROUND UP

Fumigants, Ozone, and Health

Cesar Chavez stayed up late to review court documents on the night of April 22, 1993 in the home of a former farmworker in San Luis, a small Arizona border town not far from where he had grown up. After spending the day in the Yuma County Superior Court giving testimony to defend his union in a lawsuit, he drove past some familiar places of his youth. He broke a three-day fast that night, sharing a vegetarian dinner with a few staffers and their host before retiring to his bedroom to read. He showed signs of tiredness, but nothing to raise concern. Chavez, however, never woke.[1]

Six days later, a three-mile-long procession of thirty-five thousand mourners followed Chavez and his pallbearers on the funeral march from Delano to the UFW's Forty Acres compound. Union flags, banners, chants, and songs filled the streets. Farmworkers alternated with celebrities and political allies to carry the simple white pine casket hewn by Chavez's brother Richard.[2] Luis Valdez, founder of El Teatro Campesino, closed the ceremony with a promise to Chavez. He said: "We have come to plant your heart like a seed . . . the seed of your heart will keep on singing, keep on flowering, for the cause."[3]

In the wake of his passing, the Natural Resources Defense Council commended Chavez's work on pesticides and expressed hope that cooperative efforts with the UFW to safeguard the health of farmworkers and protect the environment would continue to grow. Co-founder and executive director John Adams and attorney Al Meyerhoff, an NRDC attorney who had begun his legal career at California Rural Legal Assistance in 1972, characterized Chavez as a "visionary . . . [who] far before the concepts of 'environmental justice' became popular . . . understood that preserving human dignity and protecting the earth's resources are necessarily intertwined."[4] The organization dedicated a 1993 report entitled *After Silent Spring: The Unsolved Problems of Pesticide Use in the United States* to the memory of Chavez for his commitment "to protecting farmworkers and the rural poor—those most exposed to the hazards of pesticides."[5] The report noted that the volume of pesticides used in the United States had nearly doubled in the thirty years since publication of Carson's seminal book, climbing from an estimated annual figure of 540 million pounds to more than one billion pounds per year in 1991. It summarized the continuing health and environmental threats associated with pesticide use, arguing that the shortcomings of existent regulatory law failed to keep dangerous pesticides off the market.[6] The report maintained that regulations to "protect farmworkers are wholly inadequate and should be dramatically overhauled."[7] The NRDC asked Arturo Rodriguez, successor to Chavez, to speak at the press conference announcing the release of the report.[8]

To illustrate its point about the inadequacies of current regulations, the NRDC used the example of methyl bromide, a pesticide targeted in the Wrath of Grapes campaign. The UFW tried to force California grape growers away from the fumigant with the boycott, but that effort proved unsuccessful. Methyl bromide, in fact, remained widely used in the production of a variety of crops across California, the United States, and the world. Global usage climbed from 92 million pounds in 1984 to 139 million in 1990 with the United States accounting for more than 42 percent of the total. The pesticide, however, posed a serious threat to human and environmental health. Between 1982 and 1990, poisoning from methyl bromide caused the death of fifteen people and over 250 injuries in California alone.[9] Chronic overexposure could cause nerve damage, kidney problems, and impaired vision.[10] Animal-based studies showed it to be a mutagen and reproductive toxin. Upon breaking down in the atmosphere, methyl bromide, in combination with chlorofluorocarbons (CFCs), also deteriorates the ozone layer.[11]

After the death of Chavez, environmental groups and farmworker organizations worked to effect a methyl bromide ban. The discovery of a hole in the ozone layer in 1985 and subsequent signing of the Montreal Protocol in 1987 had committed the nation to ending usage of ozone-depleting substances, and an amendment to the international agreement in 1993 set a phase-out date for methyl bromide. Growers' associations and industry groups fiercely resisted the ban with some success. Through the 1990s and first decade of the new millennium, environmentalists and farmworker organizations worked separately and in coalitions to counter agricultural industry lobbying and to keep the United States on target for replacing methyl bromide with suitable, less toxic alternatives.

The Development of International Agreement

Some scientists grew increasingly concerned about the potential for humans to damage the ozone layer in the early 1970s. Chemists F. Sherwood Roland and Mario Molina postulated in 1974 that CFCs, a common industrial chemical, had the potential to degrade the thin protective atmospheric layer by breaking down into the compound chlorine monoxide that would attack ozone particles. The British Antarctic Survey documented a hole in the ozone layer over the continent eleven years later, a finding that was reaffirmed by NASA satellite photos.[12] The hole spanned an area as large as the United States, extending over some parts of Argentina and New Zealand.[13] Subsequent studies concluded that high concentrations of chlorine from CFC breakdowns caused the low stratospheric ozone levels. The Airborne Arctic Stratospheric Expedition detected a similar deterioration of ozone particles at the North Pole in 1989, though the thinning proved less severe.[14]

The atmospheric degradation posed a significant threat to human health and environment, since ozone helps shield the Earth from the sun's harmful ultraviolet rays. The EPA predicted that the United States would witness 40 million additional cases of skin cancer and 12 million more eye cataracts as a result of the increased shortwave ultraviolet radiation (UV-B) exposure in the next hundred years if the volume of CFC emissions remained unchanged.[15] Increased UV-B could also weaken the body's immune system and hasten the spread of infectious disease.[16] Evidence suggested that the ocean ecology could be adversely affected, with phytoplankton, a vital source of food for marine life, being unable to weather the change well. Subsequent declines in fish stocks would likely impact human life, since approximately half of the protein consumed by humans worldwide is drawn from the oceans. Scientists knew little about the effects of increased UV-B on agricultural production, though a few early tests showed a decline in yields and greater susceptibility to weeds, insects, and disease.[17]

The severity of threats associated with more UV-B rays reaching the Earth's surface sparked a global recognition that ozone deterioration needed to be promptly addressed. The United Nations Environment Programme (UNEP) Governing Council hosted a conference in April 1987 that led to the signing of the Montreal Protocol on Substances that Deplete the Ozone Layer by twenty-four industrialized and developing nations.[18] Taking effect in 1989, the accord froze production of CFCs at 1986 levels, gradually reducing the manufacture of the ozone-depleting chemicals over the next ten years. In addition, CFC-producing nations agreed to further scale back manufacturing and consumption 50 percent by 1998.[19] The protocol took a precautionary approach based on available scientific data. Recognizing that new scientific evidence could necessitate an alteration in response, the agreement included a clause that required signees to meet every few years to consider whether changes needed to be made to the restrictions.[20]

Participating nations adopted stronger resolutions in subsequent meetings. The 1990 gathering in London hastened the plan for phasing out CFCs because of the ready availability of less harmful alternatives.[21] Copenhagen hosted the next meeting, during which participants addressed the deleterious effects of methyl bromide, which breaks down into bromine in the atmosphere and destroys stratospheric ozone particles with fifty times greater efficiency than chlorine. Scientists estimated that bromine caused approximately 25 percent of the ozone depletion in 1992. Dr. Robert Watson, associate director for the environment for the Office of Science and Technology Policy, estimated that if usage ceased by 2001 the rate of ozone loss would fall by 13 percent in the fifty years following. Attendees consequently passed the Copenhagen Amendment, freezing the production and consumption of methyl bromide in 1995 at the chemical's 1991 levels of manufacture and use.[22]

Subsequent amendments set a schedule for ending use in industrialized and developing countries, though the United States planned to follow a self-imposed timeline that was even more abbreviated. The 1995 Vienna Amendment set a goal of 50 percent reduction for industrialized countries by 2005 and a complete halt in usage by 2010. A meeting in Montreal tightened the time frame by four years, although "critical use exemptions" would still allow for use in agriculture when no viable alternative existed.[23] The US Clean Air Act Amendments of 1990 accelerated the schedule for Americans. Intended to complement the Montreal Protocol, the amendments established a seven-year cancellation plan for chemicals categorized as Class 1 ozone-depleting substances. In the case of a rule discrepancy, the stricter standard took precedence. Hence, when the EPA listed methyl bromide as a Class 1 chemical in December 1993, American growers had only until 2001 to adopt alternatives. The legislative amendments carried no "critical use" exemption.[24]

American growers grew increasingly vocal in their calls to prolong the timeline as the date approached, arguing that the effectiveness of methyl bromide could not be matched. Executive manager of the California Cherry Export Association Jim Culbertson declared that the compound had been unfairly "placed in the position of public enemy No. 1 by the radical environmental community" and stressed that "methyl bromide has remained as a silver bullet in the economic control of many pests and diseases, weathering the tide of pest evolution."[25] The American Farm Bureau Federation (AFBF) reiterated the chemical's uniqueness, stating that its ability to combat a wide variety of pests in a multitude of crops differentiated it from other pesticides. It countered arguments that the pending cancellation would spark innovations, suggesting that "while government can ban certain technologies . . . it can't require scientists to invent something." The AFBF asserted that potential alternatives were not as effective as methyl bromide, cost too much, had environmental impact issues, or would not be able to be registered before 2001.[26]

The agricultural lobby also held that the accelerated schedule would put the nation's farmers at a competitive disadvantage. Industrialized nations would be able to use the fumigant for four years longer than the United States and Mexico, classified as a developing country, could continue to use the compound until 2015. The AFBF warned that this discrepancy threatened the vitality of American agriculture. It estimated that strawberry production in Florida and California would decline by 30 to 50 percent, causing prices to spike. Mexican growers could then undersell American competitors because their unrestricted access to methyl bromide allowed for the continued strong yields at low cost.[27] The Florida Farm Bureau Federation forecast that holding the nation's growers to more stringent standards would bring "no net environmental gain" because Mexico would expand planted acreage to fill the niche left by Florida growers who could no longer compete in the global marketplace.[28]

Methyl bromide proponents questioned the rationale behind the planned phase-out. Jim Culbertson argued that natural occurrences like biomass burning injected a far greater share of the substance into the atmosphere than agricultural use, complaining that the international community nonetheless continued "to concentrate our regulatory efforts on a minute portion of the methyl bromide equation that carries with it a great loss for agriculture."[29] His complaint implied that there was consensus on the percentage of methyl bromide emissions in the atmosphere that could be traced to agricultural production and that the figure was negligible. Others chose to attack the science supporting the ban. The AFBF declared that "methyl bromide's role as an ozone depleter is still uncertain" and that restrictive action was premature. It pointed to results from recent tests, funded in part by the National Oceanic and Atmospheric Administration, showing that the oceans broke down atmospheric methyl bromide more quickly than previously thought, which meant that the atmospheric lifetime of the compound was shorter than earlier estimated. The grower organization suggested that this finding should forestall regulation because the discovery proved that methyl bromide constituted less of a threat.[30]

All of the arguments for prolonging use had weaknesses. The NOAA estimated that 20 to 30 percent of the methyl bromide in the atmosphere came from crop fumigation emissions. Even as scientists revised the chemical's atmospheric lifetime in 1997, the agency still maintained that "manmade methyl bromide is responsible for 3–10% of global stratospheric ozone destruction."[31] The fumigant, furthermore, was the most easily regulated source of the compound, and soil fumigation accounted for approximately

75 percent of global use in 1998. Phasing it out in agriculture, then, would greatly reduce release of the dangerous compound into the air. Though growers applied it to over a hundred varieties of fruits and vegetables, UNEP's Methyl Bromide Technical Options Committee maintained that every crop that currently used the fumigant could be successfully produced using integrated pest management instead.[32] Field experiments in Florida, for instance, concluded that some growers might suffer a slight decline in volume, but could still produce a good yield. Some trials with integrated pest management, however, actually had higher net returns because the cost of production fell when growers did not have to pay for fumigation.[33] This evidence discounted growers' assertions that lack of viable alternatives to methyl bromide and increased foreign competition would cause the decline of American agriculture in the wake of a ban.

Linking Local to Global

As growers continued their lobbying efforts, the Farmworker Association of Florida (FWAF) partnered with Friends of the Earth, Farmworker Self-Help, Inc., the Florida Consumer Action Network, and the Legal Environmental Assistance Foundation to initiate a campaign in support of the methyl bromide ban. The organizations opted to take a largely localized approach to an international problem, focusing primarily on Florida and its tomato industry.[34] Soil fumigation in tomato production accounted for approximately 30 percent of the 35 million pounds of methyl bromide used in American agriculture in 1996.[35] Florida growers led production of fresh market tomatoes, growing nearly half of the nation's total, and used the fumigant on 93 percent of the crop.[36] The Sustainable Tomatoes/Safer Communities campaign launched by the coalition of farmworker groups and environmental organizations clearly targeted a segment of the industry that was one of the primary users of methyl bromide in the United States.

Both Friends of Earth and the Farmworker Association of Florida had a history of engagement in pesticide issues prior to forming the Sustainable Tomatoes/Safer Communities Coalition. Friends of the Earth partnered with NRDC and EDF to petition EPA in December 1991 to phase out usage of methyl bromide by 1993.[37] Friends of the Earth also worked to find replacement options for methyl bromide, funding studies and coordinating projects to identify alternatives that would ease the transition away from the ozone depleter.[38] Since former farmworker Tirso Moreno became director of FWAF in 1986, the organization had engaged in efforts to better protect farmworkers from pesticide-related injuries and diseases.[39] Moreno had previously served as a worker representative for the UFW in Florida and considered Chavez an environmental hero.[40] Like Chavez, he expressed concern about the hazardousness of pesticides and pushed for more a stringent right-to-know law in Florida.[41] FWAF also engaged in educational outreach to make farmworkers more aware of the pesticide threat and teach doctors how to better identify pesticide poisoning.[42] The groups found opportunity for collaboration in the campaign against methyl bromide in 1998. FoE health and environment director Larry Bohlen and atmosphere campaign director Jessica Vallette Revere, along

Figure 7.1. FWAF educates farmworkers, like the citrus picker pictured here, about the best practices for protecting their health and the health of their families from pesticide hazards. Such efforts aim to reduce the tens of thousands of pesticide poisonings that happen every year in the United States. Photo by Gaye Ajoy. Courtesy of the Farmworker Association of Florida.

with FWAF Pesticide Safety and Environmental Health Project coordinator Jeannie Economos and administrator Sister Gail Grimes served as the primary points of contact in the collaborative effort.[43]

The Sustainable Tomatoes/Safer Communities campaign introduced its broad-based agenda with the release of a report, *Reaping Havoc: The True Cost of Using Methyl Bromide on Florida's Tomatoes*, published jointly by the participating organizations. The coalition called on the Clinton administration, Congress, and the State of Florida to resist growers' appeals for an extension on methyl bromide and recommended the adoption of a graduated timeline for use reduction leading up to the 2001 phase-out. It additionally urged the EPA and the USDA to develop an educational program to ease growers' transition to safer alternatives. The report then narrowed its focus from the national level to Florida. To global concern about ozone deterioration, the coalition added complaints that methyl bromide threatened the health of farmworkers and people living close to agricultural fields. The groups further stated that the Florida Department of Agriculture and Consumer Services (FDACS) failed to enforce EPA Worker Protection Standards, and requested the EPA to review the regulatory program and take corrective action. The organizations also advocated for the expansion of public right-to-know laws and the promotion of sustainable pest management practices to reduce overall pesticide use.[44]

The joint campaign, in part, continued FWAF's work of educating farmworkers and their families about the risks of exposure to methyl bromide and other chemicals. *Reaping Havoc* and educational pamphlets outlined the chronic effects and short-term symptoms of poisoning. The acute effects of exposure included eye and lung irritation, shortness of breath, difficulty talking, convulsions, fainting, and vomiting. More severe cases could result in damage to the brain and other vital organs, heart attack, and death.[45] A children's coloring book entitled "Sunny's Niños Juegan Con Cuidado" (Sunny's Kids Play with Care) taught the children of farmworkers how to identify hazardous containers of pesticides, instructed them to stay away from freshly sprayed fields and agricultural chemicals, and informed them about the preventative steps that their working family members should take in the fields to protect themselves from pesticide poisoning.[46]

The coalition similarly devoted resources to an education campaign explaining the hazards associated specifically with methyl bromide. It appealed to the public on multiple levels ranging from global to local, addressing both environmental and human health concerns.[47] Friends of the Earth President Brent Blackwelder asserted: "We're talking attack of the killer tomatoes. Not only is it depleting the ozone; but if it drifts into the air, it could kill someone. It's a lethal toxic."[48] The coalition warned that Congress and the Clinton administration might cave to the agricultural lobby and extend usage until 2005. They urged the public to write congressional representatives and the president to counter pressure from grower associations and industry-related groups. The Sustainable Tomatoes/Safer Communities campaign also recommended that the public use its purchasing power to effect change by demanding that grocers carry "ozone friendly" tomatoes produced without methyl bromide.[49]

The campaign had little chance to gain momentum before Victor Fazio, a Democratic US representative from a rural California district, introduced an amendment to extend the chemical's life. Florida's Republican Representative Dan Miller had previously introduced a House bill in 1998 that would amend the Clean Air Act and set the United States on the same reduction schedule as other industrialized nations. It also included a provision, absent from the Clean Air Act, that allowed growers to continue using methyl bromide after the ban if they got an emergency use exemption.[50] Congress passed the legislation, but Clinton used the veto to keep it from becoming law.[51] Fazio then attached a similarly worded rider to the 1999 omnibus spending bill. It received little notice in the package legislation and passed with Clinton's signature.[52] Jessica Vallette voiced the sentiments of environmentalists and other proponents of the ban, stating that Fazio "sneaking in an anti-environmental amendment without hearings" was contemptible.[53] Vice President Al Gore characterized the tactic as a "sneak attack" that buried "special-interest riders deep in budget bills where they hope no one will find them."[54] The strategy proved successful nonetheless, allowing growers to continue using methyl bromide until 2005.

After the passage of the Fazio Amendment, the Sustainable Tomatoes/Safer Communities coalition tightened its focus on state-level policies. Florida's pesticide regulations provided far less protection to farmworkers and residents in surrounding communities than did laws in California. The California Department of Pesticide Regulation (CDPR) set the limit for methyl bromide exposure for farmworkers and the general public at

210 ppb (parts per billion) in a twenty-four-hour period; the EPA guidelines followed by FDACS, in contrast, raised the threshold to 5,000 ppb.
California regulations also mandated that a sixty-foot buffer zone separate spray areas from residential zones, and some counties further required
growers to notify people living within 360 feet of an application site prior to
the use. Florida growers escaped these responsibilities.[55] Florida's Department of Agriculture kept no data banks comparable to California's that
charted the volume of pesticides used, the location of application, or the
duration of use. In addition, FWAF charged that the agency showed laxity in its enforcement of existing regulations, asserting that FDACS failed
to ensure that recently fumigated fields were posted with warning signs.[56]

The coalition drew inspiration from activists in California to show that
Florida's regulatory laws did an inadequate job of protecting the public
from exposure to pesticides. California planned to ban the use of methyl
bromide in March 1996 because manufacturers had failed to submit scientific data required under the 1984 California Birth Defects Prevention
Act. After being intensely lobbied to rescind the ban and reportedly receiving nearly $100,000 from the agricultural industry, Governor Pete
Wilson called the legislature into special session in January 1996 with
virtually no notice to the public.[57] The legislature lifted the proposed ban
less than three weeks before it was to take effect.[58] The Environmental
Working Group (EWG) subsequently collaborated with a number of local
community organizations to conduct air monitoring tests to demonstrate
that methyl bromide posed a risk to residents in neighborhoods adjoin-
ing fields.[59] The group responded to complaints from Castroville residents,
who had suffered the symptoms of pesticide poisoning on several occasions after growers fumigated their crop. Silicon-lined canisters that the
organization set at an elementary school outside of the buffer zone showed
concentrations of methyl bromide at 3,700 ppb, an amount that exceeded
the allowable exposure level seventeen times.[60] The EWG also analyzed
state figures on school enrollment and reported that 68,238 children attended schools within 1.5 miles of fields that used the compound.[61] It then
joined Friends of the Earth, the Pesticide Action Network, and Pesticide
Watch to bring suit against the CDPR using the test data to force a revision
of state regulations.[62]

The Sustainable Tomatoes/Safer Communities coalition initiated
its own air monitoring campaign to demonstrate that Florida's anemic

regulatory structure was putting the members of some communities at risk as well. In fall 2000, FWAF volunteers and Florida Consumer Action Network staffers watched for growers who applied methyl bromide to the fields around the town of Homestead. Then they set out twelve test canisters in the parking lots of churches for eight to twelve hours, collecting air samples.[63] Test results revealed that drift exited the fields into surrounding areas, sometimes in concentrations reaching 625 ppb.[64] That amount was within allowable limits according to Florida regulations, but nearly three times as high as the legal limit in California. The growers provided no advance warning to people in surrounding areas because they were not required to do so by law. The coalition also reported that farmworkers did not receive proper instruction or protective equipment for using and working around methyl bromide.[65]

Results from the monitoring tests supported the coalition's arguments for stricter regulations. It held that the evidence of high drift concentrations showed the necessity of restricting where the fumigant could be applied, recommending that the state establish buffer zones around field perimeters to better protect people in surrounding residential and commercial areas. Growers, the groups maintained, should also be required to give advance notice before chemical applications. Tirso Moreno maintained that "the work we do does not have to be a cause of illness to our family, neither should we have to lose our lives to feed ourselves."[66] The Sustainable Tomatoes/Safer Communities groups urged FDACS to help growers transition to nontoxic alternative forms of pest control.[67]

News accounts of a church congregation near Homestead suffering methyl bromide poisoning combined with pressure from the Sustainable Tomatoes/Safer Communities campaign to oblige the state to respond. Reverend Gladys Herrera of Iglesia El Calvario Fuente de Vida, a church located just north of Homestead in the small town of Naranja, told reporters that some children had coughed and vomited when exposed to the chemical while others had experienced sickness, dizziness, and throat irritation.[68] The coalition urged people to sign a resolution of support and to write letters to Governor Jeb Bush demanding action to protect farmworkers and public alike.[69] A sample letter drafted by the coalition outlined health hazards and claimed that "simple measures can go a long way toward reducing risk."[70] Jeb Bush promised, in response, to investigate problems of pesticide drift in Florida.[71]

The Sustainable Tomatoes/Safer Communities campaign ultimately heralded no change in methyl bromide use by Florida growers. Though Governor Bush promised to investigate drift after the air monitoring tests drew media attention, the administration quietly dismissed the issue and did nothing to strengthen pesticide regulations.[72] The campaign did raise awareness among farmworkers and the public about associated health risks by giving presentations, publicizing monitoring test results, and distributing pamphlets and coloring books. The actions, however, did not generate the sustained public pressure necessary to convince the governor or legislature to champion additional restrictions. The coalition eventually fractured when the goal was not achieved. The Farmworker Association of Florida stayed engaged in issues relating to methyl bromide, while Friends of the Earth devoted more of their resources to genetically modified food issues.

The Persistent Fight for Less Toxic Alternatives

The passage of the Fazio Amendment as a rider on the 1999 omnibus spending bill extended the life of methyl bromide in the United States, to the chagrin of pesticide reform advocates. It modified the Clean Air Act to put the nation's growers on the same timeline for transitioning away from methyl bromide as growers in other industrialized countries. The addition of four years intended to eliminate any competitive disadvantage that American growers might face if held to an accelerated schedule. It also included a "critical use exemption" clause that provided a means for growers to extend usage beyond the phase-out date. In years following, proponents of the ban struggled to limit "critical use exemptions," wean the nation off the fumigant, and force growers to use less toxic alternatives.

Users of methyl bromide continued to press their case in the early years of George W. Bush's presidency, rehashing old arguments that the scarcity of effective alternatives required the continued availability of the favored fumigant. Requests for exemptions went through the EPA before being submitted to the UNEP's Ozone Secretariat. Senior EPA officials showed little enthusiasm for limiting the number of growers' use applications.[73] The United States ultimately submitted sixteen permission requests that ranged from strawberries and tomatoes to golf course greens. Some applications, such as the ones for orchard seedlings and orchard replants, applied to a variety of crops.[74] The volume requested totaled more than 12,500 tons, approximately 40 percent of the volume used in 1991.[75] Other nations sought "critical use exemptions" as well, but the amount sought by the United States exceeded that of all other nations combined.[76]

Many of the Montreal Protocol's participating nations doubted the legitimacy of the American claims, suspecting that viable alternatives existed in some circumstances and that not all of the requested uses were essential. European Union Environment Commissioner Margot Wallström reacted with skepticism, stating that "many farmers worldwide successfully grow crops without methyl bromide," and adding that "substitutes are available for the majority of uses."[77] Dutch consultant Marten Barel intimated that the fears of American growers were largely unfounded, saying that farmers in the Netherlands had similarly complained that "it would be the end of the world for farming" before transitioning to alternatives that produced good yields. European Union critics warned that the United States' noncooperation threatened to undermine efforts to repair the ozone layer.[78] Executive director of UNEP Klaus Toepfer held that "maintaining the integrity of the Protocol is paramount; otherwise, the world community is left with only a partial success toward a declining level of this ozone depleting substance."[79] President Bush and some members of Congress, in response, raised the possibility of vacating the international agreement if the United States was not granted the "critical use exemptions"[80]

American activists similarly opposed the actions of the Bush administration, viewing them as a threat to what had previously been a successful effort to reduce deterioration of the ozone layer.[81] The Montreal Protocol had benefited from bipartisan support in the United States and cooperation from nations around the globe. Bush and House Republicans threatened to bring a halt to those gains by backing out of the international agreement. David Doniger, director of the NRDC's Climate Center and former director of climate change policy for the Clinton administration, testified before Congress that it was in the nation's best interest to stay committed to the Montreal Protocol.[82] While admitting that the exemption was an acceptable relief when used appropriately, Doniger charged that "the Bush administration has abused the critical use exemption process by submitting a bloated application . . . padded against the possibility that absolutely every use stalls out where it is now and no further progress in reducing" use is achieved.[83] He warned that "if the Bush administration pushes too hard on this, it is going to stick its finger in the eye of yet another international treaty and risk a backlash that will imperil the health of Americans."[84]

Negotiations among parties to the Montreal Protocol broke down in November 2003 over the exemptions sought by the United States and other industrialized countries, though UNEP ultimately approved almost all of the applications submitted by the Bush administration. Developing nations in attendance at the 15th Meeting of the Parties to the Montreal Protocol in Nairobi threatened to halt efforts to reduce use, because of a seeming lack of commitment from the United States and eleven other industrialized nations.[85] Doniger also attended the 2003 conference in Nairobi and, as the only nongovernmental environmental spokesperson to take the floor, spoke out against the excessiveness of the American request. The United States wanted approval for four times more methyl bromide than the nation seeking the second largest exemption.[86] He maintained that the amount was so large that the United States, which had substantially reduced the amount of the fumigant manufactured in the years preceding, would actually increase production if the exemption were granted.[87] The Nairobi Conference ended without resolution for the first time in the history of Montreal Protocol meetings.[88]

An "extraordinary" meeting had to be called in Montreal in March 2004 to resolve the issue before the start of the 2005. At the meeting, Klaus Toepfer commented that "the high demand for exemptions to the methyl bromide phase out shows that governments and the private sector will have to work much harder to speed up the development and spread of ozone-friendly replacements," adding that "the best way for governments to protect the integrity of the Montreal Protocol . . . is to send a powerful signal to both producers and users that methyl bromide does not have a future."[89] The parties then authorized the United States to use 37.5 percent of the volume of methyl bromide used by its growers in 1991.[90] The total exemptions granted in 2005 totaled 14,713 tons, of which 9,857 tons were allocated for use in the United States. UNEP cut the allowable usage to 26.3 percent of the 1991 total for the following year.[91]

After the manufacturing of new stocks began, the NRDC filed suit against the EPA. To meet the demand for the year, delegates at the Montreal meeting authorized the manufacture of 8,443 tons of methyl bromide to supplement 1,414 tons of existing stocks. Doniger, however, found evidence in a letter from the EPA to Congress that the United States had not been forthcoming about its stockpiles. The letter revealed that Chemtura and other pesticide suppliers had stores of the compound that exceeded the volume granted in the exemption.[92] The EPA would not disclose the exact amount of suppliers' holdings when requested to do so, however, claiming that it was "confidential business information, the disclosure of which would result in a competitive disadvantage to the respective companies."[93] The NRDC sought to gain access to the withheld information with its lawsuit. Upon winning, it learned that methyl bromide holdings within the United States totaled roughly 18,500 tons, an amount well in excess of the 2005 exemption.[94]

The organization filed another suit against the EPA in 2006, arguing that the ongoing production of methyl bromide violated the conditions of the UNEP exemption. It claimed that the United States must exhaust existing supplies before engaging in manufacture, citing the clause of the UNEP decision stating that new production of methyl bromide should occur only if the fumigant "is not available in sufficient quantity and quality from existing stocks."[95] The EPA interpreted the resolution differently, maintaining that methyl bromide could be produced even if suppliers had stores of the fumigant.[96]

The appellate court offered no judgment on whether the UNEP exemption had been violated. On first hearing, the court ruled that the NRDC lacked standing to sue because it found the increased health risks posed by EPA action to be trivial, and therefore did not weigh the substance of the arguments.[97] The organization appealed, asserting that any "scientifically demonstrable increase in the threat of death or serious illness" was not trivial.[98] At a rehearing en banc, the appellate court reversed judgment on the NRDC's standing to sue, deciding that one could reasonably argue that two to four of NRDC's 500,000 members would develop cancer over the course of a lifetime as a result of the EPA rule.[99] The court, however, still ruled against the organization, holding that the stipulations in the UNEP exemption were not enforceable in a federal court because the "critical use" decision had not been ratified by Congress. Since the clause was unenforceable, the court made no ruling whether or not the EPA action was allowable under the UNEP clause.[100] The decision, therefore, did not interfere with the manufacture of methyl bromide.

Use of methyl bromide in the United States continued, but has declined every year since 2005. "Critical use exemptions" in 2005 equaled 37.5 percent of the volume used in 1991. Growers' usage of the fumigant fell to roughly 3,307 tons in 2010, approximately 12 percent of the 1991 baseline. The United States received approval for the use of nearly 416 tons of the chemical in 2015, once again going beyond the planned phase-out date. Canada and Australia received vastly smaller exemptions.[101] The elimination of methyl bromide from growers' chemical arsenal finally appears to be on the horizon. Yet, the United States remains one of only three industrialized countries that continue to seek "critical use exemptions," driven by growers' insistence on its necessity in production. The volume approved for 2015 is nearly eleven times larger than the combined total of Canada and Australia.[102]

Environmental organizations and farmworker groups continued to draw attention to the problems of methyl bromide in this period of "critical use exemptions" and take steps to further limit use within the nation. In *Latino Communities at Risk*, the Sierra Club chronicled the suffering of two disabled farmworkers, Jorge Fernández and Guillermo Ruiz, who had labored in California strawberry fields without being warned about the dangers of methyl bromide exposure and without being equipped with appropriate protective clothing. Reporting that sound alternatives existed for 95 percent of uses, it concluded that farmworkers would continue to face unnecessary health risks as a result of the extensions.[103] The two farmworkers partnered with organizations belonging to Californians for Pesticide Reform, a coalition of more than 180 labor, environmental, and citizen groups, to bring suit against the CDPR. The diverse ranks of participants included the Audubon Society of California, the Earth Island Institute, the California Rural Legal Assistance, the Sierra Club, the EDF, the Pesticide Action Network, the EWG, and the UFW.[104] The plaintiffs argued that the agency had failed to properly protect farmworkers and the public from harm when promulgating exposure standards for the fumigant, because it had failed to consult the California Office of Environmental Health Hazard Assessment (COEHHA) as required by law. The court found the CDPR at fault for not jointly developing the regulation with COEHHA, an agency better able to evaluate the health risks of chemicals.[105] Linda Krop, chief counsel for the Environmental Defense Center, responded to the verdict, stating: "Hopefully, this ruling will not only result in lower exposure to this highly toxic pesticide, but will also encourage farmers to use safer alternatives."[106]

The pesticide manufacturing industry introduced methyl iodide as an alternative, but its toxicity and threat to human health gave rise to the same sort of opposition from reformers. A contingent of fifty-four scientists and chemists, including five Nobel laureates, signed a letter urging the EPA to block the registration of the compound. They warned that it was a highly volatile mutagenic chemical that raised cancer risks. Tests conducted by the EPA showed laboratory animals developing permanent neurological damage, fetal losses, and increased thyroid toxicity when exposed to methyl iodide. The scientists stated that "as chemists and physicians familiar with the effects of this chemical, we are concerned that pregnant women and the fetus, children, the elderly, farm workers, and other people living near application sites would be at serious risk if methyl iodide is permitted for use in agriculture."[107] They added that if the agency ignored its own data or characterized the results as an acceptable risk, then it would be willingly accepting that 5 percent of persons exposed to the fumigant at the application sites would develop these health problems.[108] Nevertheless, the urging of the fifty-four scientists to deny the registration request for methyl iodide failed to sway the Bush administration's EPA. It approved use of fumigant in October 2007.[109]

Environmentalists and farmworker groups wanted growers to switch to nontoxic alternatives and opposed methyl iodide because of its associated health risks and the threat of groundwater contamination. The FWAF, the Pesticide Action Network, the Sierra Club, and other organizations pressed the EPA to reject the registration request for methyl iodide.[110] The FWAF initiated a letter-writing campaign in 2008 to oppose registration of the fumigant for use in Florida. While unsuccessful in blocking approval of the chemical, the FWAF helped convince the state to enact tougher regulations than those promulgated by the EPA.[111] When the CDPR approved methyl iodide in 2010, a coalition of environmental organizations and farmworker groups submitted comments from fifty-two thousand concerned citizens to Governor Jerry Brown requesting that he prevent use of the fumigant in California. The legal arm of the Sierra Club, Earthjustice, and CRLA then filed suit against the CDPR in an attempt to block use. They represented Pesticide Action Network North

America, the United Farm Workers, Californians for Pesticide Reform, the Pesticide Watch Education Fund, Worksafe, Communities and Children, Advocates Against Pesticide Poisoning, and farmworkers Jose Hidalgo Ramon and Zeferino Estradain in the suit. Hidalgo maintained that "it's farmworkers like me who become sick . . . it's already too dangerous in the fields, we don't need new, even more dangerous, toxins." The groups argued that registration of methyl iodide violated the California Environmental Quality Act, the California Birth Defects Prevention Act, and the Pesticide Contamination Prevention Act.[112] Faced with mounting public pressure, the manufacturer of methyl iodide halted production before the lawsuit could be decided, giving pesticide reformers some cause for optimism.[113]

Twenty-five years after the UFW first targeted methyl bromide in its Wrath of Grapes campaign, and eighteen years after the Parties to the Montreal Protocol first recognized it as an ozone-depleting substance, usage of the fumigant continues in the United States. Growers, aided by the USDA, have vigorously fought to extend usage of the chemical long after it was recognized as a threat to the environment and human health. Efforts to maintain access to methyl bromide came from other quarters of government as well. Congress slipped a rider into an omnibus budget bill extending the chemical's lifeline four years beyond the original 2001 phase-out date. Actions of the George W. Bush administration then helped ensure that 2005 would not herald the chemical's end. Instead, the date passed with the United States holding "critical use exemptions" that allowed American growers to use more methyl bromide than all other growers in the world combined. Even the EPA under Bush, an agency charged with the task of protecting environmental and human health, squirreled away information on existing stocks of methyl bromide, thus permitting more to be manufactured. From the enactment of the 1990 Clean Air Amendments until present, the United States moved from being one of the most aggressive supporters of phasing out ozone-depleting substances to being one of the most resistant to the phase-out.

Uncertainty in science, in part, enabled methyl bromide supporters to create doubt that the fumigant was a critical threat, and they used that doubt to delay the phase-out of its use. The Montreal Protocol recognized that the scientific understanding of ozone depletion and ozone-depleting particles was incomplete and adopted a strategy that allowed participating nations to consider new scientific information and make adjustments to the international agreement as necessary. Countries generally held to the precautionary principle, using the best available science to craft proactive policy to protect human and environmental health while expecting that some revision might be necessary as new research increased understanding of ozone depletion. Methyl bromide supporters, in contrast, argued that the strategy showed a careless hastiness that unnecessarily handicapped growers. They capitalized on some of the scientific uncertainty relating to the accumulation and breakdown of ozone-depleting substances in the atmosphere to cast doubt on the need for immediate action, while stressing the centrality of the fumigant in the production of a wide variety of agricultural crops.

Environmental organizations and farmworker groups acted as an important counterbalance to the aggressive lobbying of growers' associations and the agricultural industry. Historians Naomi Oreskes and Erik M. Conway note that "scientists' commitment to expertise and objectivity . . . places them in a delicate position when it comes to refuting false claims [and] if a scientist jumps into the fray on a politically contested issue, he may be accused of 'politicizing' the science and compromising his objectivity."[114] Environmentalists and farmworker advocates concerned about human and environmental health therefore served as valuable conduits of scientific information about the fumigant's risks. When they disseminated information, it was couched as an argument for precautionary action rather than the "wait-and-see" approach favored by growers and the agricultural industry. The organizations educated the public about the hazards of methyl bromide and helped build support for regulation and phase-out. Environmental and farmworker organizations also contributed to the bank of knowledge with air monitoring tests and the chronicling of pesticide poisoning incidents. While unable to keep the United States on its phase-out schedule, the groups undoubtedly helped hasten the switch to alternatives by generating public interest in the issue, scrutinizing the transition, drawing attention to questionable delays, and threatening suit when necessary.

Diversity and Unity in the Pesticide Reform Movement

In his book *Banned: A History of Pesticides and the Science of Toxicology*, Frederick Davis returns in his closing to the road metaphor employed by Rachel Carson more than fifty years ago—her admonition, mentioned also earlier in this book, that the road upon which Americans were traveling would soon split, with branches heading in very different directions; one toward a sustainable future and the other toward disaster. Davis examined signposts along the way and determined that a core component of Carson's message had not been received. What occurred as a result was less a change in direction and more of a lane change, in which growers had proceeded along the same course at an accelerated velocity using different chemical control agents.[1] Even the banned use of a pesticide did not necessarily mean that it disappeared. It could often still be manufactured in the United States and then exported, eventually completing the "circle of poison" when the pesticide residues entered the country again on imported fruits and vegetables.[2] Historian David Kinkela notes, for example, that the US Agency for International Development shipped DDT to at least six foreign countries in 1974 to be used for malarial control projects and agricultural development.[3] New toxic compounds replaced chemicals banned domestically. With the EPA reporting the use of 1.1 billion pounds of pesticides in the United States alone during 2007, 80 percent of which was in agriculture, it is clear that the pesticide problem did not get addressed in the way that Carson intended.[4]

A fight for the steering wheel broke out. Many concerned Americans from many different backgrounds—environmentalists, farmworkers, mothers, and consumers—tried to maneuver toward the less trodden route that led to a destination less fraught with danger, but growers and their allies had become path-dependent on chemical forms of pest control and did their best to hold the course. Government-funded research into pest control focused heavily on chemical solutions from 1894 onward and contributed to the narrowing of agriculturalists' vision. The introduction of DDT and other synthetic compounds to commercial markets after World War II wed growers more tightly to the idea of chemically intensive production with false promises of total control over insect pests. David Kinkela argues that Cold War politics made the marriage even closer as these chemicals came to play an important role in American campaigns to win the favor of nations in the developing world.[5] The existence of an iron triangle of interests and pesticide regulation that intended to protect growers more than the public made the challenge of pesticide reform all the greater.

After the Federal Environmental Pesticides Control Act amended FIFRA in 1972, the public had greater access into the world of pesticide governance but many problems remained. The "pesticides subgovernment," as Christopher Bosso terms it, had to grant voice and political access to interests that did not necessarily embrace the pesticide paradigm.[6] The language of the law and the regulatory structure it created provided pesticide proponents a means of postponement. Since supporters of regulation and government bore the burden of proof to remove an economic poison from the market, the agricultural industry could fall back on the defense of scientific uncertainty and calls for more research. Establishing a link between a public health problem and a particular chemical or product often proves an arduous task laden with difficulties, particularly when there is a lag between exposure to a substance and the development of a health problem. Long periods of latency expand the range of possible locations of exposure and causal agents. These complicating factors often make it difficult for scientists to conclusively link a health problem with a culpable chemical. Consequently, scientists employ the uncertain language of probability to explain their investigative findings. Industry representatives may then use the uncertain language of scientists to create doubt about a chemical's health risks and stall regulatory efforts with demands for more proof and further studies.[7] Historian Nancy Langston asserts that "the call for 'more research!' has often become a way of delaying action, keeping profitable drugs and chemicals on the market as long as possible," causing a "regulatory and judicial logjam" in the process.[8]

As the wrangling over risk and culpability occurred, toxic chemicals continued to saturate the market. Banning a single pesticide often took years, during which time numerous new toxic compounds could enter into circulation. This phenomenon led the Sierra Club's Carl Pope to draw the parallel to building a dam at the base of a waterfall to illustrate the seeming futility of the system.[9] The EDF's David Roe realized the damage done to public confidence as this occurred, recognizing that the public would place the onus of blame on the inefficiencies of government rather than the industries employing the tactics of delay.[10] The rising acceptance of "quantitative risk assessment" in the 1980s added further to the difficulties of pesticide reformers. Premised upon the idea that a certain amount of hazard would always be present in daily life, the goal for regulators became efficiently managing that risk rather than eliminating it. Nancy Langston contends that consequently, "regulators have found themselves caught in a tangle of competing voices and manipulated by increasingly powerful lobbying groups" in setting the standards of acceptable risk.[11]

Several historians recognize the 1970s as a pivotal decade: one that brought promise and pitfalls for advocates of more stringent environmental standards. Adam Rome contends that "Earth Day gave environmental activism a name" by connecting a host of issues like pollution, pesticides, population, waste, and wilderness preservation and asserting that "all were facets of a far-reaching environmental crisis."[12] The emergent political force of this new movement showed in increased recognition from officeholders and in the next electoral cycle's ballot returns.[13] Bruce Schulman maintains, however, that facing environmentalists' rising clout, Richard Nixon tried to shepherd in "a conservative version of environmentalism, sucking the wind out of his liberals opponents' sails" and minimizing the impacts of new regulation.[14] The Left also increasingly lacked cohesion.

As Jefferson Cowie so clearly demonstrates in *Stayin' Alive: The 1970s and the Last Days of the Working Class*, the "social forces" of the 1970s "tended to be centrifugal rather than unifying," a phenomenon that weakened the momentum of progressive politics.[15] Economic malaise cooled some of the enthusiasm for regulatory reform as well. The nation's economy suffered its most precipitous decline since the Great Depression mid-decade with effects that stretched beyond jobs and dollars. Noting the effect on the American psyche, Judith Stein observes that "when economies do poorly, the reigning economic paradigms are questioned."[16] A growing distrust of government after Vietnam, the bombing of Cambodia, and the Watergate scandal compounded this effect.[17] In terms of environmental politics, this translated into increased questioning about the burdens of regulation. Still, groups interested in pesticide reform pressed on both together and separately, working within traditional political channels and outside in the streets and in the fields to foster change that would better protect human and environmental health.

A Single Movement for Reform

It is important in reviewing the decades of pesticide activism to consider not just the shortcomings, but the successes as well. It is similarly important to consider not just the breaks that divide movement groups, but the bridges between them. Too often overused tropes are conjured up to show favor to one group of activists over another. The problematic specter of the elitist environmentalist who cares more about the birds in the backyard than the farmworkers in the field haunts scholarly literature. Too often a close examination of the rhetoric employed and actions undertaken in pesticide reform efforts does not clearly bear out that well-accepted characterization. Sociologist Robert Brulle and environmental engineer Jonathan Essoka maintain that "arbitrary and constructed dichotomies, such as between the 'Group of Ten' and the environmental justice movement obscure the real variation within the environmental movement, and fail to advance our understanding of the dynamics of this movement."[18] Nancy Langston writes that "histories are not just academic exercises; they are political acts."[19] If that compelling statement is taken as truth, then consider the potential effects of the widespread scholarly understanding that environmentalists exited pesticide politics the moment that DDT no longer posed a threat to wildlife. Not only is that assertion untrue, but it could also arguably complicate or forestall future collaborations between movement groups if each side is led to believe that there has been no cooperation between them for more than fifty years. New understanding could, as Robert Brulle and sociologist David Pellow suggest, overcome "obstacles to the construction of a powerful mass movement that could potentially produce the sort of structural changes associated with the goals of environmental justice."[20] Thinking of farmworker groups and environmental organizations as part of a single social movement to reform the industrial agriculture production system may spark a new analysis of both of these.

Farmworker groups and environmental organizations are typically characterized as belonging to distinct social movements. From one perspective this is true. Yet, their efforts to reform pesticide use practices place them together in a broad social movement to transform industrialized agriculture into a system with more just labor relations, less impact on the environment, sustainable crop production, and production of safe food. David Meyer defines social movements within the United States as "coalition affairs" involving "sometimes loosely negotiated alliances among groups and individuals with different agendas."[21] He adds that the combination of "different constituencies, analysis, tactical capabilities, and resources" strengthens a social movement. A diverse collection of organizations working simultaneously toward complementary goals increases the visibility of issues, improves the opportunity to involve a wider range of people in the reform effort, and enhances a movement's chance of success.[22] Viewing the organizations as part of a single social movement makes it easier to view them in less dichotomous terms and to understand that even when they are working on separate efforts, they are often working toward a common end.

The approaches employed by farmworker groups and environmental organizations to restrict pesticide use and foster the growth of a more just and sustainable agricultural production system have produced a variety of gains. Union contracts prohibited growers from using a handful of hazardous pesticides and gave farmworkers a say in decision-making processes for the duration of the contracts. Lawsuits resulted in the banning of a number of dangerous pesticides, beginning with DDT, aldrin, and dieldrin. Bills supported, and sometimes written, by environmental organizations and farmworker groups created a body of laws that together changed the intent of regulation from protecting growers' investments to safeguarding the health of workers, the public, and environment. Growers, faced with numerous restrictions, need to be much more careful in their use of pesticides today than they were in the 1960s.

During the nearly fifty years of pesticide activism, environmental organizations and farmworker groups added to the catalog of information on agricultural chemicals by conducting studies and using the data to support arguments for stronger regulations. The UFW conducted tests on grocery store grapes to prove the presence of DDT residues on produce and show consumers that they were not free of pesticide risk. Air monitoring tests conducted by the Farmworker Association of Florida, Friends of the Earth, and the Environmental Working Group showed that the fumigant methyl bromide drifted into neighborhoods surrounding fields in the process of dissipating into the atmosphere. The evidence from the tests done in California led to the creation of buffer zones around field perimeters. Friends of the Earth also helped fund research that investigated the feasibility of phasing out methyl bromide in developing countries. In Arizona, Maricopa County Organizing Project collected data to chart the sale and usage of DBCP and EDB and mapped the locations of labor camps in order to get the state Health Department to treat agricultural wells in the same way as residential wells, a change that promised to better protect farmworker health. When the beleaguered Health Department claimed to lack the resources necessary to conduct extensive testing of water supplies, M-COP coordinated a series of groundwater tests and submitted the data showing contaminated well sites to the Arizona Department of Health Services. The information-gathering efforts of environmental organizations and farmworker groups often helped advance pesticide reform efforts.

A belief that Americans should have a greater voice in decision making that potentially exposed them to environmental hazards undergirded many of the efforts undertaken by farmworker groups and environmental organizations.[23] Recognition of this motivation is common enough for farmworker groups that sought to expand industrial democracy in the fields, but it is an association not always made with environmental organizations. Sociologist Jill Lindsey Harrison notes that some environmental justice activists critique the mainstream environmental movement for its preference for litigation and lobbying in campaigns, which EJ activists believe to be "pathways to environmental change that exclude so-called non-experts from participation."[24] Environmental groups, however, lobbied for and won the inclusion of right-to-know and citizen suit provisions in the 1972 Federal Environmental Pesticide Control Act. This provides the public readier access to information and means to affect pesticide governance. Environmentalists and farmworkers alike supported passage of the 1986 Arizona Environmental Quality Act which expanded pesticide education efforts, created avenues for public participation, protected whistle-blowers, and recognized citizens' right to bring a lawsuit against a polluting industry or a state regulatory body. The right to know and a citizen suit clause composed the core of California's Prop 65 as well. Supporting environmental organizations and farmworker groups embraced what political scientists Bruce Williams and Albert Matheny characterize as the communitarian thread of American politics; a vision of governance in which "reformers challenged the ability of experts, especially those employed by government and business, to capture the values involved in protecting" environmental and human health.[25] Williams and Matheny, nevertheless, observe that the degree of direct citizen participation in decision making that affects their lives has not been realized as fully as expected by advocates of reform.[26]

More often environmental organizations and farmworker groups acted as watchdogs. The communitarian language embedded in the regulatory laws does not necessarily shift power imbalances. After the passage of new regulations, general public interest in the function of a regulatory agency wanes. The regulated industry, however, remains deeply interested, sometimes aggressively opposing agency action. With public interest relaxed, industry has greater opportunity to exert its influence on the government agency, tempering regulation and, as much as possible, preserving the status quo.[27] An example of this phenomenon occurred when growers' associations and their congressional allies pressured the Occupational Health and Safety Administration to revise its standards on organophosphates, which were intended to protect farmworkers, in 1974. Political scientist Paul Sabatier consequently argues that "the presence of an organized constituency (supportive of aggressive regulation) capable of monitoring the [regulatory] agency and mobilizing in its defense is a necessary and, within certain broad limits, even a sufficient condition for forestalling" regulatory decay.[28] In their role as watchdogs, environmental organizations and farm-worker groups have regularly filed suit when state and federal agencies have proven slack in their regulation of pesticides. The resulting court rulings have often forced the targeted governmental body to change its behavior and better fulfill its responsibility to the public. The importance of the work performed by watchdog groups cannot be understated. Consider that Samuel Epstein asserts that the EPA only took action against a small number of chemicals, some of which were no longer manufactured by the time the agency acted, and contends that the majority of actions began after public interest groups threatened legal action.[29]

Yet, as noted earlier, dangerous pesticides still remain in use after decades of engagement in pesticide politics. The problem, in part, can be traced to the way in which pesticides are conceptualized, registered, and regulated. To remove a pesticide from the market or to restrict its usage, proponents of reform must first establish that the chemical poses a significant risk to human health or the environment. This process often requires a great investment of time and resources. Hence, despite the significant achievements of environmental organizations and farmworker groups in past pesticide reform efforts, many challenges remain ahead. Prop 65 introduced another alternative for regulation to California voters that ultimately had ripple benefit effects across the nation. When passed Prop 65 fundamentally reshaped the regulatory landscape in California by shifting the burden of proof from government and the public to industry. Premised on the precautionary principle, it required industry to prove that a product was safe before selling it, rather than necessitating that regulatory proponents prove the existence of a health threat after a toxin had caused harm. Since products using a listed carcinogen or mutagen in their manufacture had to carry a warning label until the company proved that its usage in the product did not constitute a risk, the law gave industry reason to favor expediency over delay. The California Environmental Protection Agency analyzed the effect of the legislation five years after its passage and concluded that it "resulted in 100 years of progress in the areas of hazard identification, risk assessment, and exposure assessment" when compared to federal standards.[30] Replicas of the California initiative or other variations of the precautionary principle have not been widely adopted, though. Environmental organizations and farmworker groups will have to remain ever vigilant: staying abreast of new scientific studies on the adverse effects of pesticides, taking into account the experiential knowledge of communities and persons who encounter pesticides in their daily life, educating the public and government officials about pesticide threats, and monitoring regulatory agencies to ensure that they fulfill their responsibility to the public. Together and separately, environmental organizations and farmworker groups will undoubtedly continue to take action as part of a diverse social movement to reform the chemically intensive industrial agriculture system that developed in the post–World War II era and reduce the threat that dangerous pesticides pose to human health and the environment.

Notes

Confronting the Consequences of the Pesticide Paradigm

1. Christopher J. Bosso, *Pesticides and Politics: The Life Cycle of a Public Issue* (Pittsburgh: University of Pittsburgh Press, 1987), 63.

2. David Nye, *Consuming Power: A Social History of American Energies* (Cambridge, MA: MIT Press, 1998), 3; Thomas P. Hughes, *Networks of Power: Electrification in Western Society, 1880–1930* (Baltimore: Johns Hopkins University Press, 1983), 14–15, 465.

3. James E. McWilliams, *American Pests: The Losing War on Insects from Colonial Times to DDT* (New York: Columbia University Press, 2008), 170.

4. Bosso, *Pesticides and Politics*, 32, 33; Jill Lindsey Harrison, *Pesticide Drift and the Pursuit of Environmental Justice* (Cambridge, MA: MIT Press, 2011), 27.

5. Bosso, *Pesticides and Politics*, 59; see also Roger E. Meiners and Andrew P. Morriss, "Silent Spring and Silent Villages: Pesticides and the Trampling of Property Rights," in *Government vs. Environment*, ed. Donald Leal and Roger E. Meiners (Lanham, MD: Rowman & Littlefield, 2002), 17.

6. Michael Egan, *Barry Commoner and the Science of Survival: The Remaking of American Environmentalism* (Cambridge, MA: MIT Press, 2007), 6.

7. Karl Boyd Brooks, *Before Earth Day: The Origins of American Environmental Law, 1945–1970* (Lawrence: University Press of Kansas, 2009), 94.

8. Robert Gottlieb, *Forcing the Spring: The Transformation of the American Environmental Movement*, rev. ed. (Washington, DC: Island Press, 2005), 48–50, 58–59.

9. Christopher C. Sellers, *Hazards of the Job: From Industrial Disease to Environmental Health Science* (Chapel Hill: University of North Carolina Press), 7.

10. Alan Derickson, *Black Lung: Anatomy of a Public Health Disaster* (Ithaca, NY: Cornell University Press, 1998), xii, 21, 60.

11. David Rosner and Gerald Markowitz, *Deadly Dust: Silicosis and the Politics of Occupational Disease in Twentieth-Century America* (Princeton, NJ: Princeton University Press, 1993), 10.

12. Gerald Markowitz and David Rosner, *Deceit and Denial: The Deadly Politics of Industrial Pollution* (Berkeley: University of California Press, 2002), 300.

13. Samuel Epstein, *The Politics of Cancer* (San Francisco: Sierra Club Books, 1978), 430.

14. Naomi Oreskes and Erik M. Conway, *Merchants of Doubt: How a Handful of Scientists Obscured the Truth on Issues from Tobacco Smoke to Global Warming* (New York: Bloomsbury Press, 2010), 264.

15. Ibid., 264.

16. Karen T. Litfin, *Ozone Disclosures: Science and Politics in Global Environmental Cooperation* (New York: Columbia University Press, 1994), 3.

17. Ibid., 4.

18. Ibid., quote on 198.

19. Jacqueline Jones, *The Dispossessed: America's Underclasses from the Civil War to the Present* (New York: Basic Books, 1992), 70.

20. Cindy Hahamovitch, *Fruits of Their Labor: Atlantic Coast Farmworkers and the Making of Migrant Poverty, 1870–1945* (Chapel Hill: University of North Carolina Press, 1997), 138.

21. Melvin F. Hall, *Poor People's Social Movement Organizations: The Goal Is to Win* (Westport, CT: Praeger, 1995), 31.

22. Guy Burgess and Heidi Burgess, "Justice Without Violence: Theoretical Foundations," in *Justice Without Violence*, ed. Paul Wehr et al. (Boulder, CO: Lynne Rienner, 1994), 12.

23. Richard White, "'Are You an Environmentalist or Do You Work for a Living?': Work and Nature" in *Uncommon Ground: Rethinking the Human Place in Nature*, ed. William Cronon (New York: Norton, 1996), 172, 173.

24. Chad Montrie, *A People's History of Environmentalism in the United States* (New York: Continuum International, 2011), 145. For an example of how opponents of regulation employ this strategy, see James Longhurst, *Citizen Environmentalists* (Lebanon, NH: Tufts University Press, 2010), 165–67.

25. Brian Mayer, *Blue-Green Coalitions: Fighting for Safe Workplaces and Healthy Communities* (Ithaca: ILR Press of Cornell University Press, 2009), 3–4.

26. Robert Gordon, "Poisons in the Fields: The United Farm Workers, Pesticides, and Environmental Politics," *Pacific Historical Review* 68, no. 1 (February 1999): 61.

27. Laura Pulido, *Environmentalism and Economic Justice: Two Chicano Struggles in the Southwest* (Tucson: University of Arizona Press, 1996), 58.

28. Laura Pulido and Devon Peña, "Environmentalism and Positionality: The Early Pesticide Campaign of the United Farm Workers' Organizing Committee, 1965–1971," *Race, Gender and Class* 6, no. 1 (October 31, 1998): 36, 38.

29. Adam Rome, "Give Earth a Chance: The Environmental Movement and the Sixties," *Journal of American History* 90, no. 2 (September 2003): 525; see also Adam Rome, *The Genius of Earth Day: How a 1970 Teach-In Unexpectedly Made the First Green Generation* (New York: Hill & Wang, 2014), 194–205.

30. Brian Mayer refers to these individuals as bridge brokers. Mayer, *Blue-Green Coalitions*, 20, 32.

31. Sherry Cable, Tamara Mix, and Donald Hastings, "Mission Impossible? Environmental Justice Activists' Collaborations with Professional Environmentalists and with Academics," in

Power, Justice, and the Environment: A Critical Appraisal of the Environmental Justice Movement, ed. David Naguib Pellow and Robert J. Brulle (Cambridge, MA: MIT Press, 2005), 66.

32. David S. Meyer, *The Politics of Protest: Social Movements in America* (New York: Oxford University Press, 2007), 76.

1. Sowing the Seeds of Chemical Dependency

1. John H. Perkins, "The Quest for Innovation in Agricultural Entomology, 1945–1975," in *Pest Control: Cultural and Environmental Aspects*, ed. David Pimentel et al. (Boulder, CO: Westview Press, 1980), 30, 37.

2. Edmund Russell, *War and Nature: Fighting Humans and Insects from World War I to Silent Spring* (New York: Cambridge University Press, 2001), 5, 6.

3. E. O. Essig, *A History of Entomology* (New York: Macmillan, 1931), 403, 404.

4. Essig, *A History of Entomology*, 53. L. O. Howard and C. L. Marlatt, *The San Jose Scale: Its Occurrences in the United States With a Full Account of Its Life History and the Remedies to Be Used Against It* (Washington, DC: Government Printing Office, 1896), 10.

5. Thomas Dunlap, *DDT: Scientists, Citizens, and Public Policy* (Princeton, NJ: Princeton University Press, 1981), 18, 19.

6. Hubert Martin, *The Scientific Principles of Plant Protection* (New York: Longmans, Green, 1928), 6, 109.

7. "Millions of Fish and Fowl Dying: Results of the Use of Paris Green in Agriculture," *New York Times*, August 9, 1878.

8. "Killed By Paris Green," ibid., July 8, 1884; "Poisoned Grapes on Sale: Quantities of Them Destroyed by Health Officers," ibid., September 23, 1891.

9. See, for example, "Disappointed in Love," ibid., October 22, 1887; "Driven to Suicide," ibid., February 2, 1887; "Attempted Suicide by Paris Green," ibid., November 22, 1878; "Love and Paris Green," ibid. July 15, 1888.

10. Russell, *War and Nature*, 6.

11. John H. Perkins, *Insects, Experts, and the Insecticide Crisis: The Quest for New Pest Management Strategies* (New York: Plenum Press, 1982), 242–44.

12. Dunlap, *DDT*, 22, 23; Perkins, *Insects, Experts, and the Insecticide Crisis*, 243–244.

13. McWilliams, *American Pests*, 49; Martin, *The Scientific Principles of Plant Protection*, 11.

14. House of Representatives, *Adulterated or Misbranded Fungicides, Insecticides, Etc.*, 61st Cong., 2d sess., 1910, H. Rep. 990, 5.

15. Perkins, *Insects, Experts, and the Insecticide Crisis*, 4; McWilliams, *American Pests*, 97; Essig, *A History of Entomology*, 419.; Adelynne Hiller Whitaker, "A History of Federal Pesticide Regulation in the United States to 1947," (Ph.D. diss., Emory University, 1974), 2–4.

16. Martin, *The Scientific Principles of Plant Protection*, 55, 79; McWilliams, *American Pests*, 104.

17. McWilliams, *American Pests*, 55, 81.

18. J. A. Lintner, "Entomology in America in 1879," *American Entomologist* 3, no. 2 (February 1880): 33.

19. "The Use of Paris Green," *American Entomologist* 3, no. 9 (September 1880): 244.

20. McWilliams, *American Pests*, 86, 87. J. S. Wade, "Leland Ossian Howard (Obituary)," *Annals of the Entomological Society of America* 43, no. 4 (December 1950): 610.

21. McWilliams, *American Pests*, 90–91, 114.

22. Ibid., 111–13; Howard, "Two Billion Crop Loss Spurs Fight on Insects," *New York Times*, February 24, 1924.

23. McWilliams, *American Pests*, 114–19.

24. Essig, *A History of Entomology*, 522.

25. McWilliams, *American Pests*, 127–28; Perkins, *Insects, Experts, and the Insecticide Crisis*, 4.

26. House Committee on Interstate and Foreign Commerce, *Hearing on Bills Relating to Insecticides and Fungicides, Part 1*, 61st Cong., 2d sess., 1910, 15, 23; John Wargo, *Our Children's Toxic Legacy: How Science and Law Fail to Protect Us from Pesticides* (New Haven, CT: Yale University Press, 1996), 67.

27. Wargo, *Our Children's Toxic Legacy*, 67; Dunlap, *DDT*, 24.

28. Perkins, *Insects, Experts, and the Insecticide Crisis*, 4.

29. The Food, Drug, and Insecticide Administration took over regulatory responsibilities in 1926 with the abolishment of the Insecticide and Fungicide Board. Carleton R. Ball, *Federal, State, and Local Administrative Relationship in Agriculture,* vol. 1 (Berkeley: University of California Press, 1938), 319.

30. J. K. Haywood, "Report of the Insecticide and Fungicide Board," in *Annual Reports of the Department of Agriculture for the Year Ended June 30, 1913: Report of the Secretary of Agriculture: Reports of Chiefs* (Washington, DC: Government Printing Office, 1914), 331–33.

31. Whitaker, "A History of Federal Pesticide Regulation in the United States to 1947," ii.

32. McWilliams, *American Pests*, 129, 132, 142.

33. Dunlap, *DDT*, 25, 31.

34. Perkins, *Insects, Experts, and the Insecticide Crisis*, 23.

35. L. O. Howard, "Man's War with Insects," *Washington Post*, March 25, 1928.

36. Perkins, *Insects, Experts, and the Insecticide Crisis*, 211–12, 215, 219; Deborah Fitzgerald, *Every Farm a Factory: The Industrial Ideal in American Agriculture* (New Haven, CT: Yale University Press, 2003), 186–87.

37. Perkins, *Insects, Experts, and the Insecticide Crisis*, 232.

38. McWilliams, *American Pests*, 170.

39. Sellers, *Hazards of the Job*, 199; Dunlap, *DDT*, 45–47.

40. Sellers, *Hazards of the Job*, 201.

41. Wargo, *Our Children's Toxic Legacy*, 68.

42. Dunlap, *DDT*, 50, 52; *Agricultural Appropriations Bill, 1938*, 75th Cong., 1st sess., S. Rep. 537.

43. Dunlap, *DDT*, 53–55.

44. Perkins, "The Quest for Innovation in Agricultural Entomology, 1945–1978," 26–27; "Total Insect War Urged," *Science News-Letter* 47, no. 1 (January 6, 1945): 5.

45. Russell, *War and Nature*, 149, 156–57, 162.

46. Wargo, *Our Children's Toxic Legacy*, 70.

47. "Mosquitoes Resist DDT," *Science News-Letter* 56, no. 23 (December 3, 1949): 355; Perkins, *Insects, Experts, and the Insecticide Crisis*, 36.

48. Wargo, *Our Children's Toxic Legacy*, 70.

49. *Regulating the Marketing of Economic Poisons and Devices*, 80th Cong., 1st sess., S. Rep. 199, 2.

50. Senate Committee on Commerce, *Amending the Insecticide Act*, 78th Cong., 1st sess., 1943, 4, 14. Sodium fluoride is the common ingredient used in toothpaste to help remove plaque from teeth and prevent decay. It kills insects and rats in denser concentrations.

51. Ibid., 12, 30–31.

52. House Committee on Agriculture, *Federal Insecticide, Fungicide, and Rodenticide Act*, 80th Cong., 1st sess., 1947; House Committee on Agriculture, *Federal Insecticide, Fungicide, and Rodenticide Act*, 79th Cong., 2d sess., 1946.

53. Bosso, *Pesticides and Politics*, 59.

54. *Regulating the Marketing of Economic Poisons and Devices*, 5.

55. Pete Daniel, *Toxic Drift: Pesticides and Health in the Post–World War II South* (Baton Rouge: Louisiana State University, 2005), 5, 8, 130.

56. Brooks, *Before Earth Day*, 113.

57. William H. Rodgers Jr., "The Persistent Problem of Persistent Pesticides: A Lesson in Environmental Law," *Columbia Law Review* 70, no. 4 (April 1970): 572.

58. Perkins, "The Quest for Innovation in Agricultural Entomology, 1945–1975," 31, 33; Russell, *War and Nature*, 173, 198.

59. Russell, *War and Nature*, 184, 189, 190, 194.

2. Hidden Hands of the Harvest

1. Stephanie S. Pincetl, *Transforming California: A Political History of Land Use and Development* (Baltimore: John Hopkins University Press, 1999), 2, 5, 20–21; Cletus E. Daniel, *Bitter Harvest: A History of California Farmworkers, 1870–1941* (Berkeley: University of California Press, 1981), 18; Carey McWilliams, *Factories in the Field: The Story of Migratory Farm Labor in California* (1935; Berkeley: University of California Press, 2000), 15–16.

2. Pincetl, *Transforming California*, 9; Daniel, *Bitter Harvest*, 18, 21.

3. Donald Worster, *Rivers of Empire: Water, Aridity and the Growth of the American West* (New York: Oxford University Press, 1985), 193–256.

4. Steven Stoll, *The Fruits of Natural Advantage: Making the Industrial Countryside in California* (Berkeley: University of California Press, 1998), 16, 63, 64.

5. Stoll, *The Fruits of Natural Advantage*, 62; Daniel, *Bitter Harvest*, 34–35, 46; McWilliams, *Factories in the Field*, 59.

6. Stoll, *The Fruits of Natural Advantage*, 98–107.

7. Daniel, *Bitter Harvest*, 45. Historian Cindy Hahamovitch documents a comparable labor situation in vegetable and berry truck farms in the Atlantic seaboard states. See Hahamovitch, *Fruits of Their Labor*, 6, 27, 28.

8. Daniel, *Bitter Harvest*, 63, 64; Camille Guerin-Gonzales, *Mexican Workers and American Dreams: Immigration, Repatriation, and California Farm Labor, 1900–1939* (New Brunswick, NJ: Rutgers University Press, 1994), 16, 25; Greg Hall, *Harvest Wobblies: The Industrial Workers of the World and Agricultural Laborers in the American West, 1905–1930* (Corvallis: Oregon State University Press, 2001), 33, 34; Lloyd H. Fisher, "The Harvest Labor Market in California," *Quarterly Journal of Economics* 65, no. 4 (November 1951): 469.

9. McWilliams, *Factories in the Field*, 68–71, 77.

10. Douglas S. Massey, Jorge Durand, and Nolan J. Malone, *Beyond Smoke and Mirrors: Mexican Immigration in an Era of Economic Integration* (New York: Russell Sage Foundation, 2002), 27–28; McWilliams, *Factories in the Field*, 104–33.

11. McWilliams, *Factories in the Field*, 104, 118; Cletus E. Daniel, "Radicals on the Farm in California," *Agricultural History* 49, no. 4 (October 1975): 641.

12. Daniel, *Bitter Harvest*, 77–81.

13. McWilliams, *Factories in the Field*, 154–58; Daniel, *Bitter Harvest*, 81–88; Hall, *Harvest Wobblies*, 48–59, 92–97.

14. McWilliams, *Factories in the Field*, 48–50; Hall, *Harvest Wobblies*, 48–51.

15. Stoll, *The Fruits of Natural Advantage*, 150; Daniel, *Bitter Harvest*, 66, 67.

16. Guerin-Gonzales, *Mexican Workers and American Dreams*, 46.

17. Douglas C. Sackman, "'Nature's Workshop': The Work Environment and Workers' Bodies in the California Citrus Industry, 1900–1940," *Environmental History* 5 (January 2000): 45.

18. Douglas C. Sackman, *Orange Empire: California and the Fruits of Eden* (Berkeley: University of California Press, 2005), 88–89.

19. Ibid., 89.

20. Daniel, *Bitter Harvest*, 101, 102.

21. McWilliams, *Factories in the Field*, 190; Sackman, *Orange Empire*, 101.

22. John Steinbeck, *The Harvest Gypsies: On the Road to the Grapes of Wrath* (1936; Berkeley: Heyday Books, 1988), 32, 34; John Steinbeck, "Dubious Battle in California," *The Nation* 143, no. 11 (September 12, 1936): 303.

23. Steinbeck, *The Harvest Gypsies*, 35.

24. McWilliams, *Factories in the Field*, 211, 213, 215.

25. Daniel, *Bitter Harvest*, 115, 121, 143. While growers favored using deportation as a threat against Mexican unionists they did not support immigration quotas for Mexican immigrants and opposed the indiscriminate repatriation of Mexicans in the United States. Francisco E. Balderrama and Raymond Rodríguez, *Decade of Betrayal: Mexican Repatriation in the 1930s* (Albuquerque: University of New Mexico Press, 1995), 22–23.

26. See Daniel, *Bitter Harvest*, 105–257; McWilliams, *Factories in the Field*, 211–63.

27. Nelson A. Pichardo, "The Power Elite and Elite-Driven Countermovements: The Associated Farmers of California during the 1930s," *Sociological Forum* 10, no. 1 (March 1995): 29.

28. Pichardo, "The Power Elite and Elite-Driven Countermovements," 26, 27; Sackman, *Orange Empire*, 220.

29. Sackman, *Orange Empire*, 220, 221.

30. Pichardo, "The Power Elite and Elite-Driven Countermovements," 10.

31. Melvyn Dubofsky, *The State and Labor in Modern America* (Chapel Hill: University of North Carolina Press, 1994), 113.

32. Nelson Lichtenstein, *State of the Union: A Century of American Labor* (Princeton, NJ: Princeton University Press, 2002), 110, 111; Daniel, *Bitter Harvest*, 258.

33. Daniel, *Bitter Harvest*, 261.

34. Hahamovitch, *The Fruits of Their Labor*, 156; Daniel, *Bitter Harvest*, 270.

35. Fisher, "The Harvest Labor Market in California," 140.

36. Devra Weber, *Dark Sweat, White Gold: California Farm Workers, Cotton, and the New Deal* (Berkeley: University of California Press, 1994), 134–35.

37. Allen J. Matusow, *Farm Policies and Politics in the Truman Years* (Cambridge, MA: Harvard University Press, 1967), 69.

38. Hahamovitch, *The Fruits of Their Labor*, 152.

39. Matusow, *Farm Policies and Politics in the Truman Years*, 69.

40. Dubofsky, *The State and Labor in Modern America*, 171.

41. Lichtenstein, *State of the Union*, 101.

42. David Brody, *Workers in Industrial America: Essays on the Twentieth Century Struggle*, 2d ed. (New York: Oxford University Press, 1993), 160–65.

43. Ernesto Galarza, *Strangers in Our Fields* (Washington, DC: Joint United States–Mexico Trade Union Committee, 1956), 5–7; Eric V. Meeks, *Border Citizens: The Making of Indians, Mexicans, and Anglos in Arizona* (Austin: University of Texas Press), 163.

44. Daniel J. Tichenor, *Dividing Lines: The Politics of Immigration Control in America* (Princeton, NJ: Princeton University Press, 2002), 174, 175.

45. Galarza, *Strangers in Our Fields*, 23–28.

46. Ibid., 13, 32, 62.

47. Ibid., 70–71.

48. Vernon M. Briggs Jr., "Non-Immigrant Labor Policy in the United States," *Journal of Economic Issues* 17, no. 3 (September 1983): 614, 617; Hahamovitch, *The Fruits of Their Labor*, 200–201.

49. Hahamovitch, *The Fruits of Their Labor*, 200–201.

50. "Harvest of Shame," *CBS Reports*, episode 78 (originally aired November 26, 1960), http://www.cbsnews.com/video/watch/?id=7087479n&tag=related;photovideo.

51. Richard J. Schaefer, "Reconsidering Harvest of Shame: The Limitations of a Broadcast Journalism Landmark," *Journalism History* 19, no. 4 (Winter 1994): 121–32.

52. Jim Hightower, *Hard Tomatoes, Hard Times: The Original Hightower Report—and Other Recent Reports—on Problems and Prospects of American Agriculture* (Cambridge, MA: Schenkman, 1973, 1978), 35. Ingolf Vogeler, *The Myth of the Family Farm: Agribusiness Dominance of U.S. Agriculture* (Boulder, CO: Westview Press, 1981), 69, 71. Perkins, *Insects, Experts, and the Insecticide Crisis*, 211.

53. Perkins, *Insects, Experts, and the Insecticide Crisis*, 212.

3. The Budding Movement for Pesticide Reform, 1962–1972

1. Rachel Carson, *Silent Spring* (1962; Boston: Houghton Mifflin, 1994), 3.

2. Ibid., 103–28, 129–53.

3. Ibid., 22, 23, 222.

4. Ibid., 242.

5. Mark Hamilton Lytle, *The Gentle Subversive: Rachel Carson, Silent Spring, and the Rise of the Environmental Movement* (New York: Oxford University Press, 2007), 8.

6. Devon G. Peña, *Mexican Americans and the Environment: Tierra y Vida* (Tucson: University of Arizona Press, 2005), 122.

7. Linda Nash, "The Fruits of Ill-Health: Pesticides and Workers' Bodies in Post–World War II California," *Osiris* 19 (2004): 209, 211 (quote).

8. Carson, *Silent Spring*, 22, 30.

9. Frederick Rowe Davis, *Banned: A History of Pesticides and the Science of Toxicology* (New Haven, CT: Yale University Press, 2014), 161 (quote), 192, 193.

10. Carson, *Silent Spring*, 277.

11. Egan, *Barry Commoner and the Science of Survival*, 2–3, 6–7, 57 (quote); Sarah L. Thomas, "A Call to Action: Silent Spring, Public Discourse, and the Rise of Modern Environmentalism," in *Natural Protest: Essays on the History of American Environmentalism*, ed. Michael Egan and Jeff Crane (New York: Routledge, 2009), 185, 186.

12. Egan, *Barry Commoner and the Science of Survival*, 58.

13. Ibid., 58, 63.

14. Jacques E. Levy, *Cesar Chavez: Autobiography of La Causa* (New York: Norton, 1975), 97–98; Susan Ferriss and Ricardo Sandoval, *The Fight in the Fields: Cesar Chavez and the Farmworkers Movement*, ed. Diana Hembree (San Diego, CA: Harcourt Brace, 1997), 37–39.

15. Levy, *Cesar Chavez*, 101–2; Ferriss and Sandoval, *The Fight in the Fields*, 51–53.

16. F. Arturo Rosales, *Chicano! The History of the Mexican American Civil Rights Movement* (Houston, TX: Arte Público Press, 1996), 132–33; Marshall Ganz, *Why David Sometimes Wins: Leadership, Organization, and Strategy in the California Farm Worker Movement* (New York: Oxford University Press, 2009), 82.

17. Randy Shaw, *Beyond the Fields: Cesar Chavez, the UFW, and the Struggle for Justice in the 21st Century* (Berkeley: University of California Press, 2008), 17.

18. Ferriss and Sandoval, *The Fight in the Fields*, 80.

19. Ganz, *Why David Sometimes Wins*, 104–105.

20. Shaw, *Beyond the Fields*, 17.

21. Levy, *Cesar Chavez*, 182–83, 185; Ferriss and Sandoval, *The Fight in the Fields*, 86.

22. Ganz, *Why David Sometimes Wins*, 125–26.

23. Ibid., 127.

24. Fred Ross Sr., "History of the Farm Worker Movement" (lecture, Dayton, OH, October 1974), 7, UFW Information and Research Department Collection, box 26, folder 26-26, Archives of Labor and Urban Affairs, Wayne State University, Detroit; Levy, *Cesar Chavez*, 183.

25. "Editorial: Enough People With One Idea," *El Malcriado*, no. 19 (1965): 2.

26. Ganz, *Why David Sometimes Wins*, 130–31.

27. Levy, *Cesar Chavez*, 196; Ganz, *Why David Sometimes Wins*, 134. Historian Matthew Garcia also emphasizes the importance of the movement's diversity and its democratic pooling of ideas in the early success of the UFWOC. Matthew Garcia, *From the Jaws of Victory: The Triumph and Tragedy of Cesar Chavez and the Farm Worker Movement* (Berkeley: University of California Press, 2012), 3, 6, 296 (Kindle edition).

28. Ganz, *Why David Sometimes Wins*, 141. 142.

29. Levy, *Cesar Chavez*, 197.

30. Ganz, *Why David Sometimes Wins*, 10, 13 (quote).

31. "Delano Needs Doctors," *El Malcriado,* no. 26 (1965): 12; "What Is the NFWA?" ibid., no. 31 (March 17, 1966): 20.

32. "Association Strike Continues Successful," ibid., no. 17 (1965): 7; "You Can Help: 'A Crime Against All the Farm Workers of California," ibid.: 8.

33. "The Plan of Delano," (March 1966), https://libraries.ucsd.edu/farmworkermovement/ufwarchives/elmalcriado/Proclamation%201966.pdf.

34. The speech from which this quote is drawn lacks identifying information. However, references within the speech, as well as its cataloguing in the archives, allow it to be placed fairly accurately in time. Chavez states that "it is now almost 18 months since the strike . . . started," which means the speech was likely delivered in February 1967. Cesar Chavez, speech, United Farm Workers Organizing Committee Collection, box 2, folder 2-5, Archives of Labor and Urban Affairs, Wayne State University, Detroit, MI.

35. The only time that pesticides were discussed in *El Malcriado* prior to 1967 was in a report of a confrontation between a grower and farmworkers on the picket line. It reported that the eighteen-year-old son of Delano grower Jack Radovich Jr. drove along a picket with a spray rig, dousing workers with a "deadly sulfur spray" that caused temporary blindness in sixteen of the victims. The story, however, focused less on the potential health threat of exposure to the chemical and more on the insensate hostility of the act and the reluctance of local police to arrest and prosecute the grower's son. "Radovich Sprays 16 Strikers with Blinding Sulfur," *El Malcriado*, no. 21 (1965): 11. In a subsequent article, the incident received mention again, but it was used as an example of the picketers' stalwartness and commitment to the cause, rather than as an opportunity to discuss the risk of pesticide poisoning. "The Good and the Bad," ibid., no. 22 (1965): 3.

36. Nash, "The Fruits of Ill-Health," 212–13.

37. "Delano Water Bad for Babies," *El Malcriado*, no. 54 (January 13, 1967): 10. A subsequent article in *El Malcriado* carried a much angrier tone, complaining that growers continued to receive government subsidies to "grow profits . . . while the people have to drink poison." "Power, Profit and Poison," *El Malcriado* 2, no. 6 (May 15, 1968): 12.

38. Ganz, *Why David Sometimes Wins,* 141, 154–59, 195, 205.

39. Marion Moses, "'Viva la Causa!'" *American Journal of Nursing* 73, no. 5 (May 1973): 842–43.

40. Ibid., 844.

41. Marion Moses to LeRoy [Chatfield], July 14, 1968, Marion Moses, MD Collection, box 2, folder 2-3, Archives of Labor and Urban Affairs, Wayne State University, Detroit; Levy, *Cesar Chavez*, 195.

42. "Pesticide Notes," UFW Central Administration Files Collection, box 10, folder 10-29, Archives of Labor and Urban Affairs, Wayne State University, Detroit, MI.

43. Marion Moses to LeRoy [Chatfield], July 14, 1968.

44. Marion Moses to LeRoy [Chatfield], July 14, 1968; "Poisoning the Wells," *Environment* 11, no. 1 (January–February 1969): 45. The UFWOC cited the *Environment* article in petitioning the city of Delano to better address the issue. Paul Driscoll to the Delano City Council, September 2, 1969, UFW Central Administration Files Collection, box 9, folder 9-19.

45. Marion Moses to Charles Worster [*sic*], July 15, 1968, Marion Moses, MD Collection, Box 2, Folder 2-3; William A. Butler, "Opening the Washington Office," in *Acorn Days: The*

Environmental Defense Fund and How It Grew, ed. Marion Lane Rogers (New York: Environmental Defense Fund, 1990), 86.

46. Charles Wurster, "The Power of an Idea," ibid., 47.

47. Jerry Cohen, interview by Leroy Chatfield, May 19, 2009, Farmworker Movement Documentation Project, "Audio Interview: Jerry Cohen/David Averbuck/Chuck Farnsworth Discuss Legal Cases 1960's," https://libraries.ucsd.edu/farmworkermovement/ufwarchives/index.shtml; Shaw, *Beyond the Fields*, 121.

48. Jerry Cohen, interview by Leroy Chatfield, May 19, 2009.

49. "Growers Hide Facts on Poisons," *El Malcriado* 2, no. 13 (September 1, 1968): 6; "UFWOC Demands Poisons Records," ibid., no. 17 (November 1, 1968): 12.

50. Chuck Farnsworth, interview by Leroy Chatfield, May 19, 2009, Farmworker Movement Documentation Project, "Audio Interview: Jerry Cohen/David Averbuck/Chuck Farnsworth Discuss Legal Cases 1960's"; Uribe v. Howie, 19 Cal. App. 3d 194, 96 Cal. Rptr. 493 (1971).

51. "Growers Hide Facts on Poisons," 6; "UFWOC Demands Poisons Records," 12. "Growers Spurn Negotiations on Poisons," *El Malcriado* 2, no. 22 (January 15, 1969): 3.

52. Robert Van Den Bosch, *The Pesticide Conspiracy* (1978; Berkeley: University of California Press, 1989), 76; David Averbuck, interview by Leroy Chatfield, May 19, 2009, Farmworker Movement Documentation Project, "Audio Interview: Jerry Cohen/David Averbuck/Chuck Farnsworth Discuss Legal Cases 1960's."

53. Judge George A. Brown quoted in "Judge Denies UFWOC Access to Poison Info.," *El Malcriado* 3, no. 3 (April 1–15, 1969): 2.

54. David Averbuck, interview by Leroy Chatfield, May 19, 2009.

55. Ibid.

56. Wurster, "The Power of an Idea," 45.

57. Harmon Henkin, "DDT and the Constitution," *The Nation* 208, no. 10 (March 10, 1969): 308, 309.

58. Wurster, "The Power of an Idea," 45.

59. Ibid., 47; Dennis Puleston, "Birth and Early Days," in Rogers, *Acorn Days*, 23.

60. Puleston, "Birth and Early Days," 24, 25; Wurster, "The Power of an Idea," 51.

61. Puleston, "Birth and Early Days," 25; Roderick Cameron, "View From the Front Office," in Rogers, *Acorn Days*, 35.

62. Marion Lane Rogers, "Onward and Upward," in Rogers, *Acorn Days*, 42.

63. Wurster, "The Power of an Idea," 46; Puleston, "Birth and Early Days," 26; Wurster, "The Last Word," 182–85.

64. Wurster, "The Last Word," 184.

65. Henkin, "DDT and the Constitution," 309–10.

66. "Organization and Responsibilities of EDF, Inc.," Environmental Defense Fund Collection, Record Group (RG) 2, Series Group (SG) 1, Series (S) 1, Subseries (SS) 1, box 1, folder 9, Department of Special Collections, SUNY Stony Brook, Stony Brook, NY.

67. Frank Graham Jr. and Carl W. Buchhesiter, *The Audubon Ark: A History of the National Audubon Society* (New York: Knopf, 1990), 46, 47.

68. Pam Nicholls, ed., *Chapter and Group Leaders' Handbook* (San Francisco: Sierra Club, 1981), 6. Sierra Club Florida Chapter Collection, box 12, folder Group Handbooks, Manuals, and Model Bylaws, University of Florida Special Collections, Gainesville. See also Rome, "Give Earth a Chance," 527; J. Michael McCloskey, *In the Thick of It: My Life in the Sierra Club* (Washington, DC: Island Press, 2005), 101; Graham and Buchhesiter, *The Audubon Ark*, 228.

69. Graham and Buchhesiter, *The Audubon Ark*, 228.

70. Wurster, "The Power of an Idea," 52–53; Graham and Buchhesiter, *The Audubon Ark*, 231–32.

71. McCloskey, *In the Thick of It*, 87–88; Scott Thurber, "Conservation Comes of Age," *The Nation* 204, no. 9 (February 27, 1967): 273. The Sierra Club did not hire its first full-time lobbyist until 1965. Michael McCloskey, "Introduction," in "John Zierold: Environmental Lobbyist in California's Capital, 1965–1984" (interview by Ann Lage, 1984), xii, Regional Oral History Office, The Bancroft Library, University of California Berkeley; Robert A. Jones, "Fratricide in the Sierra Club," *The Nation* 208, no. 18 (May 5, 1969): 568.

72. Edgar Wayburn, "Envoi," *Sierra Club Bulletin* 54, no. 5 (May 1969): 2; Edgar Wayburn, "Elections and Electioneering," ibid., 53, no. 12 (December 1968): 2.

73. Edgar Wayburn, "The Anatomy of Positive Conservation, Part I," ibid., 53, no. 9 (September 1968): 2; Edgar Wayburn, "A Reaffirmation of Purpose," ibid., no. 5 (May 1968): 2.

74. Michael McCloskey, "A Conservation Agenda for 1969," ibid., no. 12 (December 1968): 5.

75. "Conclusion: Annual Organization Meeting Report," ibid., 54, no. 6 (June 1969): 14. More than half of the *Sierra Club Bulletin* issues published in 1969 carried such articles.

76. Pulido, *Environmentalism and Economic Justice*, 86.

77. Thomas H. Jukes to March K. Fong, March 26, 1971, Fong (March K.) Collection, LP159: 499, AB163-AB552, California State Archives, Sacramento.

78. Stephen R. Fox, *The American Conservation Movement: John Muir and His Legacy* (Madison: University of Wisconsin Press, 1981), 298.

79. *Edwards v. National Audubon Society, Inc*, 556 F.2d 113 (1977).

80. Judith Kunofsky to Mike McCloskey et al., July 9, 1980, Sierra Club Members Papers Collection, carton 80, folder 10, Bancroft Library, University of California Berkeley; Graham and Buchhesiter, *The Audubon Ark*, 232.

81. Judith Kunofsky to Mike McCloskey et al., July 9, 1980.

82. Paul Cabbell, "A Free Press Interview with Cesar Chavez," *Los Angeles Free Press* (August 22, 1969), UFW Information and Research Department Collection, box 5, folder 5-30.

83. Huerta, "Keynote Address Before the Annual Convention of the American Public Health Association," (New Orleans, October 21, 1974), UFW Information and Research Department Collection, box 5, folder 5-30.

84. "Strike!" *El Malcriado*, no. 65 (August 16, 1967): 1.

85. Meeting Minutes (n.d.), UFW Work Department Collection, box 5, folder 5-1, Archives of Labor and Urban Affairs, Wayne State University, Detroit.

86. Ganz, *Why David Sometimes Wins*, 228.

87. Jerry Cohen, interview by Leroy Chatfield, May 19, 2009.

88. "Danger-Poison!/¡Peligro-Veneno!," UFW Office of the President: Cesar Chavez Collection Part II, box 36, folder 36-20, Archives of Labor and Urban Affairs, Wayne State University, Detroit.

89. Jerry Cohen, interview by Leroy Chatfield, May 19, 2009; George Getze, "Suits Ask Ban on Use of DDT in State, Confiscation of Crops," *Los Angeles Times*, April 15, 1969.

90. UFWOC attorney David Averbuck quoted ibid.

91. Rome, "Give Earth a Chance," 527, 553.

92. Ibid., 538.

93. Juanita Brown to Boycotters, 1969, United Farmworkers Organizing Committee Collection, box 9, folder 9-29.

94. "Commentary to Go With Pesticide Slides," prepared April 21, 1970, UFW Central Administration Files, box 10, folder 10-34.

95. Juanita Brown to Boycotters, 1969; Jerry Cohen to Boycotters, August 5, 1969, UFW Information and Research Department Collection, box 24, folder 24-1.

96. "Grape Workers Are Killed and Maimed Every Year by the Pesticides You Are Eating," leaflet, UFWOC New York Boycott Collection, Box 11, Folder 11-13, Archives of Labor and

Urban Affairs, Wayne State University, Detroit; "It's a Matter of Good Health for You to Support the Grape Boycott," leaflet, United Farmworkers Organizing Committee Collection, Box 9, Folder 9–29.

97. "Growers Spurn Negotiations on Poisons," 3.

98. "Historic Break Through! Growers Offer Negotiations," *El Malcriado* 3, no. 6 (June 1–30, 1969): 3, 14.

99. "Talks Stalled on Poison Use: Chavez Speaks Out on Negotiations," ibid. no. 8 (July 15–31, 1969): 3, 13; "Blackmail!" ibid., 3, 14.

100. "UFWOC Signs Historic Pesticide Safety Clause," ibid., no. 12 (September 15–October 1, 1969): 3, 6.

101. Safeway Stores, Inc. to Customers, June, 26 1969, UFWOC New York Boycott Collection, box 11, folder 11-4; Cesar Chavez to Boycotters, September 19, 1969, UFWOC New York Boycott Collection, box 11, folder 11-4.

102. Jerry Cohen to Cesar Chavez and Marion Moses, May 30, 1969, UFW Office of the President: Cesar Chavez Collection Part II, box 36, folder 36-20.

103. Thomas J. Foley, "Grape Pesticides Finding Challenged," *Los Angeles Times*, September 30, 1969.

104. Subcommittee on Migratory Labor, *Migrant and Seasonal Farmworker Powerlessness: Pesticides and the Farmworker*, 91st Cong., 1st and 2d sess., 1969, Part 6B, 3366–67, 3379.

105. Jerry Cohen, interview by Leroy Chatfield, May 19, 2009.

106. Chuck Farnsworth to Boycotters (n.d.); Cesar Chavez to Boycotters, September 19, 1969; both UFWOC New York Boycott Collection, box 11, folder 11-4.

107. Environmental Defense Fund, Incorporated, et al., "In re: Irene Lopez, Elvira Garduno, Kathy Rake, Marilyn Vittor, Leigh Roycroft, Juan Zamora, and the Environmental Defense Fund Incorporated," "Petition for Issuance of a Proposed Regulation Repealing a Tolerance for a Pesticide on Raw Agricultural Commodities," in "Petition Requesting the Suspension and Cancellation of Registration of Economic Poisons Containing DDT," appendix B, 6, Sierra Club Records Collection, BANC 71/103 c, carton 125, folder 12, Bancroft Library, University of California Berkeley.

108. Michael D. Green, "The Politics of Pesticides," *The Nation* 209, no. 18 (November 24, 1969): 570.

109. Environmental Defense Fund Incorporated, "Leading Environmentalists Petition U.S.D.A. to Ban DDT," press release, October 31, 1969, Environmental Defense Fund Collection, RG 1, SG 1.4, S 7, SS 2, box 7, folder 22; James W. Moorman to Michael McCloskey, November 3, 1969, Sierra Club Records, BANC 81/103c, carton 125, folder 14. James W. Moorman to Michael McCloskey, October 21, 1969, Sierra Club Records, BANC 71/103 c, carton 125, folder 14.

110. Environmental Defense Fund Incorporated, "Leading Environmentalists Petition U.S.D.A. to Ban DDT."

111. Dunlap, *DDT*, 207–8.

112. James W. Moorman to Willard E. Wolfe, October 22, 1969, Sierra Club Records, BANC 71/103 c, carton 125, folder 14.

113. "Huelga Ends: Delano Struggle Concludes With Dramatic Signing," *El Malcriado* IV, no. 4 (August 1, 1970): 4.

114. "Consumer and Worker Protection Clause," UFW Information and Research Department Collection, box 24, folder 24-1.

115. "Health and Safety Portions of the Freedman Contracts," UFW Central Administration Files Collection, box 10, folder 10-34.

116. Dunlap, *DDT*, 211.

117. Van Den Bosch, *The Pesticide Conspiracy*, 54.

4. Movements in Transition

1. For a short description of various events see "And the Day After," *Science News* 97, no. 18 (May 2, 1970): 432; Richard Harwood, "Earth Day Stirs Nation," *Washington Post*, April 23, 1970; David Lowenthal, "Earth Day," *Area* 2, no. 4 (1970): 1–10. For a comprehensive account of organizational efforts, events, and persons, see Rome, *The Genius of Earth Day*.

2. Louise Durbin, "Earth Day May Not Save the World, but It's a Beginning," *Washington Post*, March 22, 1970; George C. Wilson, "Ecology: Protests to Mount," ibid., March 15, 1970.

3. Lowenthal, "Earth Day," 3 (quote); Dael Wolfle, "After Earth Day," *Science* 168, no. 3932 (8 May 1970), 657.

4. "And the Day After," 432.

5. Thomas F. Jackson, *From Civil Rights to Human Rights: Martin Luther King, Jr., and the Struggle for Economic Justice* (Philadelphia: University of Pennsylvania Press, 2007), 285, 412n.

6. Johanna Fernandez, "Between Social Service Reform and Revolutionary Politics: The Young Lords, Late Sixties Radicalism, and Community Organizing in New York City," in *Freedom North: Black Freedom Struggles Outside the South, 1940–1980*, ed. Jeanne F. Theoharis and Komozi Woodard (New York: Palgrave Macmillan, 2003), 264–69.

7. Rocky Barker, "A Lawmaker's Brainchild, Earth Day Turns 40, Having Spawned Environmental Movement," *Cleveland Plain Dealer*, April 18, 2010. For a description of Sandoval's activism in the Chicano movement and how he blended Chicano and environmental concerns, see Rome, *The Genius of Earth Day*, 83, 88, 92–93. Other staffers who helped organize Earth Day events had roots in movements for civil rights and social justice as well. See Adam Rome, "The Genius of Earth Day," *Environmental History* 15, no. 2 (April 2010): 197.

8. "Earth Day/Daughters of the American Revolution/Blacks/South Dakota," (originally aired April 23, 1970), Vanderbilt University Television News Archive, Nashville, TN.

9. Quote is from Howard University student Michael Harris. "Earth Day/Daughters of the American Revolution/Blacks/South Dakota."

10. Lowenthal, "Earth Day," 3.

11. Harwood, "Earth Day Stirs Nation."

12. Environmental Action, *Earth Tool Kit: A Field Manual for Citizen Activists*, ed. Sam Love et al. (New York: Pocket Books, 1971), 7.

13. McCloskey, *In the Thick of It*, 105–6.

14. Jim Morse and Nancy Matthews, eds., *The Sierra Club Survival Songbook* (San Francisco: Sierra Club, 1971).

15. McCloskey, *In the Thick of It*, 106, 108.

16. Carson, *Silent Spring*, 25–26.

17. Samuel S. Epstein, *The Politics of Cancer Revisited* (Freemont Center, NY: East Ridge Press, 1998), 166.

18. Ibid., 166.

19. Wargo, *Our Children's Toxic Legacy*, 88. The EDF worked to ban both chemicals simultaneously, because aldrin converted to dieldrin as it broke down in the body. For a discussion of the chemical and its effects, see Epstein, *The Politics of Cancer Revisited*, 159–66.

20. Stuart L. Spradling, "Testimony in Support of the Continued Use of Aldrin as a Corn Soil Insecticide" (testimony, Environmental Protection Agency Aldrin Dieldrin Cancellation Hearing, Kansas City, MO, August 28, 1973), Environmental Defense Fund Collection, RG 3, SG II.2, S 1, SS Aldrin & Dieldrin Suspension/Cancellation Hearings, box 46, folder 17.

21. Max Bailey, testimony, Environmental Protection Agency Aldrin Dieldrin Cancellation Hearing, Kansas City, MO, August 28, 1973, Environmental Defense Fund Collection, RG 3, SG II.2, S 1, SS Aldrin & Dieldrin Suspension/Cancellation Hearings, box 46, folder 18; Stuart L. Spradling, "Testimony in Support of the Continued Use of Aldrin as a Corn Soil Insecticide."

22. Statement of Dianna Lyons (n.d), Environmental Defense Collection, RG 3, SG II.2, S 1, SS Aldrin & Dieldrin Suspension/ Cancellation Hearings, box 39, folder 14.

23. William A. Butler to Joseph Segor, February 7, 1973, Environmental Defense Fund Collection, RG 3, SG II.2, S 1, SS Aldrin & Dieldrin Suspension/ Cancellation Hearings, box 2, folder 2.

24. Ibid.

25. Boycott Central to UFWOC Staff, February 24, 1972, UFW Central Administration Files Collection, box 26, folder 26-26.

26. Statement of Dianna Lyons (n.d).

27. William A. Butler to Joseph Segor, February 7, 1973.

28. Statement of Dianna Lyons (n.d). Her brief statement was one among many that filled the thirty-five thousand pages of testimony accumulated over a twelve-month period, so the weight that it carried in the decision-making process is difficult to determine. Wargo, *Our Children's Toxic Legacy*, 88.

29. *Environmental Defense Fund v. Environmental Protection Agency*, 510 F. 2d 1292 (2d Cir. 1975).

30. Epstein, *The Politics of Cancer Revisited*, 169.

31. The aldrin and dieldrin case was unique in addressing two chemicals at once; an approach necessitated by the fact that aldrin broke down into dieldrin.

32. Senate Subcommittee on the Environment, Committee of Commerce, *Federal Environmental Pesticide Control Act of 1971*, 92d Cong., 2d sess., 1972, 28, 42; Bosso, *Pesticides and Politics*, 144.

33. Daniel, *Toxic Drift*, 157.

34. Victor Cohn, "The 'Grim Specter,'" *Washington Post*, August 1, 1972.

35. Dunlap, *DDT*, 236.

36. Senate Subcommittee on the Environment, *Federal Environmental Pesticide Control Act of 1971*, 107. The Sierra Club began lobbying for the passage of the Toxic Substances Control Act in 1971 as well. It eventually passed in 1976. Judith Kunofsky to Mike McCloskey et al., July 9, 1980, Sierra Club Members Papers Collection, carton 80, folder 10, Bancroft Library, University of California, Berkeley.

37. Daniel, *Toxic Drift*, 130.

38. Ibid., 156–57.

39. Senate Subcommittee on the Environment, *Federal Environmental Pesticide Control Act of 1971*, 112.

40. Senate Subcommittee on the Environment, *Federal Environmental Pesticide Control Act of 1971*, 170; Senate Subcommittee on Agricultural Research and General Legislation, Committee on Agriculture and Forestry, *Federal Environmental Pesticide Control Act*, Part II, 92d Cong., 2d sess., 1972, 230.

41. Bosso, *Pesticides and Politics*, 177.

42. Epstein, *The Politics of Cancer*, 365.

43. Wargo, *Our Children's Toxic Legacy*, 89–93; Cohn, "The 'Grim Specter.'"

44. McCloskey, *In the Thick of It*, 119.

45. Senate Subcommittee on the Environment, *Federal Environmental Pesticide Control Act of 1971*, 172; Senate Subcommittee on Agricultural Research and General Legislation, *Federal Environmental Pesticide Control Act*, 230; Wargo, *Our Children's Toxic Legacy*, 89–93.

46. Epstein, *The Politics of Cancer*, 367.

47. Ganz, *Why David Sometimes Wins*, 231. The initials UFW will also be used when making a generalized statement about the period both before and after the name change.

48. *Englund v. Chavez*, 504 P. 2d 457 (Cal Supreme Court 1972); Ferriss and Sandoval, *The Fight in the Fields*, 161.

49. "Worldwide Lettuce Boycott to Resume," *Los Angeles Times*, March 16, 1972.

50. Ganz, *Why David Sometimes* Wins, 228–29; *Englund v. Chavez*.

51. *Englund v. Chavez*; Miriam J. Wells, *Strawberry Fields: Politics, Class and Work in California Agriculture* (Ithaca: Cornell University Press, 1996), 81.

52. Ganz, *Why David Sometimes Wins*, 229; "Inter-Harvest Pact: 'Best Yet,'" *El Malcriado* IV, no. 4 (1 August 1, 1970): 7; Ferriss and Sandoval, *The Fight in the Fields*, 163–68.

53. Shaw, *Beyond the Fields*, 133; "Pesticides and the Public," *El Malcriado* IV, no. 10 (November 15, 1970): 2.

54. Ferriss and Sandoval, *The Fight in the Fields*, 163, 170. "Our Strike in Salinas," *El Malcriado* IV, no. 7 (September 15, 1970): 5.

55. Ferriss and Sandoval, *The Fight in the Fields*, 170.

56. Levy, *Cesar Chavez*, 382, 383, 385; "Salinas and Santa Maria: Violence, Greed and Stupidity," *El Malcriado* IV, no. 6 (September 1, 1970): 2.

57. Ganz, *Why David Sometimes* Wins, 230; "Boycott Scab Lettuce," *El Malcriado* IV, no. 8 (October 1, 1970): 3.

58. "Cesar Jailed; Boycott Goes On," *El Malcriado* IV, no. 11 (December 15, 1970): 5, 6.

59. Bill Carder, "Bill Carder,1970–1974: UFW Attorney," Farmworker Documentation Project, http://farmworkermovement.com/essays/essays/076%20Carder_Bill.pdf.

60. "Boycott Scab Lettuce," 3.

61. "Pesticides and the Public," 2.

62. "Non-Violence vs. Greed: Who Should Be on Trial?" *El Malcriado* IV, no. 11 (December 15, 1970): 2.

63. "Cesar Jailed; Boycott Goes On," 5.

64. "Lettuce Boycott Shows Signs of Gaining after Lagging for Its First Three Months," *New York Times*, September 4, 1972.

65. Harry Bernstein, "Jailing of Chavez May Rally Support for Lettuce Boycott," *Los Angeles Times*, December 6, 1970. Joel Glick, "Joel Glick 1971–1973," Farmworker Documentation Project, http://farmworkermovement.com/essays/essays/096%20Glick_Joel.pdf.

66. "Boycott to Free Cesar," *El Malcriado* IV, no. 11 (15 December 1970): 7.

67. Levy, *Cesar Chavez*, 431–33; "Cesar Jailed; Boycott Goes On," 5, 6; "Coretta King Visits with Cesar in Jail, Asks Blacks to Boycott Lettuce," *El Malcriado* IV, no. 12 (January 1, 1971): 10.

68. Bill Carder, "Bill Carder,1970–1974: UFW Attorney."

69. Philip Hager, "Lettuce Boycott Legal, State High Court Decides," *Los Angeles Times*, April 16, 1971.

70. Farm Workers Protest at Pentagon: Department of Defense is Breaking Antle Lettuce Strike," *El Malcriado* IV, no. 12 (January 1, 1971): 3;"Farm Workers Picket to Protest DoD Use of Boycotted Lettuce" ibid. "UFWOC Files Suit Against No. 1 Scab: The Pentagon," ibid., 4, no. 13 (January 15, 1971): 4.

71. "The Republican Party Needs to be Educated," *El Malcriado* V, no. 1 (March 20, 1972): 2. "Message From Cesar Chavez: Help Stop Illegal Attack by Republican Party," ibid., 3; Joel Glick, "Joel Glick 1971–1973."

72. Joel Glick, "Joel Glick 1971–1973."

73. "Democratic Party Supports Lettuce Boycott," *El Malcriado* V, no. 5 (July 21, 1972): 8.

74. Joe Brooks, "Pesticide Poisoning: Senate Will Act to Protect Farmworkers," Assembly Environmental Quality Committee, LP159:506, California State Archives, Sacramento; "Legislative Report From Sacramento," *El Malcriado* V, 5 (July 21, 1972): 8;

75. United Farm Workers, press release, February 21, 1973, UFW Work Department Collection, box 5, folder 5-30; Environmental Protection Agency to Edward R. Roybal, March 16 1973, UFW Work Department Collection, box 5, folder 5-52.

76. Consumer advocate Ida Honoroff verified that the CDFA had destroyed 2,896 crates of contaminated lettuce, but the fate of the other 7,104 seized crates remained unknown. Assembly Select Committee on Agriculture, Food, and Nutrition, *Hearing on Monitor 4 Residues in Imperial County Lettuce Crops*, March 9, 1973, 7, 6 Belt 16-B JK, Belt 6-B dsm, Fong (March K.) Collection, LP159:553.

77. Ibid., 7 Belt A5 dsm.

78. Ibid., 1 Belt 9-A J-K.

79. Ibid., 7 Belt 8-B HRT.

80. Ibid., 1 Belt 8-B HRT.

81. Ibid., 1 Belt 16B JK.

82. Jerry Cohen, United Farm Workers, Press Release, February 20, 1973, Fong (March K.) Collection, LP159:553.

83. Assembly Select Committee on Agriculture, Food, and Nutrition, *Hearing on Monitor 4 Residues in Imperial County Lettuce* Crops, 3 Belt A5 dsm.

84. Legal Department to All Boycott Cities, February 16, 1973, UFW Information and Research Department Collection, box 24, folder 24-3; telegram to A&P, Safeway, and Director of the FDA and Minister of Public Health in Ottawa, February 13, 1973, UFW Information and Research Department Collection, box 24, folder 24-3.

85. Legal Department to All Boycott Cities, February 16, 1973; United Farm Workers, "Lettuce May be Hazardous for Your Health," pamphlet, 1973, Fong (March K.) Collection, LP159:553.

86. Legal Department to All Boycott Cities, February 19, 1973.

87. The workers also reportedly did not "recondition" the lettuce, because they got paid on a piece rate basis and the extra work would have reduced the amount of money made in a day. Legal Department to Everyone, March 16, 1973, UFW Information and Research Department Collection, box 24, folder 24-3; Assembly Select Committee on Agriculture, Food, and Nutrition, *Hearing on Monitor 4 Residues in Imperial County Lettuce Crops*, 3, Belt A5 dsm.

88. Ibid.

89. "Assembly Select Committee on Acticulture [*sic*], Food, and Nutrition Hearing on Monitor 4 Residues in Imperial County Lettuce Crops," March 9, 1973, Fong (March K.) Collection, LP159:553.

90. Robert Jones, "Monitor 4 Pesticide Banned by U.S. for Use on Head Lettuce," *Los Angeles Times,* March 7, 1973.

91. "Clergy Condemns Teamster Attacks on Union," *El Malcriado* VI, no. 8 (April 20, 1973): 2.

92. Ganz, *Why David Sometimes Wins*, 232. See also J. Craig Jenkins, *The Politics of Insurgency: The Farm Worker Movement in the 1960s* (New York: Columbia University Press, 1985), 185–92.

93. Philip Shabecoff, "Chavez Union Struggling for Survival," *New York Times*, June 27, 1973.

94. Ganz, *Why David Sometimes Wins*, 234; Jenkins, *The Politics of Insurgency*, 195–97.

95. Ganz, *Why David Sometimes Wins*, 236–37.

96. Cesar Chavez to Brook [*sic*] Evans, May 9, 1973, UFW Work Department Collection, box 3, folder 3-21.

97. The environmental organizations supporting the OCAW strike included the Center for Science in the Public Interest, the Ecology Center, Environmental Action, the Environmental Policy Center, the Environmental Defense Fund, Friends of the Earth, the Institute for Public Transportation, the National Parks and Conservation Association, the Natural Resources Defense Council, the Public Interest Economics Center, the Sierra Club, and the Wilderness Society. Environmental Action to Friend, April 2, 1973, UFW Work Department Collection, box 3, folder 3-21. For details on the OCAW-environmental alliance, see Robert Gordon, "'Shell No!': OCAW and the Labor-Environmental Alliance," *Environmental History* 3, no. 4 (October 1998): 460–77.

98. Cesar Chavez to Brook [*sic*] Evans, May 9, 1973.

99. Raymond Sherwin, "A Broader Look at the Environment," *Sierra Club Bulletin* 58, no. 4 (April 1973): 18.

100. Ibid., 18.

101. William Futrell, "The Environment and the Courts," *Sierra Club Bulletin* 58, no. 5 (May 1973): 18.

102. "Club Supports Labor Move to Improve Environment for Factory Workers," *Sierra Club Bulletin* 58, no. 4 (April 1973): 20.

103. Scott Dewey, "Working for the Environment: Organized Labor and the Origins of Environmentalism in the United States, 1948–1978," *Environmental History* 3, no. 1 (January 1998): 48–49, 56; Gordon, "'Shell No!'" 467.

104. "UAW, Conservationists Ask Stiff Pollution Law," *Los Angeles Times,* July 12, 1970; Dewey, "Working for the Environment, 52–53, 56.

105. Rome, "The Genius of Earth Day," 195, 199; Dewey, "Working for the Environment," 56.

106. Chad Montrie, "Expedient Environmentalism: Opposition to Coal Surface Mining in Appalachia and the United Mine Workers of America, 1945–1975," *Environmental History* 5, no. 1 (January 2000): 78.

107. Andrew Hurley, *Environmental Inequalities: Class, Race, and Industrial Pollution in Gary, Indiana, 1945–1980* (Chapel Hill: University of North Carolina Press, 1995), 138, 149; Gottlieb, *Forcing the Spring*, 369; Dewey, "Working for the Environment," 58.

108. Henning made the charge at a California State Federation conference co-sponsored by the Sierra Club. Gordon, "'Shell No!'" 471.

109. The Sierra Club, the Wilderness Society, the National Wildlife Federation, and Environmental Action supported the passage of OSHA, but Davidson remained dissatisfied with the organizations for failing to make the legislation a priority. Gordon, "'Shell No!'" 474. None of the organizations testified in support of the Occupational Health and Safety Act at the congressional hearings that took place between 1968 and 1970. House Select Subcommittee on Labor, Committee on Education and Labor, *Occupational Safety and Health*, 90th Cong., 2d sess., 1968; Senate Subcommittee on Labor, Committee on Labor and Public Welfare, *Occupational Safety and Health Act of 1968*, 90th Cong., 2d sess., 1968; Senate Subcommittee on Labor, Committee on Labor and Public Welfare, *Occupational Safety and Health Act, 1970, Part 1*, 91st Cong., 1st sess., 1969, 1970; House Select Subcommittee on Labor, *Occupational Safety and Health Act of 1969, Part 1*, 91st Cong., 1st sess., 1969; House Select Subcommittee on Labor, Committee on Education and Labor, *Occupational Safety and Health Act of 1969, Part 2 and Appendix*, 91st Cong., 1st sess., 1969; Senate Subcommittee on Labor, Committee on Labor and Public Welfare, *Occupational Safety and Health Act, 1970, Part 2*, 91st Cong., 1st sess., 1970.

110. Dewey, "Working for the Environment," 57.

111. John Kifner, "Earth Day Group Zeros in on Autos," *New York Times,* July 20, 1970.

112. Gordon, "'Shell No!'" 473.

113. "Club Supports Labor Move to Improve Environment for Factory Workers," 20.

114. "We Oppose Mindless Progress, McCloskey Tells Chemical Workers," *Sierra Club Bulletin* 58, no. 9 (October 1973): 35.

115. Cesar Chavez to Brook [*sic*] Evans, May 9 1973.

116. Albert J. Fritsch to Cesar Chavez, May 19, 1973, UFW Information and Research Department Collection, box 24, folder 24-3.

117. Joe Browder to Cesar Chavez, June 21, 1973, UFW Information and Research Department Collection, box 24, folder 24-3.

118. Ibid.

119. Robert Eisenbud to Cesar E. Chavez, June 14, 1973, UFW Information and Research Department Collection, box 24, folder 24-3. The UFW received the letter from the NPCA in

mid-June, at a time that the UFW was beset by violence. It is unclear whether the UFW neglected to submit an article or if the NPCA failed to print it.

120. Brock Evans to Cesar Chavez, June 5, 1973, UFW Work Department Collection, box 3, folder 3-21.

121. The Sierra Club executive committee and board of directors minutes from May through December 1973 make no mention of receipt of a request from Cesar Chavez, which indicates that neither entity ever held a discussion on supporting the UFW in its campaign. Sierra Club Records, BANC MSS 71/103 c, carton 4, folder 13 and carton 6, folder 9.

122. Linda Billings to Cesar Chavez, August 22, 1973, UFW Information and Research Department Collection, box 24, folder 24-3.

123. Benjamin W. Mintz, *OSHA: History, Law, and Policy* (Washington, DC: Bureau of National Affairs, 1984), 96, 97; "Emergency Standard for Exposure to Organophosphorous Pesticides," *Federal Register* 38, no. 83 (May 1, 1973): 10715.

124. "Emergency Standards for Exposure to Organophosphorous Pesticides," 10715; "U.S. Eases Pesticide Safeguards Under Pressure From Farmers, Hill," *Washington Post*, June 27, 1973. MLAP dropped its suit after OSHA promulgated the standards. Mintz, *OSHA*, 96.

125. "Emergency Standard for Exposure to Organophosphorous Pesticides," 10715–17.

126. *Florida Peach Growers Association, Inc. v. United States Department of Labor*, 489 F.2d 120 (2d Cir. 1974).

127. "U.S. Eases Pesticide Safeguards Under Pressure From Farmers, Hill."

128. Phillip Shabecoff, "U.S. Is Blocked From Enforcing Safeguards on Farm Pesticides," *New York Times*, July 14, 1973.

129. Harold Faber, "Fruit Growers Protest Safety Standard," *New York Times*, August 13, 1973; Linda Billings to Cesar Chavez, August 22, 1973.

130. The AFL-CIO advised Billings not to press Senator Nelson for a hearing as Chavez requested, because a good deal of political capital had been spent in the fight against the "anti-OSHA" provisions. Billings communicated the AFL recommendation to Chavez, assuring him that support for the Nelson hearings had not been abandoned. Linda Billings to Cesar Chavez, August 22, 1973. Robert Gordon uses Billings's letter to argue that the Sierra Club and other mainstream environmental organizations showed a lack of concern for the UFW and a reluctance to support pesticide reform efforts after the DDT ban. He states that Billings told Chavez that the Sierra Club could not support the UFW effort to force a congressional hearing and "offered no concrete support" to the union. Robert Gordon, "Poisons in the Fields," 70. In his otherwise sound analysis, Gordon mischaracterizes the episode by failing to note that Billings was ready to push Nelson for a hearing until the AFL-CIO dissuaded her from doing so. He also neglects to discuss Billings's efforts to get an environmentalist contingent to the OSHA hearings to defend farmworkers' health interests. On an individual level, Billings's concern for social justice can be tracked to some degree by her employment before and after working for the Sierra Club. Billings coordinated Earth Day affairs for Senator Nelson in 1970 before becoming a Sierra Club lobbyist. Gaylord Nelson with Susan Campbell and Paul Wozniak, *Beyond Earth Day: Fulfilling the Promise* (Madison: University of Wisconsin Press, 2002), 8. After working as a lobbyist, Billings became the director of the Pesticide Farm Safety Staff at the EPA. Linda M. Billings to Lupe Sanchez, May 29, 1985, MCOP Papers, ACC# 1990-00402, box 5, folder 28, Department of Archives and Special Collections, Arizona State University, Tempe.

131. Linda Billings to Cesar Chavez, August 22, 1973; Shabecoff, "U.S. Is Blocked From Enforcing Safeguards on Farm Pesticides."

132. Linda Billings to Cesar Chavez, August 22, 1973.

133. Mintz, *OSHA*, 105; "Interpreting OSHA's Preemption Clause: Farmworkers as a Case Study," *University of Pennsylvania Law Review* 128, no. 6 (June 1980): 1980.

134. "Interpreting OSHA's Preemption Clause: Farmworkers as a Case Study," 1980–1981. See *Organized Migrants in Community Action v. Brennan*, 520 F.2d 1161 (D.C. Cir 1975).

135. Senate Subcommittee on Agricultural Research and General Legislation, Committee on Agriculture and Forestry, *Extension of the Federal Insecticide, Fungicide, and Rodenticide Act*, 94th Cong., 1st sess., October 28–29, 1975, 52–53, 61.

136. Ibid., 252, 253.

137. Senate Subcommittee on Agricultural Research and General Legislation, Committee on Agriculture and Forestry, *Extension of the Federal Insecticide, Fungicide, and Rodenticide Act*, 94th Cong., 1st sess., May 12–16, 1975, 199, 200; ibid., October 28–29, 1975, 20.

138. Ibid., May 12–16, 1975, 184–85; ibid., October 28–29, 1975, 46.

139. Ibid., October 28–29, 1975, 52–54.

140. Ibid., 21, 46, 52–55.

141. Ibid., May 12–16, 1975, 200.

142. Ibid., October 28–29, 1975, 19. Alabama Senator James Allen questioned MLAP attorney Miriam Guido about whether she thought the DDT ban had worsened conditions in the fields for farmworkers, since growers had switched to more acutely toxic organophosphates. She responded that she could not agree with that logic, stating: "I do not believe the farmworker is better off dying of cancer 20 years hence than he is from having an acute organophosphate today." Organophosphates, she believed, just needed to be better regulated. Ibid., 24.

143. Ibid., May 12–16, 1975, 186–95.

144. Penelope A. Fenner-Crisp, "Risk Assessment and Risk Management: The Regulatory Process," *Handbook of Pesticide Toxicology,* vol. 2: *Principles*, 2d ed., ed. Robert Krieger et al. (San Diego, CA: Academic Press, 2001), 682.

145. Russell Train sent personal letters to both Linda Billing and Brock Evans, who was director of Sierra Club's Washington office, thanking them for the club's efforts. Russell E. Train to Brock Evans, December 18, 1975, Sierra Club National Legislative Office Records, BANC 71/289 c, carton 78, folder 27, Bancroft Library, University of California Berkeley; Russell E. Train to Linda Billings, December 18, 1975, Sierra Club National Legislative Office Records, BANC 71/289 c, carton 78, folder 27.

146. Pulido, *Environmentalism and Economic Justice*, 103.

147. *Sierra Club National News Report* 13, no. 12 (May 6, 1981): 6, Grand Canyon Chapter Sierra Club Collection, ACC# 94-1420, box 2, folder 2-5, Department of Archives and Special Collections, Arizona State University, Tempe; House Subcommittee on Department Operations, Research, and Foreign Agriculture, Committee on Agriculture, *Federal Insecticide, Fungicide, and Rodenticide Act Part 1*, 97th Cong., 1st sess., June 16, July 16, and July 22, 1981, 623–26; House Subcommittee on Department Operations, Research, and Foreign Agriculture, Committee on Agriculture, *Federal Insecticide, Fungicide, and Rodenticide Act Part 2*, 97th Cong., 1st sess., June 18 and September 4, 1981, 200–201; House Subcommittee on Department Operations, Research, and Foreign Agriculture, Committee on Agriculture, *Federal Insecticide, Fungicide, and Rodenticide Act Part 3*, 97th Cong., 2d sess., February 4, 1982, 8–10; Erik Loomis, *Out of Sight: The Long and Disturbing Story of Corporations Outsourcing Catastrophe* (New York: New Press, 2015), 91.

5. A Different Kind of Border War

1. Gordon Robbins, "Crop Dust Probe Asked," *Scottsdale Daily Progress*, November 1, 1971. Though the leased land belonged to the tribe, growers had to comply with state and federal regulation and could be investigated by state agencies. Barbara L. Nellor and Patti A. Cleary, *Arizona Agricultural Pesticide Program Evaluation, August 13–21, 1979* (San Francisco: US Environmental Protection Agency, 1981), 30.

2. "Aerial Crop Spraying Halted," *Scottsdale Daily Progress*, October 27, 1971.

3. Minutes of the Board of Pesticide Control, May 15, 1970 and September 1, 1971, Board of Pesticide Control Collection, RG 72 Board of Pesticide Control, SG Pesticide Control Board

Minutes 1968–79, Archives and Records Management Branch, Arizona State Library, Archives and Public Records, Phoenix.

4. Bob Rayburn to Board of Pesticide Control, December 3, 1971, Board of Pesticide Control Collection, RG 72 Board of Pesticide Control, SG Pesticide Control Board Minutes 1968–79.

5. Gordon Robbins, "Pesticide Effect Denied: Indians to Undergo Tests," *Scottsdale Daily Progress*, November 25, 1971.

6. Pesticide monitoring notes, 1971–72, United Farm Workers Arizona State Office Collection, box 4, folder 4-2, Archives of Labor & Urban Affairs, Wayne State University, Detroit.

7. Rosales, *Chicano!* 150.

8. Deposition of Gustavo Gutierrez, United Farm Workers Union on Behalf of Itself and Its Members v. Raul Castro, Governor of the State of Arizona, et. al, 72-445 PHX CAM (1975), 5–7, 12, RG 9 Department of Agriculture, SG 4 Boards and Commissions, SG 1 Agricultural Employment Relations Board Collection, box unprocessed, Archives and Records Management Branch, Arizona State Library, Archives and Public Records, Phoenix.

9. Deposition of Gustavo Gutierrez, 112, 113. See also letter from UFWOC organizer Mel Huey to the Pesticide Control Board, May 19, 1970, Board of Pesticide Control Collection, RG 72 Board of Pesticide Control, SG Pesticide Control Board Minutes 1968–79.

10. "We Want a Safety Law," *El Paisano*, (February 1968), UFW Office of the President: Cesar Chavez Collection Part II, box 36, folder 36-12.

11. Robbins, "Pesticide Effect Denied; Indians to Undergo Tests."

12. José A. Maldonado, "¡Sí Se Puede! The Farm Worker Movement in Arizona 1965–1979" (M.A. thesis, Arizona State University, 1995), 65.

13. Meeks, *Border Citizens*, 202–3, 205.

14. Richard Griswold del Castillo and Richard A. Garcia, *Cesar Chavez: A Triumph of Spirit* (Norman: University of Oklahoma Press, 1997), 165.

15. Guadalupe L. Sanchez to Timothy Collins, July 23, 1978, UFW Office of the President: Cesar Chavez Collection Part II, box 22, folder 22-5.

16. Maricopa County Organizing Project, *Who Is MCOP?* (El Mirage, AZ: Maricopa County Organizing Project, n.d.), folder MCOP—Maricopa County Organizing Project, Department of Archives and Special Collections, Arizona State University, Tempe.

17. "A Formal Invitation to Each Agricultural Worker to the First Historical Constitutional Convention of Farm Workers in Arizona," December 16, 1979, 2, 3 (quote), UFW Office of the President: Cesar Chavez Collection Part II, box 25, folder 25-10.

18. Marcela Cerrutti and Douglas S. Massey, "Trends in Mexican Migration to the United States, 1965–1995," in *Crossing the Border: Research From the Mexican Migration Project*, ed. Jorge Durand and Douglas S. Massey (New York: Russell Sage Foundation, 2004), 19.

19. Kenneth Juan Figueroa, "Immigrants and the Civil Rights Regime: Parens Patriae Standing, Foreign Governments and Protection From Private Discrimination," *Columbia Law Review* 102, no. 2 (2002): 409, 410, 414.

20. Jeffrey Shavelson, "Bottom-Up Populism: The Lessons for Citizen and Community Empowerment" (Ph.D. diss., University of Maryland, 1989), 36, 37; *The Plight of the Migrant*, VHS (Tucson: Arizona Center for Occupational Safety and Health, 1979).

21. Guadalupe L. Sánchez and Jesús Romo, "Organizing Mexican Undocumented on Both Sides of the Border," Working Papers in U.S.-Mexican Studies, 27 (La Jolla, CA: University of California San Diego, 1981), 3.

22. Ibid.

23. Ibid; Maldonado, "¡Sí Se Puede!," 101.

24. "Workers Picket Robert Goldwater's Ranch," *Scottsdale (AZ) Progress*, October 3, 1977; "Citrus Workers' Strike Hits Arizona Farm," *Newsday*, October 4, 1977; "IRE Reported on Aliens in March," ibid., October 4, 1977; Tom Kuhn, "Harvest Hands in Citrus Grove Out on Strike,"

Arizona Republic, October 4, 1977; "Unequal Enforcement La Migra in Arizona," *Watch Seers Weekly*, October 21–28, 1977. Folder Maricopa County Organizing Project (News Clippings), Department of Archives and Special Collections, Arizona State University, Tempe.

25. Sánchez and Romo, "Organizing Mexican Undocumented on Both Sides of the Border," 3. Border enforcement and, hence also smuggling networks have grown much more sophisticated in the years subsequent to these field "trials." The average cost of a crossing before the passage of the Immigration Reform and Control Act of 1986 ran around four hundred dollars, roughly one-third the amount spent by an undocumented migrant in 2002. Douglas S. Massey and Fernando Riosmena, "Undocumented Migration in an Era of Rising U.S. Enforcement," *Annals of the American Academy of Political and Social Science*, no. 630 (July 2010): 297. As the profit potential of human smuggling has grown, criminal syndicates have increasingly capitalized off the opportunity. Wendy A. Vogt, "Crossing Mexico: Structural Violence and the Commodification of Undocumented Central American Migrants," *American Ethnologist* 40, no. 4 (November 2013): 769, 772-75. The greater involvement of the gangs in human smuggling across the border would likely make the labor organizers' trust-building strategy of "prosecuting" exploitative coyotes less feasible in the present than in the 1970s. Former M-COP organizer Gustavo Gutiérrez recognized the border as changed place, stating "now with the mafia, with the cartels, it's very dangerous." Gustavo Gutiérrez, interview by Judy Lentine, Tempe Historical Museum Oral History Project, July 19, 2012, 20, http://www.tempe.gov/Home/ShowDocument?id=30249.

26. Shavelson, "Bottom Up Populism," 40.

27. Sánchez and Romo, "Organizing Mexican Undocumented On Both Sides of the Border," 5, 6; José A. Maldonado, "¡Sí Se Puede!," 101.

28. Massey, Durand, and Malone, *Beyond Smoke and Mirrors*, 12; Margarita Mooney, "Migrants' Social Capital and Investing Remittances in Mexico," in Durand and Massey, *Crossing the Border*, 45, 61.

29. Sánchez and Romo, "Organizing Mexican Undocumented On Both Sides of the Border," 5, 6.

30. Ibid.

31. Tom Kuhn, "Harvest Hands in Citrus Grove Out on Strike."

32. Tom Barry, "Ghosts Strike Goldwater Ranch," *In These Times*, October 19–25, 1977, folder Arrowhead Ranch Strike, Department of Archives and Special Collections, Arizona State University, Tempe.

33. "Unequal Enforcement La Migra in Arizona."

34. Barry, "Ghosts Strike Goldwater Ranch"; Michael Kiefer, "Carl Muecke, Retired Judge, Dies in His Sleep at 89," *Arizona Republic*, September 24, 2007.

35. "Unequal Enforcement La Migra in Arizona."

36. "Laborers and Ranch Reach Pact," *Phoenix Gazette*, November 25, 1977, folder Maricopa County Organizing Project (News Clippings).

37. Maricopa County Organizing Project, "Maricopa County Organizing Project 1977–1988" (El Mirage, AZ: Maricopa County Organizing Project, 1988), 3, folder Maricopa County Organizing Project; 1987, Department of Archives and Special Collections, Arizona State University, Tempe; Shavelson, "Bottom-Up Populism," 57.

38. "M-COP Helps Farmworkers Win Victories," *MCOP*, March 1979, 4. folder MCOP—Maricopa County Organizing Project; Maricopa County Organizing Project, *Who Is MCOP?*

39. *Cooperativa Sin Fronteras: El Primer Paso*, VHS, directed by Juan Farre (New York: West Glen Productions, 1987); Maricopa County Organizing Project, "Maricopa County Organizing Project 1977–1988," 3; Ted Conover, "A Cooperative Between Borders," *Grassroots Development* 9, no. 2 (1985): 43, 49.

40. "Laborers and Ranch Reach Pact."

41. "Goldmar Workers Win Contract," *MCOP*, March 1979, 3, folder MCOP—Maricopa County Organizing Project; Maldonado, "¡Sí Se Puede!," 106.

42. Kathleen Stanton, "Farm Workers; Chronic Pesticide Exposure Tied to Health Woes," *Arizona Republic*, April 4, 1984; *The Plight of the Migrant*.

43. Bruce Babbitt to Douglas Costle, November 23, 1979, folder Environmental Protection Agency, U.S. General Correspondence, RG: Governor's Office, 1979, S: Federal Files, box 103, Archives and Records Management Branch, Arizona State Library, Archives and Public Records, Phoenix; U.S Environmental Protection Agency, "Notice of Intent to Suspend Registrations of Dibromochloropropane (DBCP): Direct Testimony of Mr. Frank L. Davido," FIFRA Docket no. 485, 1–5, MCOP Papers, ACC #1990-00402, box 36, folder 2; Otto Wong, M. Donald Whorton, Nancy Gordon, and Robert W. Morgan, "An Epidemiologic Investigation of the Relationship Between DBCP Contamination in Drinking Water and Birth Rates in Fresno County, California," *American Journal of Public Health* 78, no. 1 (January 1988): 43.

44. "Well Water Sampling for DBCP in Maricopa County, Arizona," MCOP Papers, ACC #1990-00402, box 39, folder 14.

45. Kathleen Stanton, "Pesticide Level in Citrus Farm's Wells Has Risen Since 1980, State Reports," *Arizona Republic*, July 25, 1984; Kathleen Stanton, "Some Farm Workers Still Rely on Tainted Wells," ibid., May 21, 1985.

46. Don Devereux to Friends of Arizona Farm Labor Movement, January 6, 1984, MCOP Papers, ACC #1990-00402, box 3, folder 6.

47. Ibid.

48. L. M. [Laurie Martinelli] to Frieda Christie (n.d.), MCOP Papers, ACC #1990-00402, box 56, folder 7.

49. Ibid; Don Devereux to Friends of Arizona Farm Labor Movement, January 6, 1984.

50. M-COP meeting notes, November 3, 1983,; Paul Bullis to AFW, MCOP, and farmworker staff, November 7, 1983; both MCOP Papers, ACC #1990-00402, box 1, folder 26.

51. Don Devereux to James Sarn, February 9, 1981, MCOP Papers, ACC #1990-00402, box 39, folder 14.

52. Ibid.

53. Karen S. Kincaid to Boyd Dover, April 17, 1984, MCOP Papers, ACC #1990-00402, box 3, folder 6.

54. Environmental Protection Agency, "EPA Acts to Ban EDB Pesticide," press release, September 30, 1983, http://www2.epa.gov/aboutepa/epa-acts-ban-edb-pesticide.

55. Ken Klein, "Need to Eat vs. Clean Water: Worries Rise Over EDB Contamination," *Los Angeles Times*, September 22, 1983.

56. Environmental Protection Agency, "EPA Acts to Ban EDB Pesticide."

57. Karen S. Kincaid to Boyd Dover, April 17, 1984.

58. Stanton, "Some Farm Workers Still Rely on Tainted Wells"; Maricopa County Organizing Project, "Maricopa County Organizing Project 1977–1988," 7; Don Devereux to Richard W. Sweet, MCOP Papers, ACC #1990-00402, box 3, folder 6; Karen S. Kincaid to Boyd Dover, April 17, 1984; Arizona Farm Worker Committee on Pesticides, "Sizeable EDB Sales Disclosed, Water Tests Needed," press release, April 17, 1984, MCOP Papers, ACC #1990-00402, box 3, folder 6.

59. Maricopa County Organizing Project, "Maricopa County Organizing Project 1977–1988," 7; Stanton, "Some Farm Workers Still Rely on Tainted Wells."

60. Maricopa County Organizing Project, "Maricopa County Organizing Project 1977–1988," 7; Charles Anders to Owner or Manager, April 29, 1986, MCOP Papers, ACC #1990-00402, box 32, folder 3. M-COP helped establish the Centro Adelante Campesino in 1978. "M-COP Helps Farmworkers Win Victories"; Karen Kincaid to María Transito Sánchez, July 23, 1980, MCOP Papers, ACC #1990-00402, box 7, folder 14.

61. Maricopa County Organizing Project, "Maricopa County Organizing Project 1977–1988," 7. "¡Cuidado!" Pesticide Bulletin 2 (n.d.), MCOP Papers, ACC #1990-00402, box 1, folder 2.

62. Kathleen Stanton, "Pesticide Containers in Valley Farm Dump Spark Probe by State," *Arizona Republic*, March 8, 1984.

63. Maricopa County Organizing Project, "Maricopa County Organizing Project, 1977–1988," 7.

64. Adam Tompkins, "A Different Kind of Border War: Conflicts Over Pesticides in Arizona's Agricultural/Urban Interface, 1977-1986," *Journal of the West* 50, no. 1 (2011): 59–60.

65. Behavior Research Center, *Survey of Urban Arizonans [sic] Attitudes Toward Agriculture Industry*, vol. 1 (Phoenix: Behavior Research Center, 1979), Arizona Cotton Growers Association Collection, box 4, folder 1, Arizona Historical Foundation, Arizona State University, Tempe.

66. Bradford Luckingham, *Phoenix: The History of a Southwestern Metropolis* (Tucson: University of Arizona Press, 1989), 77, 125, 135, 159, 188.

67. Behavior Research Center, *Survey of Urban Arizonans [sic] Attitudes Toward Agriculture Industry*, 1:ii, iii, 21, 33.

68. Bob Rayburn to Board of Pesticide Control, October 5 1970, Board of Pesticide Control Collection, RG 72 Board of Pesticide Control, SG Pesticide Control Board Minutes 1968–79.

69. Bob Rayburn to Board of Pesticide Control, December 4, 1970, Board of Pesticide Control Collection, RG 72 Board of Pesticide Control, SG Pesticide Control Board Minutes 1968–79.

70. Ibid.

71. Bob Rayburn to Board of Pesticide Control, April 26, 1972, Board of Pesticide Control Collection, RG 72 Board of Pesticide Control, SG Pesticide Control Board Minutes 1968–79.

72. Sun City Town Meeting Association to Bruce Babbitt, March 22, 1979, RG 1 Governor's Office, 1979, SG Departments, Boards, Commissions, box 93, folder Pesticide Control Board General Correspondence.

73. Residents of Ellsworth Mini-Farms subdivision to Bruce Babbitt, petition, July 13, 1979, RG 1 Governor's Office, 1979, SG Departments, Boards, Commissions, box 93, folder Pesticide Control Board General Correspondence.

74. "Testimony of Pete Slater," in US Environmental Protection Agency Region IX, Public *Hearing on the Use of Agricultural Pesticides in Arizona: September 6–8, 1979 Adam's Hotel, Navajo Room, Central and Adams Streets, Phoenix, Arizona/ United States*, vol. 1 (San Francisco: Smythe and Wilson, 1979), 346.

75. See RG 1 Governor's Office, 1978, SG Departments, Boards, and Commissions, box 93, folders Pesticide Control Board and Pesticide Control Board General Correspondence, Archives and Records Management Branch, Arizona State Library, Archives and Public Records, Phoenix.

76. Pamela C. Newton to Bruce Babbitt, March 17, 1979, RG Governor's Office, 1979 SG Departments, Board, Commissions, box 93, folder Pesticide Control Board General Correspondence.

77. Grace Alonso to Governor Bruce Babbitt (n.d.), RG 1 Governor's Office, 1978, SG Departments, Boards, and Commissions, box 93, folder Pesticide Control Board; Environmental Protection Agency Region IX, "Testimony of People's Environmental Organization for Pesticide Legislation and Enforcement member Joanne Tolman," *Public Hearing on the Use of Agricultural Pesticides in Arizona*, 1:259.

78. Catherine A. Kury to Bruce Babbitt, October 18, 1978, RG 1 Governor's Office, 1978, SG Departments, Boards, and Commissions, box 93, folder Pesticide Control Board.

79. Minutes of the Board of Pesticide Control, November 14, 1978, 10, 11, Board of Pesticide Control Collection, RG 72 Board of Pesticide Control, SG Pesticide Control Board Minutes 1968–79.

80. Minutes of the Board of Pesticide Control, November 14, 1978, 11.

81. House Subcommittee on Oversight and Investigations, Committee on Interstate and Foreign Commerce, *Involuntary Exposure to Agent Orange and Other Toxic Spraying*, 96th Cong., 1st

sess., June 26 and 27, 1979, 114; Jana Bommersbach, "September Brought Clouds of Poison: Scottsdale Housewives Took On Pesticides—and All Hell Broke Loose," *New Times* (Phoenix), June 10–16, 1981, 12, 13.

82. Minutes of the Board of Pesticide Control, August 12, 1979, 9, Board of Pesticide Control Collection, RG 72 Board of Pesticide Control, SG Pesticide Control Board Minutes 1968–79; Environmental Protection Agency, "Environmental News," July 26, 1979, Arizona Cotton Growers Association Collection, box 11, folder 2; Bommersbach, "September Brought Clouds of Poison," 12, 13.

83. Minutes of the Board of Directors Meeting Arizona Cotton Growers Association, September 25, 1979, Arizona Cotton Growers Association Collection, box 33, folder 3.

84. Environmental Protection Agency Region IX, "Testimony of Arizona Farm Bureau Federation Representative Ralph Baskett, Jr.," *Public Hearing on the Use of Agricultural Pesticides in Arizona*, 1:59, 60.

85. Environmental Protection Agency Region IX, "Testimony of People's Environmental Organization for Pesticide Legislation and Enforcement members Suzanne Prosnier and Dennis Stadel," *Public Hearing on the Use of Agricultural Pesticides in Arizona*, 1:103, 104, 786–96.

86. Environmental Protection Agency Region IX, "Testimony of Department of Health Director Suzanne Dandoy," *Public Hearing on the Use of Agricultural Pesticides in Arizona*, 1:424–25, 432, 446.

87. Environmental Protection Agency Region IX, "Testimony of Governor Bruce Babbitt," *Public Hearing on the Use of Agricultural Pesticides in Arizona*, 1:8–9.

88. Nellor and Cleary, *Arizona Agricultural Pesticide Program Evaluation, August 13–21, 1979*, 13.

89. Environmental Protection Agency Region IX, "Testimony of Administrator of the Board of Pesticide Control Bill Blackledge," *Public Hearing on the Use of Agricultural Pesticides in Arizona*, 1:256.

90. Steven D. Jellinek, "On the Inevitability of Being Wrong," speech delivered to the New York Academy of Sciences Workshop on Management of Assessed Risk for Carcinogens, New York, March 17, 1980, 3, Arizona Cotton Growers Association Collection, box 11, folder 3.

91. Environmental Protection Agency, "Advisory Opinion Concerning the Application of Cotton Insecticides and Defoliants (Draft)," July 23, 1980, 12–13, 18–19, Arizona Cotton Growers Association Collection, box 4, folder 1.

92. William T. Keane to Bill Blackledge, August 4, 1980, Arizona Cotton Growers Association Collection, box 12, folder 1.

93. Bob Stump to Douglas M. Costle, September 5, 1980, See also letters from Eldon Rudd, Thomas J. Foley, and Morris K. Udall to the EPA on behalf of growers' associations. Arizona Cotton Growers Association Collection, box 20, folder 2.

94. Steven D. Jellinek to Eldon Rudd, September 16, 1980, Arizona Cotton Growers Association Collection, box 20, folder 2.

95. Behavior Research Center, *Survey of Urban Arizonans [sic] Attitudes Toward Agriculture Industry*, 1:19, 20.

96. Minutes of the Committee on Law and Rules, Board of Pesticide Control, October 26, 1984, 3, 4, Board of Pesticide Control Collection, RG 72 Board of Pesticide Control, SG Pesticide Control Board Minutes 1984/86; Kathleen Stanton and Christia Johnson, "Ills Blamed on Spraying, Babbitt Urges Control," *Arizona Republic*, October 12, 1984.

97. Tom Beatty to Bill Blackledge, May 7, 1979, Arizona Cotton Growers Association Collection, box 11, folder 1.

98. Joanne Ralston & Associates, Inc., "News Release: Pesticide Bans Threaten Food and Fiber Production" (n.d.), Arizona Cotton Growers Association Collection, box 6, folder 4; Ronald Rayner, "1982 Annual Meeting Public Relations Committee Report," Arizona Cotton Growers Association Collection, box 34, folder 2.

99. Gila River Industries, Inc. Custom Applicator License no. 68 and Samuel D. Radoman Agricultural Aircraft Pilot License no. 2052 and Samuel D. Radoman Certified Commercial
Applicator Credential no. 9738C Before the State of Arizona Board of Pesticide Control, Order
no. 8410-11-1 (Arizona State Board of Pesticide Control 1985), 4, Board of Pesticide Control Collection, RG 72 Board of Pesticide Control, box 1, folder Official Actions, Warnings, etc. 1984–85;
letter from Governor Bruce Babbitt to Board of Pesticide Control Bill Embree, October 12, 1984,
Board of Pesticide Control Collection, RG 72 Board of Pesticide Control, SG Pesticide Control
Board Minutes 1984/86.

100. Minutes of the Board of Pesticide Control Emergency Meeting and Hearing, October
13, 1984, 6, Board of Pesticide Control Collection, RG 72 Board of Pesticide Control, SG Pesticide Control Board Minutes 1984/86; Stanton and Johnson, "Ills Blamed on Spraying, Babbitt
Urges Control."

101. Herb Drinkwater to State Pesticide Control Board (n.d.), Board of Pesticide Control
Collection, RG 72 Board of Pesticide Control, SG Pesticide Control Board Minutes 1984/86.

102. Bruce Babbitt to Bill Embree, October 12, 1984, Board of Pesticide Control Collection,
RG 72 Board of Pesticide Control, SG Pesticide Control Board Minutes 1984/86.

103. Gila River Industries, Inc. Custom Applicator License no. 68 and Samuel D. Radoman Agricultural Aircraft Pilot License no. 2052 and Samuel D. Radoman Certified Commercial
Applicator Credential no. 9738C Before the State of Arizona Board of Pesticide Control, Order
no. 8410-11-1.

104. Several BPC decisions drew criticism from the EPA upon review. State of Arizona
Office of the Auditor General, *A Performance Audit of the Board of Pesticide Control: A Report to the
Arizona State Legislature* ([Phoenix]: Office of the Auditor General, 1983), 11, 36–37.

105. State of Arizona Office of the Auditor General, *A Performance Audit of the Board of Pesticide Control*, i–ii, 19, 29, 31.

106. Minutes of the Board of Pesticide Control, April 3, 1984, 1, 2, Board of Pesticide Control Collection, RG 72 Board of Pesticide Control, SG Pesticide Control Board Minutes 1984/86.

107. Minutes of the Board of Pesticide Control, April 3, 1984, May 3, 1984, March 15, 1985,
Board of Pesticide Control Collection, RG 72 Board of Pesticide Control, SG Pesticide Control
Board Minutes 1984/86.

108. "Introduction," *Arizona Farmworkers Committee on Pesticides (AFCP) v. Arizona Board
of Pesticide Control (ABPC),* Case no. C535639, Maricopa County Superior Court records, Phoenix, AZ, 2.

109. Nellor and Cleary, *Arizona Agricultural Pesticide Program Evaluation, August 13–21, 1979,* 4.

110. "Introduction," *Arizona Farmworkers Committee on Pesticides (AFCP) v. Arizona Board of
Pesticide Control (ABPC)*, 2.

111. Ibid., 12, 13, 15, 18.

112. Ibid., 14–15.

113. Ibid., 12–16, 18.

114. Draft letter to editor, October 13, 1984, MCOP Papers, ACC #1990-00402, box 1, folder 27.

115. Gutierrez's speech was made sometime in 1982 before the Laborers' Union Local 383
election, in which he was a candidate. He spoke specifically about worker concerns about nuclear
power, but framed the value of a labor-environmental coalition in broader terms. "Dissident Candidates Plan to Challenge Incumbents in Laborers' Local Election," *Arizona Republic*, April 14,
1982; Gustavo Gutierrez, speech (n.d., 1982?), MCOP Papers, ACC #1990-00402, box 43, folder
26 (quotes pp. 2, 7).

116. Meeting notes, December 20, 1984; "Potential Additional Plaintiffs"; both MCOP
Papers, ACC #1990-00402, box 36, folder 10.

117. "Introduction," *Arizona Farmworkers Committee on Pesticides (AFCP) v. Arizona Board of
Pesticide Control (ABPC)*, 15, 16.

118. "Judgment," ibid.

119. Laurie Martinelli to MCOP board of directors, November 6, 1984, MCOP Papers, ACC #1990-00402, box 1, folder 3.

120. Laurie Martinelli to MCOP Board of Directors, November 6, 1984.

121. Tompkins, "A Different Kind of Border War," 62.

122. Andy Zipser, "How Much Poison is Enough?: When It Comes to Arizona's Groundwater Initiative, the Politics of the Possible Spells Business as Usual," *New Times* (Phoenix), February 12–18, 1986, 22.

123. Tom Kuhn, "State Powerless to Close Poisoned Wells," *New Times Weekly* (Phoenix*)*, November 28–December 4, 1979, 15; Ambient Water Quality Surveys and Data Management Office of Emergency Response and Environmental Analysis, *Results of Ethylene Dibromide (EDB) Sampling in Arizona* ([Phoenix]: Division of Environmental Health Services, 1984); Gordon Meeks Jr., *Arizona Groundwater: Negotiating an Environmental Quality Act* (Denver: National Conference of State Legislatures, 1987), 16.

124. Andy Zipser, "How Much Poison is Enough?" 22; Meeks, *Arizona Groundwater*, 16.

125. John Anderson to Winton Dahlstrom, June 14, 1984, Arizona Common Cause Collection, box 51, folder 1C, Department of Archives and Special Collections, Arizona State University, Tempe.

126. Initiative Meeting Attendance Sheet, June 13, 1984, Arizona Common Cause Collection, box 51, folder 1B; John Anderson to Winton Dahlstrom, June 14, 1984. The second Phoenix meeting drew representatives from the United Auto Workers and the AFL-CIO. Initiative Meeting Attendance Sheet, July 9, 1984, Arizona Common Cause Collection, box 51, folder 1B.

127. John Anderson to Winton Dahlstrom, June 14, 1984; Nadine Wettstein to the *Arizona Daily Star* (draft), December 6, 1985, Arizona Common Cause Collection, box 51, folder 1.

128. "Statement of John Anderson, For Arizona Common Cause, to the Senate Water Quality Study Committee and the House Study Committee on Groundwater Protection," October 24, 1984, 3, Arizona Common Cause Collection, box 51, folder 3.

129. "Statement of John Anderson, For Arizona Common Cause, to the Senate Water Quality Study Committee and the House Study Committee on Groundwater Protection," 3; John Anderson to Winton Dahlstrom, June 14, 1984.

130. Nadine Wettstein to David Yetman, August 15, 1985, Arizona Common Cause Collection, box 51, folder 1C.

131. Arizona Common Cause, press release, March 26 1985, Arizona Common Cause Collection, box 51, folder 3.

132. "Water Quality Initiative Coalition Information Sheet" (n.d.), Arizona Common Cause Collection, box 51, folder 1B; Nadine Wettstein to *Arizona Daily Star* (draft), December 6, 1985, Arizona Common Cause Collection, box 51, folder 1.

133. Minutes of Arizona Clean Water Advocates, August 22, 1985, Arizona Common Cause Collection, box 51, folder 1B.

134. "Arizona Clean Water Advocates Budget Proposal" (n.d.), Arizona Common Cause Collection, box 51, folder 1B.

135. Minutes of the Arizona Clean Water Advocates, August 12, 1985, Arizona Common Cause Collection, box 51, folder 1B.

136. "The Arizona Clean Water and Pesticide Control Act, A Citizens' Initiative: A Brief Analysis Prepared by Members of ACWA," 3, Arizona Common Cause Collection, box 51, folder 1.

137. "Clean Water Issue: Special Survey for Central Arizona Labor Council," (Phoenix: Behavior Research Center, Inc., 1986), Arizona Common Cause Collection, box 51, folder 1B.

138. Meeks, *Arizona Groundwater*, 18, 24; David S. Baron, "Arizona's New Environmental Quality Act—An Overview," in *Arizona's New Environmental Quality Act* (Phoenix: State Bar of Arizona, 1986), 21.

139. Nelson Beeman to Governor's Water Quality Group, January 22, 1986, Arizona Common Cause Collection, box 51, folder 1B.

140. Meeks, *Arizona Groundwater*, 24; Baron, "Arizona's New Environmental Quality Act—An Overview," 19; Nadine K. Wettstein, "Pesticide Control and Worker Safety Provisions of the Environmental Quality Act," in *Arizona's New Environmental Quality Act*, 231.

141. Arizona Clean Water Advocates to supporters (n.d), Arizona Common Cause Collection, box 51, folder 1.

142. Baron, "Arizona's New Environmental Quality Act—An Overview," 19, 25.

143. Wettstein, "Pesticide Control and Worker Safety Provisions of the Environmental Quality Act," 252–53, 268, 272.

144. Baron, "Arizona's New Environmental Quality Act—An Overview," 23, 25.

145. Wettstein, "Pesticide Control and Worker Safety Provisions of the Environmental Quality Act," 269.

146. Tompkins, "A Different Kind of Border War," 64.

147. US Census Bureau, 2000 Census of Population and Housing, *Population and Housing Unit Counts* PHC-3-4, Arizona (Washington, DC: Government Printing Office, 2003), 1.

148. Meeks, *Arizona Groundwater*, 16.

149. Tompkins, "A Different Kind of Border War," 64.

150. Ibid.

6. Resisting Rollbacks

1. "The Second 1980 Debate: Part IV," *Debating Our Destiny: The Second 1980 Presidential Debate October 28, 1980,* http://www.pbs.org/newshour/debatingourdestiny/80debates/cart4.html (accessed October 19, 2010); David S. Broder, "Carter Yields Early in Night," *Washington Post*, November 5, 1980.

2. Martin Schram, "Carter Goes into Debate with Lead in New Poll," *Washington Post,* October 28, 1980; Broder, "Carter Yields Early in Night."

3. Sean Wilentz, *The Age of Reagan: A History 1974–2008* (New York: Harper Perennial, 2008), 124.

4. David S. Broder, "Reagan Makes Pitch to Labor, but First He Changes the Key," *Washington Post,* October 9, 1980; Adam Clymer, "Anderson to Conduct Poll on Impact of Third Party," *New York Times*, April 9, 1980; Colman McCarthy, "Reagan: An Old Political Dog Learns No New Tricks," *Los Angeles Times*, January 17, 1980.

5. Joanne Omang, "Reagan Criticizes Clean Air Laws and EPA as Obstacles to Growth," *Washington Post*, October 9, 1980; "Mr. Reagan v. Nature," ibid., October 10, 1980.

6. Wilentz, *The Age of Reagan*, 140; Peter Behr and Joanne Omang, "Impact of Regulation Freeze Is Unclear," *Washington Post*, January 30, 1981.

7. Donald T. Critchlow, *The Conservative Ascendancy: How the GOP Right Made Political History* (Cambridge, MA: Harvard University Press, 2007), 189, 190.

8. Joanne Omang, "Denver Lawyer Reagan's Choice to Head EPA," *Washington Post*, February 21, 1981.

9. Warren Brown, "Administration Takes Muscle Out of Labor," *Washington Post*, October 28, 1981; Peter Behr and Joanne Omang, "DOE, FTC, Other Agency Payrolls Slashed," ibid., March 11, 1981.

10. Peter Behr and Joanne Omang, "White House Targets 27 More Regulations for Review," ibid., March 26, 1981; Wilentz, *The Age of Reagan*, 140.

11. Joe Fontaine, "Speech to Industrial Union Department of the AFL/CIO," Detroit, October 26, 1982, 1, Sierra Club Members Papers Collection, carton 80, folder 1.

12. Ibid.

13. Sierra Club, "Poisons on the Job: The Reagan Administration and American Workers," press release, Sierra Club Members Papers Collection, carton 80, folder 1.

14. Fontaine, "Speech to Industrial Union Department of the AFL/CIO," 2, 4.

15. David S. Broder, "A Sharp Right Turn: Republicans and Democrats Alike See New Era in '80 Returns," *Washington Post*, November 6, 1980.

16. Wilentz, *The Age of Reagan*, 124, 125.

17. Pincetl, *Transforming California*, 240.

18. George Deukmejian, speech, United Way Center of Santa Clara County, CA, September 8, 1982, Environmental Affairs Agency Collection R284, box 5, folder 16, California State Archives, Sacramento, CA.

19. George Deukmejian, speeches to California Republican Party Convention, San Diego, CA, September 18, 1982; United Way Center of Santa Clara County, CA, September 8, 1982; League of California Cities (n.p.), October 19, 1982; Environmental Affairs Discussion," January 24, 1983; all Environmental Affairs Agency Collection R284, box 5, folder 16.

20. George Deukmejian, speech, Annual Convention of Agricultural Leadership Associates, Sacramento, CA, February 10, 1982, Environmental Affairs Agency Collection R284, box 5, folder 16.

21. Keith Love, "Agriculture Ranks as No. 1 Industry: State Farmers Cultivate Clout at Capitol," *Los Angeles Times*, May 5, 1982.

22. Harry Bernstein, "Growers Eager for New Face in Sacramento," *Los Angeles Times*, September 20, 1982.

23. George Deukmejian, speech, Annual Convention of Agricultural Leadership Associates, Sacramento, CA, February 10, 1982; Nancy Skelton, "George Deukmejian as Candidate: A Cautious Man Counters a Dull Image," *Los Angeles Times*, October 18, 1982.

24. "California Farmworkers: Back to the Barricades?" *Businessweek*, September 26, 1983, 86.

25. Mark Baldassare, Bruce E. Cain, D.E. Apollonio, and Jonathan Cohen, *The Season of Our Discontent: Voters' Views on California Elections* (San Francisco: Public Policy Institute of California, 2004), 8, http://www.ppic.org/content/pubs/report/R_1004MBR.pdf.

26. Harry Bernstein, "Deukmejian's Appointments to Key Posts Forecast Changes: State's Organized Labor Can Look Forward to Four Rough Years," *Los Angeles Times*, January 26, 1983; Harry Bernstein, "Dispute Grows in Farm Labor Board Ranks," ibid., February 22, 1983.

27. Harry Bernstein, "Charges, Countercharges Fly at Farm Labor Board," ibid., March 28, 1983.

28. Internal letter to the members of the Agricultural Labor Relations Board (signed by nine board members), April 20, 1983, UFW New York Boycott Collection (unprocessed, Acc. Date 06/01), box 2, folder Press Release Originals, Archives of Labor and Urban Affairs, Wayne State University, Detroit.

29. Harry Bernstein, "Governor Withdraws Threat after Settlement with ALRB," *Los Angeles Times*, June 23, 1983; Harvey Bernstein, "Rebellion Rocks Farm Labor Board," ibid., August 1, 1983.

30. Harry Bernstein, "27% Budget Cut Will Cripple Farm Board, Member Says," ibid., July 23, 1983.

31. Carl Ingram, "Former Grower Renamed to Farm Board: Democrat is 1st Deukmejian Appointee to Embattled Labor Panel," ibid., February 16, 1984; Harry Bernstein, "Woman Is Named New Farm Labor Board Chief," ibid., July 26, 1984. The AFL-CIO had previously accused James-Massengale's firm Seyfarth, Shaw, Fairweather, and Geraldson of "union busting." "L.A. Attorney Selected to Head Farm Labor Board," ibid., July 25, 1984.

32. Douglas Shuit, "Farm Labor Board's Case Backlog Grows: Legislative Analyst Says Staff Cuts are Causing Unsettled Disputes to Pile Up," ibid., February 24, 1984.

33. Ibid.; "California Farmworkers: Back to the Barricades," 86.

34. Internal letter to the members of the Agricultural Labor Relations Board (signed by nine of the eleven board members), April 20, 1983.

35. Cesar E. Chavez to National Executive Board Members et al., July 13, 1977, Cesar Chavez (unprocessed, Acc. Date 04/07/86), box 15, folder Masters, Archives of Labor and Urban Affairs, Wayne State University, Detroit; Cesar Chavez, "General Discussion on the Union and its Struggles," (presentation, Department Re-Organization Conference, Pilgrim Pines, Yacaipa, California, July 6–8, 1976), Cesar Chavez (unprocessed, Acc. Date 04/07/86), box 15, folder Organizing 1976.

36. Cesar E. Chavez to National Executive Board Members et al., July 13, 1977.

37. David Rosenzweig, "Union Leader Uses Synanon 'Game' Regularly at Headquarters," *Los Angeles Times*, December 29, 1978; Miriam Pawal, *The Union of Their Dreams: Power, Hope, and Struggle in Cesar Chavez's Farm Worker Movement* (New York: Bloomsbury Press, 2009), 203.

38. Ganz, *Why David Sometimes Wins*, 245.

39. Ibid., 245–47; Robert Lindsey, "Glory Days are Fading for Chavez and U.F.W.," *New York Times*, December 23, 1984; Garcia, *From the Jaws of Victory*, 294–95.

40. Harry Bernstein, "Target is Governor: The Boycott: Chavez Gets a Slow Start," *Los Angeles Times*, July 25, 1985; "Changing ALRB Worries Chavez's Union," ibid., July 31, 1985; "Grape Boycott Renewed," *Washington Post*, July 12, 1984.

41. "Boycott Grapes Planning Session," meeting notes, March 16, 1985, 221-UFW (unprocessed, Acc. Date 04/10/95), box 4, folder Boycott Information, Archives of Labor and Urban Affairs, Wayne State University, Detroit.

42. Bernstein, "Target is Governor: The Boycott: Chavez Gets a Slow Start."; "Changing ALRB Worries Chavez's Union."

43. "Program Strategies," meeting notes, May 16, 1985, 221-UFW (unprocessed, Acc. Date 04/10/95), box 4, folder Boycott Information; "Chavez Tries a Computerized Grape Boycott," *Businessweek*, September 9, 1985, 35.

44. "Chavez Tries a Computerized Grape Boycott," 35.

45. "Program Strategies," meeting notes, May 16, 1985; "PR: Strat/Tactics," meeting notes, December 19, 1987, 221-UFW (unprocessed, Acc. Date 04/10/95), box 4, folder Boycott Information.

46. "Chavez Tries a Computerized Grape Boycott," 35.

47. Lindsey, "Glory Days are Fading for Chavez and U.F.W."; Bernstein, "Target is Governor."

48. Harry Bernstein, "UFW Shifting Focus in Table Grape Boycott," *Los Angeles Times*, September 4, 1985.

49. Robert Lindsey, "Cesar Chavez Tries New Direction for United Farm Workers," *New York Times*, September 19, 1983.

50. Jerome Cohen, "UFW Must Get Back to Organizing: Despite Opposition, Farm-Labor Law Is Still a Potent Weapon," *Los Angeles Times*, January 15, 1986.

51. Bernstein, "Target is Governor."

52. Bernstein, "Target is Governor."; Evan T. Barr, "Sour Grapes: Cesar Chavez 20 Years Later," *New Republic*, November 25, 1985, 23.

53. Arturo Rodriguez to Cesar E. Chavez, December 27, 1980, Cesar Chavez (unprocessed, Acc. Date 04/17/86), box 39, (no folder); Cesar E. Chavez to Marion Moses, February 4, 1981, Cesar Chavez (unprocessed, Acc. Date 04/17/86), box 45, folder Moses, Marion, (M.D.); William W. Monning to Cesar Chavez, March 16, 1982, Cesar Chavez (unprocessed, Acc. Date 04/17/86), box 38, (no folder).

54. Cesar Chavez's personal notes, Shaver Lake, CA, June 3, 1983, Cesar Chavez (unprocessed, Acc. Date 04/17/86), box 26, folder Cesar Chavez's personal notes.

55. Ibid.

56. Marion Moses to Cesar Chavez, October 5, 1985, UFW New York Boycott Collection (unprocessed, Acc. Date 06/01), box 1, (blue folder, no number/title).

57. Early issues of the UFW's new publication *Food And Justice* discussed pesticide-related issues, but the union did not immediately address pesticides in the early phase of the boycott campaign. See for example, "Pesticide Poisoning is More than an Accident," *Food and Justice* 1, no. 3 (December 1984): 8–10; " Dr. Marion Moses and Agriculture's 'Deadly Dozen,'" ibid., 2, no. 2 (February 1985): 11–14; Marion Moses, "Pesticides Which Cause Birth Defects and Kill Workers," ibid., no. 3 (April/May 1985): 10–12.

58. Philipp Gollner and Peter H. King, "Watermelons Slowly Reappear in Area Markets," *Los Angeles Times*, July 12, 1985; Cathleen Decker, "Watermelons Recalled as 18 Become Ill," ibid., July 5, 1985; Ronald B. Taylor, "Watermelons Sweet, Feelings Bitter After Poisonous '85 Crop," ibid., July 6, 1986.

59. Taylor, "Watermelons Sweet, Feelings Bitter After Poisonous '85 Crop."

60. King and Weintraub, "State Sees Illegal Use of Pesticides." *Los Angeles Times*, July 9, 1985; Taylor, "Watermelons Sweet, Feelings Bitter After Poisonous '85 Crop."

61. Gollner and King, "Watermelons Slowly Reappear in Area Markets."

62. Bruce Keppel, "Aftermath of Pesticide Contamination: Consumers Shun Melons to the Dismay of Growers," *Los Angeles Times*, July 19, 1985; Daniel P. Puzo, "Consumers More Wary About Food: Many Fear Chemical Hazards, Tampering, Survey Finds," ibid., May 14, 1987.

63. "2 Small Towns' Mysterious 'Clusters' of Cancer," *San Francisco Chronicle*, October 31, 1985.

64. David B. Cohen and Gerald W. Bowes, *Water Quality and Pesticides: A California Risk Assessment Program*, vol. 1 (Sacramento: State Water Resources Control Board, 1984), 28.

65. Lloyd G. Connelly, "'Leaching Fields' Report Reveals Pesticide Threat to State's Groundwater," press release, April 16, 1985, Assembly Agriculture Committee Collection, LP254:208, folder Bill Files, AB1890–2047, 1985–86, California State Archives, Sacramento.

66. David B. Cohen, "Ground Water Contamination by Toxic Substances: A California Assessment," ACS Symposium Series (Washington, DC: American Chemical Society, 1986), 499–503, 513; "2 Small Towns' Mysterious 'Clusters' of Cancer."

67. Cohen, "Ground Water Contamination by Toxic Substances," 520.

68. Ibid.

69. Dr. Beverly Paigen, interview by Kim Lawson, March 1986, Oakland Children's Hospital, (n.d); Connie Rosales, interview by Kim Lawson, McFarland, CA, March 18, 1986, 1, 2; Rosemary Esparza, interview by Kim Lawson, McFarland, CA, March 1986, 1; Joyce Johnson, interview by Kim Lawson, Tom Doogan's office, [n.d], 2; all UFW New York Boycott Collection (unprocessed, Acc. Date 06/01), box 1, folder (no title, black 3-ring binder).

70. Connie Rosales, interview by Kim Lawson, McFarland, CA, March 18, 1986, 1, 2.

71. "2 Small Towns' Mysterious 'Clusters' of Cancer."

72. Russell Clemings, "Town Where Cancer Lives," *Fresno Bee*, February 14, 1988.

73. California Legislature, Senate Committee on Toxics and Public Safety Management, *Childhood Cancer Incidences—McFarland* (Sacramento: Joint Publications, 1985), 32.

74. Ibid., 8.

75. Russell Clemings, "Cancer Cluster Still Not Solved; McFarland Health Study Inconclusive," *Fresno Bee*, October 30, 1986. For a more thorough analysis of the McFarland cancer cluster and the investigation into its causes, see Adam Tompkins, "Cancer Valley, California: Pesticides, Politics, and Childhood Disease in the Central Valley," in *Natural Protest: Essays on the History of American Environmentalism*, edited by Michael Egan and Jeff Crane (New York: Routledge, 2009), 275–300; Fred Setterberg and Lonny Shavelson, *Toxic Nation: The Fight to Save Our Communities from Chemical Contamination* (New York: Wiley, 1993); Linda Nash, *Inescapable Ecologies: A History of Environment, Disease, and Knowledge* (Berkeley: University of California Press, 2006), 181–208.

76. California Legislature, Senate Committee on Toxics and Public Safety Management, *Childhood Cancer Incidences—McFarland*, 27.

77. Leo C. Wolinsky, "Senate OKs Shield on State's Pesticide Use," *Los Angeles Times*, September 12, 1985.

78. Ibid.; Leo Wolinsky, "Plan to Curb Pesticide Challenges Revived," *Los Angeles Times*, September 14, 1985; Leo Wolinsky, "Pesticide Spraying Bill Caught in Legislative Cross Fire," ibid., September 11, 1985; Wolinsky, "Senate OKs Shield on State's Pesticide Use."

79. Lisa Petrillo, "County Farm Workers to Get Funds to Improve Housing," *San Diego Union*, October 4, 1985; "Growers Must Post Warnings; Stricter Controls Set on Pesticide Spraying," *San Jose Mercury News*, September 14, 1985; Wolinsky, "Pesticide Spraying Bill Caught in Legislative Crossfire."

80. California Legislature, Senate Committee on Toxics and Public Safety Management, *Childhood Cancer Incidences—McFarland*, 2; Jim Dufur, "Governor OKS Bill to Have All Counties Keep Cancer Figures," *Sacramento Bee*, September 24, 1985; Richard C. Paddock, "Governor Dips Into Surplus to Finance Spending Bills," *Los Angeles Times*, October 6, 1985.

81. Ronald B. Taylor, "Pesticide Regulations: Is State Too Strict or Too Permissive?" *Los Angeles Times*, February 19, 1983.

82. California Assembly Agriculture Committee, *AB 1525 (N. Waters) Hearing*, September 9, 1985, 3, Assembly Agriculture Committee Collection, LP254:205, folder Bill Files, AB1525-AB1605, 1985–86; Rick Rodriguez, "Comeback Try for Farm-Safety Bill," *Sacramento Bee*, September 11, 1985.

83. Petrillo, "County Farm Workers to Get Funds to Improve Housing."

84. "Duke Urged to Seek Poison-Melon Probe," *Sacramento Bee*, July 25, 1985.

85. California Assembly Committee on Agriculture, *AB 2021 (Connelly) Hearing*, May 14, 1985, 5, Assembly Agriculture Committee Collection, LP254:208, folder Bill Files, AB1890–2047, 1985–86.

86. Connelly, "'Leaching Fields' Report Reveals Pesticide Threat to State's Groundwater."

87. California State Assembly, "Concurrence in Senate Amendments: AB 1511 (Connelly)," September 10, 1985, 2, Assembly Agriculture Committee Collection, LP254:208, folder Bill Files, AB1890–2047, 1985–86.

88. Lawrie Mott to Assemblyman Norman Waters, May 10, 1985, Assembly Agriculture Committee Collection, LP254:208, folder Bill Files, AB1890–2047, 1985–86.

89. Michael Paparian to Norman Waters, May 13, 1985, Assembly Agriculture Committee Collection, LP254:208, folder Bill Files, AB1890–2047, 1985–86; Sierra Club Legislative Office, "Pesticides Threaten Groundwater: Your Help Needed," Sierra Club California Legislative Office Records Collection, box 7, folder 5, Bancroft Library, University of California Berkeley; California Assembly Committee on Agriculture, *AB 2021 (Connelly) Hearing*, 5.

90. "Grape Pesticides Worse Than Watermelons," *Food and Justice* 2, no. 4 (September 1985): 6, 7.

91. Cesar Chavez, "Deterioration of Farm Law Led UFW Back to Boycott," *Los Angeles Times*, January 10, 1986.

92. "Grape Pesticides Worse Than Watermelons," 6.

93. "Farm Workers March Against Pesticides on Boycott Anniversary," *San Jose Mercury News*, September 8, 1985; "'65 Delano Strike Observed: Farm Workers Protest Pesticide Peril," *Food and Justice* 2, no. 5 (October 1985): 3, cover.

94. Cesar Chavez, "Delano Speech–Pesticide March," Delano, California, September 8, 1985, 5, UFW New York Boycott Collection (unprocessed, 06/01), box 1, folder (no title, blue 3-ring binder), 6, 9.

95. "Wrath of Grapes Campaign to Counter Grape Growers' Natural Snack Theme," *Food and Justice* 3, no. 2 (February/March 1986): 3; "'The Wrath of Grapes'—The Tragedy of Pesticide Poisoning," ibid., 4; Chavez, "Deterioration of Farm Law Led UFW Back to Boycott."

96. "'The Wrath of Grapes'—The Tragedy of Pesticide Poisoning," 6.

97. Ibid., 4.

98. *The Wrath of Grapes*, VHS, narrated by Mike Farrell, produced by Lorena Parlee and Lenny Bourin, United Farm Workers of America, AFL-CIO, production of Volunteer Staff of UFWofA, 1986 (all quotes in next two paragraphs from this source)

99. Ibid.

100. United Farm Workers of America, AFL-CIO, Mid-Atlantic Grape Boycott, "Wrath of Grapes Video and Film Marketing Plan," January 10, 1987, UFW New York Boycott Collection (unprocessed, Acc. Date 06/01), box 5, folder Wrath of Grapes Mktg Plan (1987).

101. David Roe was the principle author of Prop 65. Carl Pope contributed greatly as well. Journalists tended to quote Pope more than Roe in the weeks preceding the election. David Roe, "An Incentive-Conscious Approach to Toxic Chemical Controls," *Economic Development Quarterly* 3, no. 3 (August 1989): 179; David Roe, "Prop. 65 Kit: A Quick Reference Guide to California's Proposition 65," http://www.edf.org/article.cfm?ContentID=3376 (accessed December 2, 2010); Robert P. Studer, "Prop. 65 Safe Water Fight Is 'How,' not 'If,'" *San Diego Union*, October 19, 1986; Dirk Werkman, "Big Five Might Steal Election Show," *Daily News of Los Angeles*, July 27, 1986; Elliot Diringer, "Safe Tap Water–Risk vs. Cost-Issues Behind the Toxics Initiative," *San Francisco Chronicle*, October 28, 1986; "Art Torres Wants to Make Government Work For People!" *El Malcriado* 5, no. 2 (June 6, 1972): 2; "Why do Farmworkers Support Art Torres?" ibid.; Cesar Chavez, "Cesar Chavez: 'Farmworkers Support Art Torres for Assemblyman!" ibid.; California Legislature, Senate Committee on Toxics and Public Safety Management, *Childhood Cancer Incidences—McFarland*.

102. Werkman, "Big Five Might Steal Election Show"; Studer, "Prop. 65 Safe Water Fight Is 'How,' Not 'If.'"

103. Tom Hayden's Campaign California was the largest donor. "Top Contributors in Prop. 65 Toxics Race," *Fresno Bee*, October, 19, 1986.

104. The UFW did not rank among the top ten contributors to the campaign: ibid. A review of articles in several California newspapers—including the *Los Angeles Times*, *Fresno Bee*, *San Francisco Chronicle*, *San Diego Union*, and the *Sacramento Bee*—did not show the UFW as an endorser of Prop 65. The union's *Food and Justice* magazine did not mention Prop 65 in 1986 either. It kept a closer focus on pesticides and the McFarland cancer cluster. See *Food and Justice* 3, no. 7 (August 1986) and no. 11 (November 1986).

105. Pope, "An Immodest Proposal," *Sierra* 70, no. 5 (September/October 1985): 45.

106. Roe, "An Incentive-Conscious Approach to Toxic Chemical Controls," 181.

107. Pope, "An Immodest Proposal," 45.

108. Roe, "An Incentive-Conscious Approach to Toxic Chemical Controls," 181.

109. Mitchel Benson, "87% in County Favor Prop. 65, Supporters Say," *San Jose Mercury News*, September 10, 1986; Jay Matthews, "California Uses 'Legal Judo' on Toxics," *Washington Post*, July 30, 1991; *Safe Drinking Water and Toxic Enforcement Act of 1986*, Chapter 6.6, http://www.edf.org/documents/3379_65original.pdf (accessed December 2, 2010).

110. Roe, "An Incentive-Conscious Approach to Toxic Chemical Controls," 181.

111. Pope, "An Immodest Proposal," 46.

112. Ibid.; Roe, "An Incentive-Conscious Approach to Toxic Chemical Controls," 183.

113. Roe, "An Incentive-Conscious Approach to Toxic Chemical Controls," 181, 182.

114. John Marelius, "Toxic Issue Draws Much Heat—Proposition 65 is Central Topic in California Campaigns," *San Diego Union,* November 2, 1986; Robert Knowles, "Prop. 65 Supporters Challenge Chevron to Debates—Memo Urges Workers Not to Discuss Waste Measure," *Daily Breeze* (Torrance, CA), August 13, 1986.

115. Donna Prokop, "Farmers Take Prop. 65 Protest to Los Angeles City Hall," *Daily Breeze* (Torrance, CA), October 23, 1986.

116. William Endicott, "Duke Opposes AIDS Initiative Pay Limit, Clean Water Proposals also Criticized," *Sacramento Bee*, September 3, 1986; "Rebuttal to Argument in Favor of Proposition 65," http://www.edf.org/documents/3386_ArgueFor.pdf (accessed December 2, 2010).

117. Marc Lifsher, "Panel Disagrees on List of What to Ban in Water—Scientific Testimony Conflicts on Which Chemicals Are Most Harmful," *Orange County Register*, April 1, 1987.

118. Ann Cony, "Duke's Toxic List Called Too Short," *Sacramento Bee*, February 28, 1987.

119. "Argument Against Proposition 65," http://www.edf.org/documents/3385_Argue-Against.pdf (accessed December 2, 2010)

120. Leslie Roberts, "A Corrosive Fight Over California's Toxic Law," *Science*, no. 230 (January 20, 1989): 306–7.

121. Elliot Diringer, "'It's an Act of Sabotage'—Prop. 65 Foe on Toxics Panel," *San Francisco Chronicle*, February 27, 1987; Robert N. Proctor, *Cancer Wars: How Politics Shapes What We Know and Don't Know about Cancer* (New York: Basic Books, 1995), 150.

122. *AFL-CIO v. George Deukmejian*, 212 Cal.App.3d 425, 260 Cal. Rptr. 479 (Cal. 1989); Ann Cony, "Duke's Toxics List Called Too Short," *Sacramento Bee*, February 28, 1987.

123. Sandra Steingraber, *Living Downstream: An Ecologist Looks at Cancer and the Environment* (Reading, MA: Addison-Wesley, 1997), 125.

124. *AFL-CIO v. George Deukmejian*, 212 Cal.App.3d 425, 260 Cal. Rptr. 479; Mitchel Benson, "Governor Releases Toxics List but Coalition Says Roster is Incomplete," *San Jose Mercury News*, February 28, 1987.

125. "Toxic List," *Daily News of Los Angeles*, February 28, 1987; "Prop 65 Backers Sue Deukmejian Over Toxic-Chemicals List," *Orange County Register*, February 28, 1987; Paul Pringle, "Deukmejian Defends Toxins List," *Daily Breeze* (Torrence, CA), March 4, 1987; Environmental Protection Agency, "DDT Ban Takes Effect," press release, December 31, 1972, http://www2.epa.gov/aboutepa/ddt-ban-takes-effect; Environmental Protection Agency, "EPA Acts to Ban EDB Pesticide."

126. Elliot Diringer, "State's Own Experts Ignored on Prop. 65," *San Francisco Chronicle*, March 25, 1988; Mathews, "California Uses 'Legal Judo' on Toxics"; David Roe, "An Incentive-Conscious Approach to Toxic Chemical Controls," 183–84.

127. *Safe Drinking Water and Toxic Enforcement Act of 1986*, Chapter 6.6.

128. William Kahrl, "Will Deukmejian Be Poison for Prop. 65? (An Update)," *Sacramento Bee*, April 19, 1987.

129. *AFL-CIO v. George Deukmejian*, 212 Cal.App.3d 425, 260 Cal. Rptr. 479.

130. Ibid.

131. California Health and Welfare Agency, Department of Health Services, *Guidelines for Chemical Carcinogen Risk Assessments and Their Scientific Rationale* (November 1985), C-20, quoted in *AFL-CIO v. George Deukmejian*, 212 Cal.App.3d 425, 260 Cal. Rptr. 479.

132. Ibid.

133. Richard C. Paddock, "Toxics Law Exemption to Be Lifted," *Los Angeles Times*, December 29, 1992.

134. Clemings, "Cancer Cluster Still Not Solved."

135. Amy Pyle, "State Will Expand McFarland Probe: Duke Requests Further Study of Cancer Cluster," *Fresno Bee*, December 17, 1987.

136. New York State Department of Health, "Love Canal: A Special Report to the Governor & Legislature: April 1981," revised October 2005, www.nyhealth.gov/environmental/investigations/love_canal/lcreport.htm.

137. Pyle, "State Will Expand McFarland Probe"; Russell Clemings, "McFarland Parents Demand New Childhood-Cancer Study," *Fresno Bee*, October 17, 1987.

138. "Pesticides Studied in Town's Cancers: Large Quantities of Four Chemicals Used in Kern Community's Fields," *Sacramento Bee*, January 30, 1988.

139. "McFarland Cancer Panel Will Look at Other Towns," *Fresno Bee*, April 9, 1988.

140. Elliot Diringer, "5 Children of Farm Workers: New Cancer Cluster in Farm Town," *San Francisco Chronicle*, September 14, 1989.

141. United Farm Workers, "Boycott Grapes For Your Sake . . . and Ours," n.d., 1988?, UFW New York Boycott Collection (unprocessed, Acc. Date 06/01), box 4, folder Boycott Grapes for Your Sake . . . and Ours; Lawrie Mott and Karen Snyder, *Pesticide Alert: A Guide to Pesticides in Fruits and Vegetables* (San Francisco: Sierra Club Books, 1987), vii–viii.

142. United Farm Workers, "Boycott Grapes For Your Sake . . . and Ours"; Lily Leung, "Three Decades of Environmental Activism," *San Diego Union Tribune*, October 17, 2010.

143. United Farm Workers, "Boycott Grapes For Your Sake . . . and Ours"; Jennifer Bowles, "Environmental Crusaders Celebrate 30 Years Strong," *Press-Enterprise* (Riverside, CA), December 7, 2007; Gottlieb, *Forcing the Spring*, 221.

144. United Farm Workers, "Boycott Grapes For Your Sake . . . and Ours"; "Walter G. Hooke (obituary)," *Post Star* (Glen Falls, NY), May 24, 2010.

145. Ethel Kennedy, interview by Paradigm Productions, 1995/1996. http://www.farmworkermovement.us/media/oral_history/ParadigmTranscripts/KennedyEthel.pdf. Paradigm Productions conducted this interview when making the documentary *The Fight in the Fields: Chavez and the Farmworkers' Struggle*, VHS, directed by Ray Telles and Rick Tejada-Flores (Sparks, NV: Paradigm Productions, 1996).

146. "Nader and Friends Dump Grapes," *Food and Justice* 5, no. 2 (February 1988): 4.

147. See, for example, Western New York Grape Boycott Coalition, "Boycott Grapes," pamphlet, October 1988, UFW New York Boycott Collection (unprocessed, Acc. Date 06/01), box 5, folder Grape Boycott Leaflets. This pamphlet included the Center for Science in the Public Interest, Environmental Action, and Friends of the Earth in its partial list of supporters.

148. "Join Actor Ed Asner in the Human Billboard," pamphlet, October 20, 1988, UFW New York Boycott Collection (unprocessed, Acc. Date 06/01), box 3, folder Fast for Life/Grape Boycott Celebrity Support.

149. Wendy Gordon Rockefeller to Artie Rodriguez, June 6, 1989; Mothers and Others Against Pesticides meeting notes, May 25, 1989; both UFW New York Boycott Collection (unprocessed, Acc. Date 06/01), box 2, folder Mothers and Others Against Pesticides.

150. "Chavez Begins Fast," *Food and Justice* 5, no. 5 (July 1988): 8.

151. ". . . and on the 36th, Bread," ibid., no. 6 (September 1988): 11, 12; Louis Sahagun, "After 36 Days Chavez Halts Protest Fast," *Los Angeles Times*, August 22, 1988; Louis Sahagun, "Chavez Ailing as He Completes 17th Day of Fast," ibid., August 4, 1988.

152. "'Today I Pass On the Fast for Life . . . ,'" *Food and Justice* 5, no. 6 (September 1988): 14.

153. Ibid.

154. "National Fast for Life," ibid., no. 7 (October 1988): 6; United Farm Workers of America, AFL-CIO, "Impact of Boycott Activity," (n.d., 1988?), UFW New York Boycott Collection (unprocessed, Acc. Date 06/01), box 2, folder Press Releases 1988.

155. "'A Multitude of Simple Deeds,'" *Food and Justice* 5, no. 7 (October 1988): 5.

156. United Farm Workers of America, AFL-CIO, "Impact of Boycott Activity."

157. California Table Grape Commission, "Boycotts Are Supposed to Protect Us. But Who Will Protect Us From Boycotts?" (n.d), UFW New York Boycott Collection (unprocessed, Acc. Date 06/01), box 3, folder Grower Boycott Propaganda.

158. "Testimony of Avan Ortega," California Table Grape Commission v. United Farm Workers of America, AFL-CIO, Agricultural Labor Relations Board Case No: 91-CL-5-ED (SD), 91-CL-5–1-ED(SD), and 91-CL-1-VI (April 6, 1992), 54, 64–68, 71, 104; "Testimony of Carlos Arambula," ibid., (April 7, 1992), 142–45, 150, 158; both UFW New York Boycott Collection (unprocessed, Acc. Date 06/01), box 5, folder Rees Lloyd Letter and Trial Transcript.

159. Proctor, *Cancer Wars*, 90–91, 150.

160. *Big Fears, Little Risk: A Report of Chemicals in the Environment*, VHS, narrated by Walter Cronkite, produced by Film Counselors Associates, Inc., American Council on Science and Health, 1989.

161. John Tweedy Jr., "Coalition Building and the Defeat of California's Proposition 128," *Stanford Environmental Law Journal* 11 (1992): 117; John Balzar, "Environmental Groups Offer Their Dream List California: Advocates and Politicians Propose a Sweeping Initiative Enforced by a Conservation Cop," *Los Angeles Times*, October 11, 1989; Marla Cone, "Prop 128 Might Double Most Sewer Bills in O.C.," ibid., October 31, 1990; Maura Dolan and Richard C. Paddock, "Proposition 128: 'Big Green' Reached Too Far, Backers Say," ibid., November 8, 1990; Scott Reeves, "Initiative Called 'Scare Tactics'," *Fresno Bee*, October 26, 1900.

162. Tweedy, "Coalition Building and the Defeat of California's Proposition 128," 117; Al Meyerhoff, "Perspectives on Proposition 128: Is it Practical and Forward-Looking, or Is It the Big Green Con Job?" *Los Angeles Times*, October 27, 1990; Cesar Chavez, "Farm Workers at Risk," in *Toxic Struggles: The Theory and Practice of Environmental Justice*, ed. Richard Hofrichter (Philadelphia: New Society Publishers, 1993), 167; Ferriss and Sandoval, *The Fight in the Fields*, 250; Dan Morain and Mark Arax, "Once-Powerful Union Declines in Influence," *Los Angeles Times*, April 24, 1993.

163. Art Torres, *Proposition 128: Analysis of Pesticide Use and Regulation* (Sacramento: Senate Committee on Toxics and Public Safety Management, 1990), 2–4, 10.

164. Senate Toxics and Public Safety Management Committee, *Proposition 128: Environmental Protection Act of 1990* (Sacramento: Senate Office of Research, 1990), 1, 6, 7.

165. Richard C. Paddock, "California Elections Proposition 128: Deukmejian Says 'Big Green' Will Jeopardize Jobs," *Los Angeles Times*, September 9, 1990.

166. Rudy Abramson, "Growers Fear Pesticide Controls in 'Big Green'," *Los Angeles Times*, July 11, 1990.

167. Paddock, "California Elections Proposition 128: Deukmejian Says 'Big Green' Will Jeopardize Jobs."

168. Nancy Rivera Brooks, "Expensive Victory for Businesses," *Los Angeles Times*, November 8, 1990.

169. Richard C. Paddock, "3 Environment Issues Lose; Prop. 140 Ahead," ibid., November 7, 1990.

170. Al Meyerhoff, "Greening California, by Initiative"; Daniel P. Puzo, "A Growing Lack of Credibility," *Los Angeles Times*, May 24, 1990.

171. Paddock, "3 Environment Issues Lose; Prop. 140 Ahead."

172. Clifford E. Gladstein, "Affidavit of the Events at the March 4, 1990 Focus Rally Buena Vista Park, Burbank,"1–3, Senator Tom Hayden Collection, LP322:384, folder Subject Files: Pesticide, Malathion (part 1), California State Archives, Sacramento.

173. Jack Cheevers, "California Elections Propositions 128 and 135: Farmers Try to Harvest Votes for 'Big Green' Rival," *Los Angeles Times*, October 28, 1990.

174. Mervin Field and Mark DiCamillo, "Voter Preferences on Prop. 128 (Big Green), Prop 134 (Nickel a Drink) and Prop. 130 (Forests Forever) Vary Considerably Depending on Awareness of Fiscal Impact of Each Initiative," *California Poll*, no. 1563 (October 16, 1990): 2, http://ucdata.berkeley.edu/pubs/CalPolls/1563.pdf.

175. Voters defeated "Big Brown" by an even larger margin than "Big Green"; Paddock, "3 Environment Issues Lose."

176. Dolan and Paddock, "Proposition 128."

177. Chavez, "Effective Protest Doesn't Require a Majority."

178. Ibid.

179. Dan Levy, "UFW Abandons '84 Boycott Against California Grapes," *San Francisco Gate*, November 22, 2000.

180. Randolph B. Smith, "California Spurs Reformulated Products," *Wall Street Journal*, November 1, 1990.

7. From The Ground Up

1. Tony Perry, "Chavez Died Near Birthplace, Site of Property Lost in Depression," *Los Angeles Times*, April 24, 1993.

2. Patt Morrison, "For the Final Time, They March for Chavez Memorial: From the Famous to the Field Workers, 35,000 Turn Out to Pay Tribute to the Late Labor Leader," ibid., April 30, 1993.

3. Ibid. The future of the farmworkers' movement remained uncertain following Chavez's death, particularly since recurrent legal fees pushed the union to the brink of bankruptcy and anemic membership rolls paled in comparison to the number of dues-paying members in the 1970s. Richard Steven Street, "Richard Steven Street 1988, 1993," Farmworker Documentation Project, http://farmworkermovement.com/essays/essays/194%20Street_Richard%20Steven.pdf; Frank Bardacke, "Cesar's Ghost," *The Nation* 257, no. 4 July 26, 1993, 130–35.

4. Adams and Meyerhoff wrote that the death of Chavez "refocused the nation's attention on the plight of our more than two million farmworkers" who labored for substandard wages and ranked among the highest for occupational illness and death as a result of "intolerable working conditions and daily exposure to the range of toxic chemicals that now characterize much of American agriculture." John Adams and Al Meyerhoff, "Recalling Cesar Chavez," UFW PR Dept: Jocelyn Sherman (unprocessed, Acc. No. 779, Acc. Date 10/28/97), box 3, folder NRDC, Archives of Labor and Urban Affairs, Wayne State University, Detroit; Steven Greenhouse, "Al Meyerhoff, Legal Voice for the Poor, Dies at 61," *New York Times*, December 24, 2008.

5. Jennifer Curtis, Tim Profeta, and Lawrie Mott, *After Silent Spring: The Unsolved Problems of Pesticide Use in the United States* (New York: Natural Resources Defense Council, 1993), dedication page. The NRDC sent an advance draft of this report to new UFW president Arturo Rodriguez that bore the title *Thirty Years Since Silent Spring: A Record of Inaction and Neglect*; UFW PR Dept: Jocelyn Sherman (unprocessed, Acc. No. 779, Acc. Date 10/28/97), box 3, folder NRDC.

6. Curtis, Profeta, and Mott, *After Silent Spring*, 3–5.

7. Ibid., 39 (quote), 43, 49.

8. Judy E. Martinez to Arturo Rodriguez, May 12, 1993, UFW PR Dept: Jocelyn Sherman (unprocessed, Acc. No. 779, Acc. Date 10/28/97), box 3, folder NRDC.

9. Curtis, Profeta, and Mott, *After Silent Spring*, 43.

10. California Department of Health Services, "Methyl Bromide," *Fact Sheet* (May 1990), http://www.cdph.ca.gov/programs/hesis/Documents/mebr.pdf.

11. R. F. Hertel, T. Kielhorn, World Health Organization, International Labour Organisation, and United Nations Environmental Programme, *Methyl Bromide: First Draft Prepared by R. F. Hertel and T. Kielhorn* (Geneva: World Health Organization, 1995), 23, 81–84, 206–11.

12. Oreskes and Conway, *Merchants of Doubt*, 107, 112, 118–20.

13. Mostafa K. Tolba and Iwona Rummel-Bulska, "The Story of the Ozone Layer," in *The Montreal Protocol: Celebrating 20 Years of Environmental Progress*, ed. Donald Kaniaru (London: Cameron May and United Nations Environment Programme, 2007), 28.

14. Oreskes and Conway, *Merchants of Doubt*, 118–24.

15. Tolba and Rummel-Bulska, "The Story of the Ozone Layer," 29.

16. Arjun Makhijani and Kevin R. Gurney, *Mending the Ozone Hole: Science, Technology, and Policy* (Cambridge, MA: MIT Press, 1995), 59–63.

17. Ibid., 77, 79–82.

18. Tolba and Rummel-Bulska, "The Story of the Ozone Layer," 29.

19. By 1995, 145 nations ratified the protocol. Makhijani and Gurney, *Mending the Ozone Hole*, 219–20.

20. Oreskes and Conway, *Merchants of Doubt*, 122.

21. Makhijani and Gurney, *Mending the Ozone Hole*, 222–225.

22. Ibid., 226; The Copenhagen Amendment also restricted hydrochlorofluorocarbons and hydrobromofluorocarbons. Senate Committee on Foreign Relations, *Environmental Treaties*, 103d Cong., 1st sess., October 26, 1993, 11.

23. Arnold W. Reitze Jr., *Air Pollution Control Law: Compliance and Enforcement* (Washington, DC: Environmental Law Institute, 2001), 400.

24. House Subcommittee on Oversight and Investigations, Committee on Commerce, *Clean Air Act Amendments*, 104th Cong., 1st sess., August 1, 1995, 2; House Subcommittee on Health and Environment, Committee on Commerce, *Implementation of Title VI of the 1990 Clean Air Act Amendments and Plans for the Upcoming Meeting of the Parties to the Montreal Protocol in Montreal in September 1997*, 105th Cong., 1st sess., July 30, 1997, 34, 41.

25. House Subcommittee on Livestock and Horticulture, Committee on Agriculture, *The Implications of Banning Methyl Bromide for Fruit and Vegetable Production*, 106th Cong., 2d sess., July 13, 2000, 14.

26. House Subcommittee on Forestry, Resource Conservation, and Research, Committee on Agriculture, *Review of the Phaseout of Methyl Bromide* 105th Cong., 2d sess., June 10, 1998, 86–88, quote on p. 88.

27. Ibid., 86.

28. House Subcommittee on Livestock and Horticulture, *The Implications of Banning Methyl Bromide for Fruit and Vegetable Production*, 53.

29. Ibid., 56.

30. House Subcommittee on Forestry, Resource Conservation, and Research, *Review of the Phaseout of Methyl Bromide*, 87; Shari A. Yvon-Lewis and James Butler, "The Potential Effect of Oceanic Biological Degradation on the Lifetime of Atmospheric CH3Br," *Geophysical Research Letters* 24, no. 10 (May 15, 1997): 1227–30; National Oceanic and Atmospheric Administration, press release, "Oceans Remove More Ozone-Depleting Methyl Bromide From Atmosphere Than Previously Estimated, Research Shows," May 22, 1997, http://www.publicaffairs.noaa.gov/pr97/may97/noaa97-31.html.

31. National Oceanic and Atmospheric Administration, "Oceans Remove More Ozone-Depleting Methyl Bromide From Atmosphere Than Previously Estimated, Research Shows."

32. United Nations Environment Programme Ozone Secretariat, *Synthesis of the Reports of the Scientific, Environmental Effects, and Technology and Economic Assessment Panels of the Montreal Protocol: A Decade of Assessments for Decision Makers Regarding the Protection of the Ozone Layer: 1988–1999*, ed. Daniel L. Albritton and Lambert Kuijpers (Nairobi: UNON Printshop, 1999), 17; House Subcommittee on Forestry, *Review of the Phaseout of Methyl Bromide*, 66, 93, 104.

33. D. O. Chellemi, "Field Validation of Methyl Bromide Alternatives in Florida Fresh Market Vegetable Production Systems," in *Global Report on Validated Alternatives to the Use of Methyl Bromide for Soil Fumigation*, ed. R. Labrada and L. Fornasari, FAO Plant Production and Protection Paper 166 (Rome: Food and Agriculture Organization of the United Nations and United Nations Environment Programme, 2001), 27–29.

34. Corinna Gilfillan, *Reaping Havoc: The True Cost of Methyl Bromide on Florida's Tomatoes* (Washington, DC: Friends of the Earth, 1998).

35. Economic Research Service, US Department of Agriculture, "Facing the Phaseout of Methyl Bromide," *Agricultural Outlook* (August 1999): 24, http://www.ers.usda.gov/publications/agoutlook/aug1999/ao263h.pdf(accessed February 20, 2011).

36. Chellemi, "Field Validation of Methyl Bromide Alternatives in Florida Fresh Market Vegetable Production Systems," 27; House Subcommittee on Livestock and Horticulture, *The Implications of Banning Methyl Bromide for Fruit and Vegetable Production*, 5.

37. Reitze, *Air Pollution Control Law*, 395; David D. Doniger, "An Emergency Phase-Out Schedule" (lecture, Hyatt Regency, Baltimore, MD, December 3, 1991), 1, quote on 3–4, Legacy

Tobacco Documents Library, University of California San Francisco, https://industrydocuments. library.ucsf.edu/tobacco/docs/#id=xylb0120.

38. Melanie Miller, ed. *The Technical and Economic Feasibility of Replacing Methyl Bromide in Developing Countries: Case Studies in Zimbabwe, Thailand and Chile*(Washington, DC: Friends of the Earth, 1996).

39. "Becoming a Standout in the Field: Farmworker Association Co-Founder Aids Laborers With Migrant Headaches," *Orlando Sentinel,* February 4, 1991.

40. "The Not-So-Funny Farm: Tirso Moreno, Farmworker Organizer, Answers Questions," *Grist,* March 20, 2006, http://www.grist.org/article/moreno.

41. Jerry Jackson, "Farm Workers Seek More," *Orlando Sentinel,* August 23, 1993.

42. Tom Moore, "Farm Workers Will Learn Work Hazard," ibid., May 28, 1992; Farmworker Association of Florida, "¡La Amenaza de los Pesticidas!" (n.d), folder MBA and Sustainable Tomato Campaign, Farmworker Association of Florida private collection, Apopka, FL.

43. Friends of the Earth, "Congress Poised to Weaken Clean Air Act and Ozone Protection: Rep. Fazio's Amendment Would Delay Ban of Toxic Pesticide Methyl Bromide," press release, September 29, 1998; Friends of the Earth, "Methyl Bromide Red Alert!!" press release, September 2, 1998; both folder Methyl Bromide, Farmworker Association of Florida private collection; Mark Johnson to Farmworker Association of Florida, November 17, 2000, folder Methyl Bromide Test Results, Farmworker Association of Florida private collection; "How to Conduct Air Test" (n.d.), folder MB Originals, Farmworker Association of Florida private collection.

44. Gilfillan, *Reaping Havoc*, 2, 35–36; "Reaping Havoc Released," *Atmosphere* (Friends of the Earth), September 1999, 5, folder Methyl Bromide Alternatives, Farmworker Association of Florida private collection.

45. Gilfillan, *Reaping Havoc*, 11–13; Farmworker Association of Florida, "Your Informational Booklet on Methyl Bromide" (February 2001), folder Methyl Bromide, Farmworker Association of Florida private collection.

46. Alisa Roberson and La Asociación Campesina de Florida, Inc. (Farmworker Association of Florida), *Sunny's Niños Juegan Con Cuidado* (Apopka, FL: Farmworker Association of Florida, 2002). Copy in possession of the author, courtesy of Farmworker Association of Florida.

47. Friends of the Earth, "I Say Tomáto, You Say Tomäto," pamphlet (n.d.), folder Methyl Bromide, Farmworker Association of Florida private collection.

48. "Some Say Time Ripe for Tomato Changes," *Orlando Sentinel*, March 8, 1998.

49. Friends of the Earth, "I Say Tomáto, You Say Tomäto."

50. "Methyl Bromide Phase-Out Focus of Agriculture Subcommittee," *California Capitol Hill Bulletin* 5, no. 20 (June 11, 1998): 6, http://www.calinst.org/bulletins/bull520.pdf; House Subcommittee on Forestry, *Review of the Phaseout of Methyl Bromide*, 13–14.

51. Pesticide Action Network North America, press release, "Action Alert: Stop Delay of U.S. Methyl Bromide Ban," October 7, 1998, http://www.sare.org/sanet-mg/archives/htmlhome/28-html/0260.html; "Methyl Bromide Ban Delayed," *Grain News* (October 21, 1998), http://www.grainnet.com/articles/methyl_bromide_ban_delayed-2408.html.

52. Martha Groves, "Gas Ban Creates a Cloud of Discontent: Both Growers, Environmentalists Unhappy," *Los Angeles Times,* November 12, 1998; "Easy Riders: Attempting to Push an Anti-Environmental Agenda, Congress Goes Into Stealth Mode," *E: The Environmental Magazine*, December 31, 1998, http://www.emagazine.com/archive/57; "Methyl Bromide Ban Delayed."

53. Friends of the Earth, "Congress Poised to Weaken Clean Air Act and Ozone Protection."

54. "Easy Riders"; "A Stealth Assault on the Environment," *San Francisco Chronicle*, October 2, 1998.

55. Friends of the Earth, "Methyl Bromide Health Effects and Exposure Level Standards" (n.d.), folder Packet of Info from FOE, Farmworker Association of Florida private collection.

56. Tirso Moreno to Jeb Bush, April 16, 2001, folder Methyl Bromide Sustainable Tomatoes, Farmworker Association of Florida private collection.

57. Michael G. Wagner, "Activists Urge Ban on Methyl Bromide Use," *Los Angeles Times*, July 29, 1996; Methyl Bromide Alternatives Network, "After Taking Almost $100,000 from the Methyl Bromide Lobby: Gov. Pete Wilson Just Called a Special Session of the Legislature to Unleash a Deadly Pesticide," advertisement, *New York Times*, January 19, 1996; United Farm Workers, "Saturday, News Conference in Oakland: UFW's Dolores Huerta Joined by Local CA. Democrats to Denounce Possible Methyl Bromide Use Extension as Lawmakers Debate Extending the Use of This Birth Defect-Causing Toxic Pesticide," press release, January 20, 1996, UFW PR Dept: Jocelyn Sherman (unprocessed, Acc. No. 779, Acc. Date 10/28/97), box 3, folder Methyl Bromide (pink folder).

58. "Wilson OKs Methyl Bromide Extension," *Los Angeles Times*, March 13, 1996.

59. Bill Walker, "California Study Admits Methyl Bromide Safety Standard Inadequate: Analysis," Environmental Working Group, June 1997, http://www.ewg.org/research/california-study-admits-methyl-bromide-safety-standard-inadequate/analysis.

60. Environmental Working Group, "High Levels of Methyl Bromide Discovered Near Elementary School," October 29, 2007, http://www.ewg.org/news/testimony-official-correspondence/high-levels-methyl-bromide-discovered-near-elementary-school.

61. Zev Ross and Bill Walker, *An Ill Wind: Methyl Bromide Use Near California Schools* (Washington, DC: Environmental Working Group, 1998), 1, 21–29, http://www.ewg.org/files/anillwind_illwind.pdf (accessed March 1, 2011).

62. Environmental Working Group, Friends of the Earth, Pesticide Action Network, Pesticide Watch, and Western Environmental Law Center, "California Court Ruling: State's Lax Guidelines for Pesticide Violate Law," press release, March 19, 1999, folder MBA and Sustainable Tomato Campaign, Farmworker Association of Florida private collection; Environmental Working Group, "California Ordered to Adopt Methyl Bromide Regulations," *San Diego Earth Times*, May 1999, http://www.sdearthtimes.com/et0599/et0599s2.html; Environmental Working Group, "High Levels of Methyl Bromide Discovered Near Elementary School."

63. "Methyl Bromide Drift in Homestead, Florida"; Friends of the Earth, Florida Consumer Action Network, and Farmworker Association of Florida, press release, "Toxic Pesticide Drifts onto Church Properties in Homestead" (n.d., 2000); both folder Methyl Bromide, Farmworker Association of Florida private collection.

64. Mark Johnson to Florida Consumer Action Network, October 13, 2000; Mark Johnson to Farm Worker Association of Florida, November 17, 2000; both folder Methyl Bromide Test Results, Farmworker Association of Florida private collection.

65. "Methyl Bromide Drift in Homestead, Florida"; Friends of the Earth, Florida Consumer Action Network, and Farmworker Association of Florida, "Toxic Pesticide Drifts onto Church Properties in Homestead."

66. Friends of the Earth, "Quotes from Five TV News Stories on the Pesticide Drift News Conference Convened by Friends of the Earth, Farmworker Association of Florida and Florida Consumer Action Network," press release, February 22, 2001, folder Methyl Bromide, Farmworker Association of Florida private collection.

67. Friends of the Earth, Florida Consumer Action Network, and Farmworker Association of Florida, "Toxic Pesticide Drifts onto Church Properties in Homestead."

68. Friends of the Earth, *Annual Report 2001* (Washington, DC: Friends of the Earth, 2001), 7, http://www.foe.org/about/PDF_Annual_Reports/ar2001.pdf (accessed March 2, 2011); "Methyl Bromide Drift in Homestead, Florida"; Sara Olkon, "Pesticide Drift to Be Investigated: Churches Fear Effect of Toxin," *Miami Herald*, February 22, 2001; Friends of the Earth, "Quotes from Five TV News Stories on the Pesticide Drift News Conference Convened by Friends of the Earth, Farmworker Association of Florida and Florida Consumer Action Network." The quote can be

found in Friends of Earth's *Annual Report 2001* and "Quotes from Five TV News Stories on the Pesticide Drift News Conference."

69. Tirso Moreno to Colleagues, June 19, 2001, folder MB Originals, Farmworker Association of Florida private collection.

70. "Sample Letter," folder MB Originals, Farmworker Association of Florida private collection.

71. Friends of the Earth, *Annual Report 2001*, 7.

72. "The Not-So-Funny Farm." A review of Jeb Bush's records at the State Archives of Florida failed to turn up any information on an investigation of methyl bromide drift after the Homestead incident in 2001. Governor (1999–2007: Bush) Collection, State Archives of Florida, Tallahassee.

73. United Nations Environment Programme, "Ozone: Bush Administration Seeks Exemption for Pesticide Banned in Treaty," *The Environment in the News*, January 31, 2003, 4, www.unep.org/cpi/briefs/Brief31Jan.doc; Andrew C. Revkin, "Bush Administration to Seek Exemptions to 2005 Ban of a Pesticide," *New York Times*, January 30, 2003.

74. "U.S. Government Nominates Critical Use Exemptions for Methyl Bromide—Materials Submitted to Ozone Secretariat of the United Nations," press release, February 7, 2003, http://yosemite.epa.gov/opa/admpress.nsf/7ebdf4d0b217978b852573590040443a/f555074ef18e1f3085256cc9005aeb17!OpenDocument.

75. Wayne A. Morrissey, "Methyl Bromide and Stratospheric Ozone Depletion," *CRS Report for Congress* (December 11, 2006), 4; House Subcommittee on Energy and Air Quality, Committee on Energy and Commerce, *The Status of Methyl Bromide Under the Clean Air Act and the Montreal Protocol*, 108th Cong., 1st sess., June 3, 2003, 13.

76. Andrew C. Revkin, "At Meetings, U.S. to Seek Support for Broad Ozone Exemptions," *New York Times*, November 10, 2003; Joan Lowy, "U.S. Seeks to Boost Production of Toxic Pesticide," *The Environment in the News*, March 25, 2004, www.unep.org/cpi/briefs/Brief25March04.doc (accessed March 5, 2011).

77. Revkin, "At Meetings, U.S. to Seek Support for Broad Ozone Exemptions."

78. Ibid. Alternative pest control methods included steam sterilization, using artificial and natural growth substrates, developing resistant plant species, rotating crops, and employing chemical substitutes. Open-Ended Working Group of the Parties to the Montreal Protocol, "The 1994 Science, Environmental Effects, and Technology and Economic Assessments," (Nairobi, Kenya, May 8–12, 1995), 17, ozone.unep.org/Meeting_Documents/oewg/11oewg/11oewg-3.e.doc.

79. Alan Crosby, "Rich States' Demands Threaten Environment Policy," *The Environment in the News*, November 26, 2004, www.unep.org/cpi/briefs/Brief26Nov04.doc.

80. Morrissey, "Methyl Bromide and Stratospheric Ozone Depletion," 5; Revkin, "At Meetings, U.S. to Seek Support for Broad Ozone Exemptions"; John Heilprin, "House GOPs Want Out of Pesticide Treaty," *Seattle Post-Intelligencer*, July 21, 2004.

81. Revkin, "At Meetings, U.S. to Seek Support for Broad Ozone Exemptions"; Carl Pope, "Alone in the World: Bush Ends an Era of Environmental Treaties," *Sierra* 88, no. 1 January/February 2003, http://vault.sierraclub.org/sierra/200301/ways.asp.

82. House Subcommittee on Energy and Air Quality, *The Status of Methyl Bromide Under the Clean Air Act and the Montreal Protocol*, 73; Crosby, "Rich States' Demands Threaten Environmental Treaty."

83. House Subcommittee on Energy and Air Quality, *The Status of Methyl Bromide Under the Clean Air Act and the Montreal Protocol*, 73.

84. Ibid., 74. Doniger, in mentioning "another international treaty," was most likely referring to the Kyoto Protocol. In 2001, Bush announced that the United States would not adhere to its provisions. Andrew C. Revkin, "Bush's Shift Could Doom Air Pact, Some Say," *New York Times*, March 17, 2001.

85. Wallstrom, "Global Efforts to Repair Ozone Layer Are in Jeopardy"; Lowy, "U.S. Seeks to Boost Production of Toxic Pesticide."

86. "Global Methyl Bromide Exemptions Over 13,000 Tons," Environment News Service, March 29, 2004, http://www.ens-newswire.com/ens/mar2004/2004–03–29–04.asp.

87. David Doniger, "Hole-y Ozone, Batman," *Switchboard: Natural Resources Defense Council Staff Blog: David Doniger's Blog*, September 14, 2007, http://switchboard.nrdc.org/blogs/ddoniger/yesterday_i_told_the_story.html).

88. Wallstrom, "Global Efforts to Repair Ozone Layer are in Jeopardy."

89. United Nations Environment Programme, press release, "Methyl Bromide Approved for Temporary Uses after Montreal Protocol Phase-Out Deadline," March 26, 2004, http://www.unep.org/ozone/Press_Releases/26March_2004.pdf (accessed March 6, 2011).

90. Wayne A. Morrissey, "Methyl Bromide and Stratospheric Ozone Depletion," 5.

91. Terra Daily, "World Bickers Over Use of Ozone-Harming Methyl Bromide After 2005," *The Environment in the News*, November 29, 2004, www.unep.org/cpi/briefs/Brief29Nov04.doc; Andrew Olson, "Methyl Bromide Loophole for U.S. Prolongs Ozone Hole," Pesticide Action Network, http://panna.org/print/1131; *Natural Resources Defense Council v. Environmental Protection Agency*, 440 F.3d 476, 370 U.S.App.D.C.154 (3rd Cir. 2006).

92. Doniger, "Hole-y Ozone, Batman."

93. *Natural Resources Defense Council v. Michael Leavitt*, 2006 WL 667327 (D.D.C.) (2nd Cir. 2006).

94. Doniger, "Hole-y Ozone, Batman"; *Natural Resources Defense Council v. Michael Leavitt*, 2006 WL 667327.

95. *Natural Resources Defense Council v. Environmental Protection Agency*, 464 F.3d 1, 373 U.S.App.D.C. 223 (3rd Cir. 2006).

96. Ibid.; *Natural Resources Defense Council v. Environmental Protection Agency*, 440 F.3d 476, 370 U.S.App.D.C. 154.

97. *Natural Resources Defense Council v. Environmental Protection Agency*, 440 F.3d 476, 370 U.S.App.D.C. 154.

98. *Natural Resources Defense Council v. Environmental Protection Agency*, 464 F.3d 1, 373 U.S.App.D.C. 223.

99. Ibid.

100. The "critical use exemption" was an adjustment to the Montreal Protocol rather than an amendment. Congress only heard and consented to new amendments, so it did not consider the "critical use exemption." Because of this, the court reasoned, the exemption could not be considered law in a US court without raising serious constitutional problems. *Natural Resources Defense Council v. Environmental Protection Agency*, 464 F.3d 1, 373 U.S.App.D.C. 223; John H. Knox, "Natural Resources Defense Council v. Environmental Protection Agency. 464 F.3d 1," *American Journal of International Law* 101, no. 2 (April 2007): 471–72.

101. United Nations Environment Programme Ozone Secretariat, "Decision XXV/4: Critical-Use Exemptions for Methyl Bromide for 2015," http://ozone.unep.org/new_site/en/Treaties/treaties_decisions-hb.php?dec_id=1058.

102. Ibid.

103. Sierra Club, *Latino Communities at Risk: How Bush Administration Policies Harm Our Community* (Washington, D.C.: Sierra Club, 2004), 4, 8, http://www.sierraclub.org/ecocentro/downloads/comunidades.pdf (accessed March 4, 2011), 8.

104. California Rural Legal Assistance, Environmental Defense Center, and California Rural Legal Assistance Foundation, "State Appeals Court Affirms Trial Court Ruling: State Pesticide Agency Failed to Adequately Protect Public and Farmworkers from Dangerous Pesticide," press release, July 16, 2008, http://www.edcnet.org/news/PressReleases/08–07–16.pdf (accessed March 8, 2011); Californians for Pesticide Reform, "Californians for Pesticide Reform Member

Organizations," *CPR Resource*, no. 16 (March 2006): 5, http://www.pesticidereform.org/downloads/CPRnewsletterMar06.pdf.

105. California Rural Legal Assistance et al., "State Appeals Court Affirms Trial Court Ruling"; *Jorge Fernandez v. California Department of Pesticide Regulation*, 164 Cal.App.4th 1214, 80 Cal.Rptr.3d 418 (Cal. App. 4th 2008).

106. California Rural Legal Assistance et al., "State Appeals Court Affirms Trial Court Ruling."

107. Robert G. Bergman et al. to Stephen Johnson, September 24, 2007, folder Methyl Iodide, Farmworker Association of Florida private collection.

108. Ibid.

109. Environmental Protection Agency, "Extension of Conditional Registration of Iodomethane (Methyl Iodide), http://www.epa.gov/pesticides/factsheets/iodomethane_fs.htm.

110. Jeanne Economos to Bill Nelson, October 2, 2007, folder Methyl Iodide, Farmworker Association of Florida private collection; "The Not-So-Funny Farm"; Pesticide Action Network North America, press release, "PAN Alert: Help Stop Carcinogenic Methyl Iodide! EPA Considers Legalizing Methyl Iodide for Food Production" (n.d., February 2006?), folder Methyl Iodide, Farmworker Association of Florida private collection; Sierra Club, "Keep Methyl Iodide Out of California," Sierra Club, https://secure2.convio.net/sierra/site/Advocacy?alertId=3387&pg=make ACall (accessed March 9, 2011).

111. Farmworker Association of Florida, press release, "Cancer and Birth Defects Could Threaten Floridians if New Pesticide is Approved," January 10, 2008, folder Methyl Iodide, Farmworker Association of Florida private collection; Farmworker Association of Florida, "Fumigant Pesticide Bad for Florida and for Farmworkers," Farmworker Association of Florida, http://www.floridafarmworkers.org/index.php?limitstart=16.

112. Peter Fimrite, "Methyl Iodide's Use in State Challenged by Suit: Environmental Groups, Farmworkers Contend that Methyl Iodide is Poisonous," *San Francisco Gate*, January 4, 2011; Earthjustice, "Coalition Sues California Over Approval of Cancer-Causing Strawberry Pesticide," press release, January 3, 2011, Earthjustice, http://earthjustice.org/news/press/2011/coalition-sues-california-over-approval-of-cancer-causing-strawberry-pesticide (quote). An independent panel of experts completed a risk assessment of methyl iodide for the CDPR prior to the registration of the fumigant. The panel concluded: "use of this agent would result in exposures to a large number of the public and thus would have a significant adverse impact on public health. Due to the potent toxicity of methyl iodide, its transport in and ultimate fate in the environment, adequate control of human exposure would be difficult if not impossible." "Petition for Writ of Mandate and Complaint for Declaratory and Injunctive Relief," *Pesticide Action Network North America v. California Department of Pesticide Regulation*, Alameda County (CA) Superior Court RG10553804 (Alameda Sup. Court 2011), http://earthjustice.org/sites/default/files/mei-final-petition-filestamped.pdf.

113. Earthjustice, "Cancer-Causing Methyl Iodide Pulled," press release, March 21, 2012, Earthjustice, http://earthjustice.org/news/press/2012/cancer-causing-methyl-iodide-pulled.

114. Oreskes and Conway, *Merchants of Doubt*, 264.

Diversity and Unity in the Pesticide Reform Movement

1. Davis, *Banned*, 206, 216–20, 223.

2. David Weir and Mark Schapiro, *Circle of Poison: Pesticides and People in a Hungry World* (San Francisco: Institute for Food and Development Policy, 1981), 3–6.

3. David Kinkela, *DDT and the American Century: Global Health, Environmental Politics, and the Pesticide That Changed the World* (Chapel Hill: University of North Carolina Press, 2011), 174–75.

4. Environmental Protection Agency, "Pesticide News Story: EPA Release Report Containing Latest Estimates of Pesticide Use in the United States," http://www.epa.gov/oppfead1/cb/csb_page/updates/2011/sales-usage06-07.html.

5. Kinkela, *DDT and the American Century*, 8.

6. Bosso, *Pesticides and Politics*, 176–77.

7. Sylvia Nobel Tesh, *Uncertain Hazards: Environmental Activists and Scientific Proof* (Ithaca: Cornell University Press, 2000), 5; Tompkins, "Cancer Valley, California," 277.

8. Nancy Langston, *Toxic Bodies: Hormone Disrupters and the Legacy of DES* (New Haven, CT: Yale University Press, 2010), Location 2074, 2927, Kindle edition.

9. Pope, "An Immodest Proposal," 45.

10. Roe, "An Incentive-Conscious Approach to Toxic Chemical Controls," 181.

11. Langston, *Toxic Bodies*, Location 2455, Kindle edition.

12. Rome, *The Genius of Earth Day*, 9.

13. Ibid., 166, 210, 215.

14. Bruce J. Schulman, *The Seventies: The Great Shift in American Culture, Society, and Politics* (New York: The Free Press, 2001), 26.

15. Jefferson Cowie, *Stayin' Alive: The 1970s and the Last Days of the Working Class* (New York: The New Press, 2010), 71.

16. Judith Stein, *Pivotal Decade: How the United States Traded Factories for Finance in the Seventies* (New Haven, CT: Yale University Press, 2010), Location 2337, Kindle edition.

17. Schulman, *The Seventies*, 51; Cowie, *Last Days of the Working Class*, 272.

18. Robert J. Brulle and Jonathan Essoka, "Whose Environmental Justice? An Analysis of the Governance Structure of Environmental Organizations in the United States," in *Power, Justice, and the Environment: A Critical Appraisal of the Environmental Justice Movement*, ed. David Naguib Pellow and Robert J. Brulle (Cambridge, MA: MIT Press, 2005), 215.

19. Langston, *Toxic Bodies*, Location 2839, Kindle edition.

20. Robert J. Brulle and David Naguib Pellow, "The Future of Environmental Justice Movements," in Pellow and Brulle, *Power, Justice, and the Environment*, 299.

21. Meyer, *The Politics of Protest*, 73.

22. Ibid., 75.

23. See for example, Pulido and Peña, "Environmentalism and Positionality," 38–39, 46–47.

24. Harrison, *Pesticide Drift and the Pursuit of Environmental Justice*, 10.

25. Bruce A. Williams and Albert R. Matheny, *Democracy, Dialogue, and Environmental Disputes: The Contested Language of Social Regulation* (New Haven, CT: Yale University Press, 1995), 27, 28.

26. Ibid., 28.

27. Paul Sabatier, "Social Movements and Regulatory Agencies: Toward a More Adequate—and Less Pessimistic—Theory of 'Clientele Capture,'" *Policy Sciences* 6, no. 3 (September 1975): 303; Williams and Matheny, *Democracy, Dialogue, and Environmental Disputes*, 33.

28. Sabatier, "Social Movements and Regulatory Agencies," 318.

29. Epstein, *The Politics of Cancer*, 367.

30. California EPA, Proposition 65 Review Panel, "Accomplishments," apps.edf.org/documents/3394_EPA_5year.pdf; David Roe, "Little Labs Lost: An Invisible Success Story," *The Green Bag* (Spring 2012): 280, http://www.greenbag.org/v15n3/v15n3_articles_roe.pdf.

BIBLIOGRAPHY

Archival Collections

Archives and Records Management Branch, Arizona State Library,
Archives and Public Records, Phoenix

Agricultural Employment Relations Board Collection
Board of Pesticide Control Collection
Governor's Office, 1978 Record Group, Series Departments, Boards, and Commissions.
Governor's Office, 1979 Record Group, Series Departments, Boards, Commissions
Governor's Office, 1979 Record Group, Series Federal Files

Arizona State University, Department of Archives and Special Collections, Tempe

Arizona Common Cause Collection
Folder Maricopa County Organizing Project; 1987
Folder MCOP—Maricopa County Organizing Project
Grand Canyon Chapter Sierra Club Collection, ACC# 94–1420
MCOP Papers, ACC# 1990–00402

Arizona State University, Arizona Historical Foundation, Tempe

Arizona Cotton Growers Association Collection

California State Archives, Sacramento
Assembly Agriculture Committee Collection
Assembly Environmental Quality Committee
Environmental Affairs Agency Collection
Fong (March K.) Collection
Senator Tom Hayden Collection

Farmworker Association of Florida private collection, Apopka

State Archives of Florida, Tallahassee
Governor (1999–2007: Bush) Collection

SUNY Stony Brook, Department of Special Collections
Environmental Defense Fund Collection.

University of California Berkeley, The Bancroft Library
Regional Oral History Office
Sierra Club California Legislative Office Records Collection
Sierra Club Members Papers Collection
Sierra Club National Legislative Office Records
Sierra Club Records Collection

University of Florida Special Collections, Gainesville
Sierra Club Florida Chapter Collection

Wayne State University, Archives of Labor and Urban Affairs, Detroit
221-UFW Collection (unprocessed, Acc. Date 04/10/95)
Cesar Chavez Collection (unprocessed, Acc. Date 04/07/86)
Cesar Chavez Collection (unprocessed, Acc. Date 04/17/86)
Marion Moses, MD Collection
UFW Central Administration Files Collection
UFW Information and Research Department Collection
UFW New York Boycott Collection (unprocessed, Acc. Date 06/01)
UFW Office of the President: Cesar Chavez Collection Part II
UFW PR Dept: Jocelyn Sherman (unprocessed, Acc. No. 779, Acc. Date 10/28/97)
UFW Work Department Collection
UFWOC New York Boycott Collection
United Farm Workers Arizona State Office Collection
United Farmworkers Organizing Committee Collection

Newspapers and Newsletters

Arizona Republic, Phoenix
California Capitol Hill Bulletin, Washington
Cleveland Plain Dealer

CPR Resource, San Francisco
Daily Breeze, Torrance, CA
Daily News of Los Angeles
El Malcriado, Delano, CA
El Paisano, Tolleson, AZ
Environment News Service, Eugene, OR
Fresno Bee
Los Angeles Times
Miami Herald
New Times, Phoenix, AZ
New York Times
Orange County Register, Santa Ana, CA
Orlando Sentinel
Phoenix Gazette
Post Star, Glen Falls, NY
Press-Enterprise, Riverside, CA
Sacramento Bee
San Diego Earth Times
San Diego Union
San Francisco Chronicle
San Francisco Gate
San Jose Mercury
Science News-Letter, Washington
Scottsdale Daily Progress
Seattle Post-Intelligencer
Washington Post
Wall Street Journal

Public Documents

Agricultural Appropriations Bill, 1938. 75th Cong., 1st sess., S. Rep. 537.
Ambient Water Quality Surveys and Data Management Office of Emergency Response and Environmental Analysis. *Results of Ethylene Dibromide (EDB) Sampling in Arizona*. [Phoenix]: Division of Environmental Health Services, 1984.
"Argument Against Proposition 65." http://www.edf.org/documents/3385_ArgueAgainst.pdf (accessed December 2, 2010).
California Department of Health Services, "Methyl Bromide." *Fact Sheet*. May 1990. http://www.cdph.ca.gov/programs/hesis/Documents/mebr.pdf.
California EPA, Proposition 65 Review Panel. "Accomplishments." apps.edf.org/documents/3394_EPA_5year.pdf.
California Legislature. Senate Committee on Toxics and Public Safety Management. *Childhood Cancer Incidences—McFarland*. Sacramento: Joint Publications, 1985.
California Safe Drinking Water and Toxic Enforcement Act of 1986. Chapter 6.6. http://www.edf.org/documents/3379_65original.pdf (accessed December 2, 2010).
California Senate Toxics and Public Safety Management Committee. *Proposition 128: Environmental Protection Act of 1990*. Sacramento: Senate Office of Research, 1990.

Cohen, David B. "Ground Water Contamination by Toxic Substances: A California Assessment." ACS Symposium Series. Washington: American Chemical Society, 1986.

Cohen, David B., and Gerald W. Bowes. *Water Quality and Pesticides: A California Risk Assessment Program.* Vol. 1. Sacramento: State Water Resources Control Board, 1984.

Crosby, Alan. "Rich States' Demands Threaten Environment Policy." *The Environment in the News.* November 26, 2004, www.unep.org/cpi/briefs/Brief26Nov04.doc.

Chellemi, D. O. "Field Validation of Methyl Bromide Alternatives in Florida Fresh Market Vegetable Production Systems." In *Global Report on Validated Alternatives to the Use of Methyl Bromide for Soil Fumigation,* edited by. R. Labrada and L. Fornasari. FAO Plant Production and Protection Paper 166. Rome: Food and Agriculture Organization of the United Nations and United Nations Environment Programme, 2001.

Daily, Terra. "World Bickers Over Use of Ozone-Harming Methyl Bromide After 2005." *The Environment in the News.* November 29, 2004. www.unep.org/cpi/briefs/Brief29Nov04.doc.

Economic Research Service, US Department of Agriculture. "Facing the Phaseout of Methyl Bromide." *Agricultural Outlook* (August 1999): 24. http://www.ers.usda.gov/publications/agoutlook/aug1999/ao263h.pdf (accessed February 20, 2011).

"Emergency Standard for Exposure to Organophosphorous Pesticides." *Federal Register* 38, no. 83 (May 1, 1973).

Environmental Protection Agency. "Pesticide News Story: EPA Release Report Containing Latest Estimates of Pesticide Use in the United States." http://www.epa.gov/oppfead1/cb/csb_page/updates/2011/sales-usage06–07.html.

Haywood, J. K. "Report of the Insecticide and Fungicide Board." In *Annual Reports of the Department of Agriculture for the Year Ended June 30, 1913: Report of the Secretary of Agriculture: Reports of Chiefs.* Washington, DC: Government Printing Office, 1914.

Hertel, R. F., T. Kielhorn, World Health Organization, International Labour Organisation, and United Nations Environmental Programme. *Methyl Bromide: First Draft Prepared by R. F. Hertel and T. Kielhorn.* Geneva: World Health Organization, 1995.

Howard, L. O., and C. L. Marlatt. *The San Jose Scale: Its Occurrences in the United States With a Full Account of Its Life History and the Remedies to Be Used Against It.* Washington, DC: Government Printing Office, 1896.

Lowy, Joan. "U.S. Seeks to Boost Production of Toxic Pesticide." *The Environment in the News.* March 25, 2004. www.unep.org/cpi/briefs/Brief25March04.doc.

Meeks, Gordon, Jr. *Arizona Groundwater: Negotiating an Environmental Quality Act.* Denver: National Conference of State Legislatures, 1987.

Morrissey, Wayne A. "Methyl Bromide and Stratospheric Ozone Depletion." *CRS Report for Congress.* December 11, 2006.

National Oceanic and Atmospheric Administration. "Oceans Remove More Ozone-Depleting Methyl Bromide from Atmosphere than Previously Estimated, Research Shows." Press release. May 22, 1997. http://www.publicaffairs.noaa.gov/pr97/may97/noaa97–31.html.

Nellor, Barbara L., and Patti A. Cleary. *Arizona Agricultural Pesticide Program Evaluation, August 13–21, 1979.* San Francisco: US Environmental Protection Agency, 1981.

New York State Department of Health. "Love Canal: A Special Report to the Governor & Legislature: April 1981." revised October 2005. www.nyhealth.gov/environmental/investigations/love_canal/lcreport.htm.

Open-Ended Working Group of the Parties to the Montreal Protocol. "The 1994 Science, Environmental Effects, and Technology and Economic Assessments." Nairobi, Kenya, May 8–12, 1995. ozone.unep.org/Meeting_Documents/oewg/11oewg/11oewg-3.e.doc.

"Rebuttal to Argument in Favor of (California) Proposition 65." http://www.edf.org/documents/3386_ArgueFor.pdf (accessed December 2, 2010).

Regulating the Marketing of Economic Poisons and Devices. 80th Cong., 1st sess. S. Rep. 199.

State Bar of Arizona. *Arizona's New Environmental Quality Act.* Phoenix: State Bar of Arizona, 1986.

State of Arizona. Office of the Auditor General. *A Performance Audit of the Board of Pesticide Control: A Report to the Arizona State Legislature.* [Phoenix]: Office of the Auditor General, 1983.

Tolba, Mostafa K., and Iwona Rummel-Bulska. "The Story of the Ozone Layer." In *The Montreal Protocol: Celebrating 20 Years of Environmental Progress,* edited by Donald Kaniaru, 27–42. London: Cameron May and United Nations Environment Programme, 2007.

Torres, Art. *Proposition 128: Analysis of Pesticide Use and Regulation.* Sacramento, CA: Senate Committee on Toxics and Public Safety Management, 1990.

United Nations Environment Programme. "Methyl Bromide Approved for Temporary Uses After Montreal Protocol Phase-Out Deadline." press release. March 26, 2004. http://www.unep.org/ozone/Press_Releases/26March_2004.pdf (accessed March 6, 2011).

———. "Ozone: Bush Administration Seeks Exemption for Pesticide Banned in Treaty." *The Environment in the News,* January 31, 2003. www.unep.org/cpi/briefs/Brief31Jan.doc.

United Nations Environment Programme Ozone Secretariat. "Decision XXV/4: Critical-Use Exemptions for Methyl Bromide for 2015." http://ozone.unep.org/new_site/en/Treaties/treaties_decisions-hb.php?dec_id=1058.

———. *Synthesis of the Reports of the Scientific, Environmental Effects, and Technology and Economic Assessment Panels of the Montreal Protocol: A Decade of Assessments for Decision Makers Regarding the Protection of the Ozone Layer: 1988–1999,* edited by Daniel L. Albritton and Lambert Kuijpers. Nairobi: UNON Printshop, 1999.

US Census Bureau. 2000 Census of Population and Housing. *Population and Housing Unit Counts.* PHC-3-4, Arizona. Washington, DC: Government Printing Office, 2003.

US Congress. House. *Adulterated or Misbranded Fungicides, Insecticides, Etc.* 61st Cong., 2d sess., 1910. H. Rep. 990.

———. Committee on Agriculture. *Federal Insecticide, Fungicide, and Rodenticide Act.* 79th Cong., 2d sess., 1946.

———. Committee on Agriculture. *Federal Insecticide, Fungicide, and Rodenticide Act.* 80th Cong., 1st sess., 1947.

———. Committee on Interstate and Foreign Commerce. *Hearing on Bills Relating to Insecticides and Fungicides, Part 1.* 61st Cong., 2d sess., 1910.

———. Select Subcommittee on Labor, Committee on Education and Labor. *Occupational Safety and Health*. 90th Cong., 2d sess., 1968.

———. Select Subcommittee on Labor. *Occupational Safety and Health Act of 1969, Part 1.* 91st Cong., 1st sess., 1969.

———. Select Subcommittee on Labor, Committee on Education and Labor. *Occupational Safety and Health Act of 1969, Part 2 and Appendix.* 91st Cong., 1st sess., 1969.

———. Subcommittee on Department Operations, Research, and Foreign Agriculture, Committee on Agriculture. *Federal Insecticide, Fungicide, and Rodenticide Act Part 1.* 97th Cong., 1st sess., June 16, July 16, and July 22, 1981.

———. Subcommittee on Department Operations, Research, and Foreign Agriculture, Committee on Agriculture. *Federal Insecticide, Fungicide, and Rodenticide Act Part 2.* 97th Cong., 1st sess., June 18 and September 4, 1981.

———. Subcommittee on Department Operations, Research, and Foreign Agriculture, Committee on Agriculture. *Federal Insecticide, Fungicide, and Rodenticide Act Part 3.* 97th Cong., 2d sess., February 4, 1982.

———. Subcommittee on Energy and Air Quality, Committee on Energy and Commerce. *The Status of Methyl Bromide Under the Clean Air Act and the Montreal Protocol.* 108th Cong., 1st sess., June 3, 2003.

———. Subcommittee on Forestry, Resource Conservation, and Research, Committee on Agriculture. *Review of the Phaseout of Methyl Bromide.* 105th Cong., 2d sess., June 10, 1998.

———. Subcommittee on Health and Environment, Committee on Commerce. *Implementation of Title VI of the 1990 Clean Air Act Amendments and Plans for the Upcoming Meeting of the Parties to the Montreal Protocol in Montreal in September 1997.* 105th Cong., 1st sess., July 30, 1997.

———. Subcommittee on Livestock and Horticulture, Committee on Agriculture. *The Implications of Banning Methyl Bromide for Fruit and Vegetable Production.* 106th Cong., 2d sess., July 13, 2000.

———. Subcommittee on Oversight and Investigations, Committee on Interstate and Foreign Commerce. *Involuntary Exposure to Agent Orange and Other Toxic Spraying.* 96th Cong., 1st sess., June 26 and 27, 1979.

———. Subcommittee on Oversight and Investigations, Committee on Commerce. *Clean Air Act Amendments.* 104th Cong., 1st sess., August 1, 1995.

US Congress. Senate. Committee on Commerce. *Amending the Insecticide Act.* 78th Cong., 1st sess., 1943.

———. Committee on Foreign Relations. *Environmental Treaties.* 103d Cong., 1st sess., October 26, 1993.

———. Subcommittee on Agricultural Research and General Legislation, Committee on Agriculture and Forestry. *Federal Environmental Pesticide Control Act.* Part II. 92d Cong., 2d sess., 1972.

———. Subcommittee on Agricultural Research and General Legislation, Committee on Agriculture and Forestry. *Extension of the Federal Insecticide, Fungicide, and Rodenticide Act.* 94th Cong., 1st sess., May 12–16, October 28–29, 1975.

———. Subcommittee on Labor, Committee on Labor and Public Welfare. *Occupational Safety and Health Act of 1968.* 90th Cong., 2d sess., 1968.

———. Subcommittee on Labor, Committee on Labor and Public Welfare. *Occupational Safety and Health Act, 1970, Part 1.* 91st Cong., 1st sess., 1969, 1970.

———. Subcommittee on Labor, Committee on Labor and Public Welfare. *Occupational Safety and Health Act, 1970, Part 2.* 91st Cong., 1st sess., 1970.

———. Subcommittee on the Environment, Committee of Commerce. *Federal Environmental Pesticide Control Act of 1971.* 92d Cong., 2d sess., 1972.

———. Subcommittee on Migratory Labor, Committee on Labor and Public Welfare. *Migrant and Seasonal Farmworker Powerlessness: Pesticides and the Farmworker, Part 6B.* 91st Cong., 1st and 2d sess., 1969.

US Environmental Protection Agency. "DDT Ban Takes Effect." Press release. December 31, 1972, http://www.epa.gov/history/topics/ddt/01.htm (accessed December 24, 2010).

———. "EPA Acts to Ban EDB Pesticide." Press release. September 30, 1983. http://www.epa.gov/history/topics/legal/02.htm(accessed September 7, 2010).

———. "Extension of Conditional Registration of Iodomethane (Methyl Iodide)." http://www.epa.gov/pesticides/factsheets/iodomethane_fs.htm.

———. "U.S. Government Nominates Critical Use Exemptions for Methyl Bromide—Materials Submitted to Ozone Secretariat of the United Nations." Press release. February 7, 2003. http://yosemite.epa.gov/opa/admpress.nsf/7ebdf4d0b217978b852573590040443a/f555074ef18e1f3085256cc9005aeb17!OpenDocument.

US Environmental Protection Agency Region IX. *Public Hearing on the Use of Agricultural Pesticides in Arizona: September 6–8, 1979 Adam's Hotel, Navajo Room, Central and Adams Streets, Phoenix, Arizona/United States.* Vol. 1. San Francisco: Smythe and Wilson, 1979.

———. *Public Hearing on the Use of Agricultural Pesticides in Arizona: September 6–8, 1979 Adam's Hotel, Navajo Room, Central and Adams Streets, Phoenix, Arizona/ United States, Environmental Protection Agency.* Vol. 3. San Francisco: Smythe & Wilson, 1979.

Wallstrom, Margot. "Global Efforts to Repair Ozone Layer are in Jeopardy." *Environment in the News*, March 25, 2004. www.unep.org/cpi/briefs/Brief25March04.doc.

Other Published Primary Sources

"'65 Delano Strike Observed: Farm Workers Protest Pesticide Peril." *Food and Justice* 2, no. 5 (October 1985): 3–7.

". . . and on the 36th, Bread." *Food and Justice 2, no.* 6 (September 1988): 10–13.

"'A Multitude of Simple Deeds.'" *Food and Justice* 5, no. 7 (October 1988): 5.

Big Fears, Little Risk: A Report of Chemicals in the Environment. VHS. Narrated by Walter Cronkite. Produced by Film Counselors Associates. American Council on Science and Health. 1989.

Butler, William A. "Opening the Washington Office." In Rogers, *Acorn Days*, 86–92.

California Rural Legal Assistance, Environmental Defense Center, and California Rural Legal Assistance Foundation. "State Appeals Court Affirms Trial Court Ruling: State Pesticide Agency Failed to Adequately Protect Public and Farmworkers from Dangerous Pesticide." press release. July 16, 2008. http://www.edcnet.org/news/PressReleases/08–07–16.pdf (accessed March 8, 2011).

Californians for Pesticide Reform. "Californians for Pesticide Reform Member Organizations." *CPR Resource*, No. 16, March 2006. http://www.pesticidereform.org/downloads/CPRnewsletterMar06.pdf.

Cameron, Roderick. "View from the Front Office." In Rogers, *Acorn Days*, 34–39.

"Chavez Begins Fast." *Food and Justice* 5, no. 5 (July 1988): 8–9.

Chavez, Cesar. "Farm Workers at Risk." In *Toxic Struggles: The Theory and Practice of Environmental Justice*, edited by Richard Hofrichter, 163–70. Philadelphia: New Society Publishers, 1993.

"Club Supports Labor Move to Improve Environment for Factory Workers." *Sierra Club Bulletin*, 58, no. 4 (April 1973): 18.

"Conclusion: Annual Organization Meeting Report." *Sierra Club Bulletin* 54, no. 6 (June 1969): 14.

Cooperativa Sin Fronteras: El Primer Paso. VHS. Directed by Juan Farre. New York: West Glen Productions, 1987.

Curtis, Jennifer, Tim Profeta, and Lawrie Mott. *After Silent Spring: The Unsolved Problems of Pesticide Use in the United States*. New York: Natural Resources Defense Council, 1993.

Doniger, David. "An Emergency Phase-Out Schedule." Lecture, Hyatt Regency, Baltimore, MD, December 3, 1991. Legacy Tobacco Documents Library, University of California San Francisco. https://industrydocuments.library.ucsf.edu/tobacco/docs/#id=xylb0120.

——. "Hole-y Ozone, Batman." *Switchboard: Natural Resources Defense Council Staff Blog: David Doniger's Blog*, September 14, 2007. http://switchboard.nrdc.org/blogs/ddoniger/yesterday_i_told_the_story.html.

"Dr. Marion Moses and Agriculture's 'Deadly Dozen.'" *Food and Justice* 2, no. 2 (February 1985):11–14.

"Earth Day/Daughters of the American Revolution/Blacks/South Dakota." (NBC newscast, originally aired April 23, 1970). Vanderbilt University Television News Archive, Nashville, TN.

Earthjustice. "Coalition Sues California Over Approval of Cancer-Causing Strawberry Pesticide." Press release. January 3, 2011. http://earthjustice.org/news/press/2011/coalition-sues-california-over-approval-of-cancer-causing-strawberry-pesticide.

Environmental Working Group. "High Levels of Methyl Bromide Discovered Near Elementary School." Environmental Working Group. http://www.ewg.org/node/8675 (accessed March 1, 2011).

Farmworker Association of Florida. "Fumigant Pesticide Bad for Florida and for Farmworkers." Farmworker Association of Florida. http://www.floridafarmworkers.org/index.php?limitstart=16.

Farmworker Movement Documentation Project. Compiled/ Published by Leroy Chatfield. http://www.farmworkermovement.org/ (accessed November 15, 2010).

Field, Mervin, and Mark DiCamillo. "Voter Preferences on Prop. 128 (Big Green), Prop 134 (Nickel a Drink) and Prop. 130 (Forests Forever) Vary Considerably Depending on Awareness of Fiscal Impact of Each Initiative." *California Poll*. October 16, 1990. http://ucdata.berkeley.edu/pubs/CalPolls/1563.pdf.

Friends of the Earth. *Annual Report 2001*. Washington, D.C.: Friends of the Earth, 2001. http://www.foe.org/about/PDF_Annual_Reports/ar2001.pdf (accessed March 2, 2011).

Futrell, William. "The Environment and the Courts." *Sierra Club Bulletin* 58, no. 5 (May 1973): 18.

Gilfillan, Corinna. *Reaping Havoc: The True Cost of Methyl Bromide on Florida's Tomatoes*. Washington, DC: Friends of the Earth, 1998.

"Grape Pesticides Worse Than Watermelons." *Food and Justice* 2, no. 4 (September 1985): 6–7.

Gutiérrez, Gustavo. Interview by Judy Lentine. *Tempe Historical Museum Oral History Project*. City of Tempe. July 19, 2012. http://www.tempe.gov/Home/ ShowDocument?id=30249.

"Harvest of Shame." *CBS Reports*, episode 78 (originally aired November 26, 1960). http://www.cbsnews.com/video/watch/?id=7087479n&tag=related;photovideo.

McCloskey, Michael. "A Conservation Agenda for 1969." *Sierra Club Bulletin* 53, no. 12 (December 1968): 5.

Miller, Melanie, ed. *The Technical and Economic Feasibility of Replacing Methyl Bromide in Developing Countries: Case Studies in Zimbabwe, Thailand and Chile*. Washington, DC: Friends of the Earth, 1996.

Morse, Jim, and Nancy Matthews, eds. *The Sierra Club Survival Songbook*. San Francisco: Sierra Club, 1971.

Moses, Marion. "Pesticides Which Cause Birth Defects and Kill Workers." *Food and Justice* 2, no. 3 (April/May 1985): 10–11.

"Nader and Friends Dump Grapes." *Food and Justice,* February 1988: 3–4.

"National Fast for Life," *Food and Justice* 5, no. 7 (October 1988): 6–7.

"The Not-So-Funny Farm: Tirso Moreno, Farmworker Organizer, Answers Questions." *Grist*, March 20, 2006, http://www.grist.org/article/moreno.

Pesticide Action Network North America. "Action Alert: Stop Delay of U.S. Methyl Bromide Ban." Press release. October 7, 1998. http://www.sare.org/sanet-mg/ archives/html-home/28-html/0260.html.

"Pesticide Poisoning is More than an Accident." *Food and Justice* 1, no. 3 (December 1984): 8–10.

The Plight of the Migrant. VHS. Tucson: Arizona Center for Occupational Safety and Health, 1979.

"Poisoning the Wells." *Environment* 11, no. 1 (January–February 1969): 16.

Pope, Carl. "Alone in the World: Bush Ends an Era of Environmental Treaties." *Sierra,* 88, no. 1 (January/February 2003). http://vault.sierraclub.org/sierra/200301/ways.asp.

———. "An Immodest Proposal." *Sierra* 70, no. 5 (September/October 1985): 43–48.

Prop. 65 Kit: A Quick Reference Guide to California's Proposition 65. Prepared by David Roe. http://www.edf.org/article.cfm?ContentID=3376 (accessed December 2, 2010).

Puleston, Dennis. "Birth and Early Days." In Rogers, *Acorn Days*, 23–29.

Roberson, Alisa, and La Asociación Campesina de Florida, Inc. (Farmworker Association of Florida). *Sunny's Niños Juegan Con Cuidado*. Apopka, FL: Farmworker Association of Florida, 2002.

Roe, David. "Little Labs Lost: An Invisible Success Story." *The Green Bag,* (Spring 2012): 275–90, http://www.greenbag.org/v15n3/v15n3_articles_roe.pdf.

Rogers, Marion Lane, ed. *Acorn Days: The Environmental Defense Fund and How It Grew.* New York: Environmental Defense Fund, 1990.

———. "Onward and Upward." In Rogers, *Acorn Days,* 40–43.

Ross, Zev, and Bill Walker. *An Ill Wind: Methyl Bromide Use Near California Schools.* Washington, DC: Environmental Working Group, 1998. http://www.ewg.org/files/anillwind_illwind.pdf (accessed March 1, 2011).

Sánchez, Guadalupe L., and Jesús Romo. "Organizing Mexican Undocumented on Both Sides of the Border." Working Papers in U.S.-Mexican Studies, 27. La Jolla, CA: University of California San Diego, 1981.

Steinbeck, John. *The Harvest Gypsies: On the Road to the Grapes of Wrath.* 1936; Berkeley: Heyday Books, 1988.

"The Second 1980 Debate: Part IV." *Debating Our Destiny: The Second 1980 Presidential Debate October 28, 1980.* http://www.pbs.org/newshour/debatingourdestiny/80 debates/cart4.html (accessed October 19, 2010).

Sherwin, Raymond. "A Broader Look at the Environment." *Sierra Club Bulletin*, April 1973: 18.

Sierra Club. "Keep Methyl Iodide Out of California." https://secure2.convio.net/sierra/site/Advocacy?alertId=3387&pg=makeACall (accessed March 9, 2011).

———. *Latino Communities at Risk: How Bush Administration Policies Harm Our Community.* Washington, D.C.: Sierra Club, 2004. http://www.sierraclub.org/ecocentro/downloads/comunidades.pdf (accessed March 4, 2011).

Steinbeck, John. "Dubious Battle in California." *The Nation*, September 12, 1936: 302–4.

"'Today I Pass On the Fast for Life . . .'" *Food and Justice* 5, no. 6 (September 1988): 14–15.

Walker, Bill. "California Study Admits Methyl Bromide Safety Standard Inadequate." Environmental Working Group. June 1997. http://www.ewg.org/reports/dprweb (accessed March 1, 2011).

Wayburn, Edgar. "A Reaffirmation of Purpose." *Sierra Club Bulletin* 53, no.9 (May 1968): 2.

———. "Elections and Electioneering." *Sierra Club Bulletin* 53, no. 12 (December1968): 2, 12.

———. "Envoi." *Sierra Club Bulletin*53, no. 12 (May 1969): 2.

———. "The Anatomy of Positive Conservation, Part I." *Sierra Club Bulletin* 53, no. 9 (September 1968): 2.

"We Oppose Mindless Progress, McCloskey Tells Chemical Workers." *Sierra Club Bulletin*58, no. 9 (October 1973): 35–36.

The Wrath of Grapes. VHS. Narrated by Mike Farrell. Produced by Lorena Parlee and Lenny Bourin, United Farm Workers of America, AFL-CIO. Production of Volunteer Staff of UFWofA. 1986.

"Wrath of Grapes Campaign to Counter Grape Growers' Natural Snack Theme." *Food and Justice* 3, no. 2 (February/March 1986): 3.

"'The Wrath of Grapes'—The Tragedy of Pesticide Poisoning." *Food and* Justice 3, no. 2 (February/ March 1986): 4–6.

Wurster, Charles. "The Last Word." In Rogers, *Acorn Days*, 178–87.

——. "The Power of an Idea." In Rogers, *Acorn Days*, 44–55.

Secondary Sources

Baldassare, Mark, Bruce E. Cain, D. E. Apollonio, and Jonathan Cohen. *The Season of Our Discontent: Voters' Views on California Elections*. San Francisco: Public Policy Institute of California, 2004. http://www.ppic.org/content/pubs/report/R_1004MBR. pdf (accessed March 27, 2011).

Balderrama, Francisco E., and Raymond Rodríguez. *Decade of Betrayal: Mexican Repatriation in the 1930s*. Albuquerque: University of New Mexico Press, 1995.

Ball, Carleton R. *Federal, State, and Local Administrative Relationship in Agriculture*. Vol. 1. Berkeley: University of California Press, 1938.

Bardacke, Frank. "Cesar's Ghost." *The Nation*, 257, no. 4, (July 26, 1993): 130–35.

Barr, Evan T. "Sour Grapes: Cesar Chavez 20 Years Later." *New Republic*, 192, no. 20 (November 25, 1985): 20–22.

Bosso, Christopher J. *Pesticides and Politics: The Life Cycle of a Public Issue*. Pittsburgh: University of Pittsburgh Press, 1987.

Briggs, Vernon M., Jr. "Non-Immigrant Labor Policy in the United States," *Journal of Economic Issues* 17, no. 3 (September 1983): 609–30.

Brody, David. *Workers in Industrial America: Essays on the Twentieth Century Struggle*. 2d ed. New York: Oxford University Press, 1993.

Brooks, Karl Boyd. *Before Earth Day: The Origins of American Environmental Law, 1945–1970*. Lawrence: University Press of Kansas, 2009.

Brulle, Robert J., and David Naguib Pellow. "The Future of Environmental Justice Movements." In Pellow and Brulle, *Power, Justice, and the Environment*, 293–300.

Brulle, Robert J., and Jonathan Essoka. "Whose Environmental Justice? An Analysis of the Governance Structure of Environmental Organizations in the United States." In Pellow and Brulle, *Power, Justice, and the Environment*, 293–300.

Burgess, Guy, and Heidi Burgess. "Justice Without Violence: Theoretical Foundations." In *Justice Without Violence*, edited by Paul Wehr, Heidi Burgess, and Guy Burgess, 7–36. Boulder, CO: Lynne Rienner, 1994.

Cable, Sherry, Tamara Mix, and Donald Hastings. "Mission Impossible? Environmental Justice Activists' Collaborations with Professional Environmentalists and with Academics." In Pellow and Brulle, *Power, Justice, and the Environment*, 55–75.

"California Farmworkers: Back to the Barricades?" *Businessweek*, (September 26, 1983): 86.

Carson, Rachel. *Silent Spring*. 1962; Boston: Houghton Mifflin, 1994.

Cerrutti, Marcela, and Douglas S. Massey. "Trends in Mexican Migration to the United States, 1965–1995." In Durand and Massey, *Crossing the Border*, 17–44.

"Chavez Tries a Computerized Grape Boycott." *Businessweek*, (September 9, 1985): 35.

Conover, Ted. "A Cooperative Between Borders." *Grassroots Development* 9, no. 2 (1985): 43–52.

Cowie, Jefferson. *Stayin' Alive: The 1970s and the Last Days of the Working Class*. New York: The New Press, 2010.

Critchlow, Donald T. *The Conservative Ascendancy: How the GOP Right Made Political History*. Cambridge, MA: Harvard University Press, 2007.

Daniel, Cletus E. *Bitter Harvest: A History of California Farmworkers, 1870–1941*. Berkeley: University of California Press, 1981.

Daniel, Cletus E. "Radicals on the Farm in California." *Agricultural History* 49, no. 4 (October 1975): 629–46.

Daniel, Pete. *Toxic Drift: Pesticides and Health in the Post–World War II South*. Baton Rouge: Louisiana State University Press, 2005.

Davis, Frederick Rowe. *Banned: A History of Pesticides and the Science of Toxicology*. New Haven, CT: Yale University Press, 2014.

Derickson, Alan. *Black Lung: Anatomy of a Public Health Disaster*. Ithaca: Cornell University Press, 1998.

Dewey, Scott. "Working for the Environment: Organized Labor and the Origins of Environmentalism in the United States, 1948–1978." *Environmental History* 3, no. 1 (January 1998): 45–63.

Dubofsky, Melvyn. *The State and Labor in Modern America*. Chapel Hill: University of North Carolina Press, 1994.

Dunlap, Thomas. *DDT: Scientists, Citizens, and Public Policy*. Princeton, NJ: Princeton University Press, 1981.

Durand, Jorge, and Douglas S. Massey, eds. *Crossing the Border: Research from the Mexican Migration Project*. New York: Russell Sage Foundation, 2004.

Earthjustice. "Cancer-Causing Methyl Iodide Pulled." Press release. March 21, 2012. Earthjustice. http://earthjustice.org/news/press/2012/cancer-causing-methyl-iodide-pulled.

"Easy Riders: Attempting to Push an Anti-Environmental Agenda, Congress Goes Into Stealth Mode." *E: The Environmental Magazine*, December 31, 1998. http://www.emagazine.com/archive/57.

Egan, Michael. *Barry Commoner and the Science of Survival: The Remaking of American Environmentalism*. Cambridge, MA: MIT Press, 2007.

Egan, Michael, and Jeff Crane, eds. *Natural Protest: Essays on the History of American Environmentalism*. New York: Routledge, 2009.

Environmental Action. *Earth Tool Kit: A Field Manual for Citizen Activists*, edited by Sam Love, Peter Hamik, and Avery Taylor. New York: Pocket Books, 1971.

Epstein, Samuel S. *The Politics of Cancer*. San Francisco: Sierra Club Books, 1978.

——. *The Politics of Cancer Revisited*. Freemont Center, NY: East Ridge Press, 1998.

Essig, E. O. *A History of Entomology*. New York: Macmillan, 1931.

Fenner-Crisp, Penelope A. "Risk Assessment and Risk Management: The Regulatory Process." In *Handbook of Pesticide Toxicology*, vol. 2: *Principles*, 2d ed., edited by Robert Krieger, John Doull, Donald Ecobichon, Derek Gammon, Ernest Hodgson, Larry Reiter, and John Ross, 681–90. San Diego, CA: Academic Press, 2001.

Fernandez, Johanna. "Between Social Service Reform and Revolutionary Politics: The Young Lords, Late Sixties Radicalism, and Community Organizing in New York City." In *Freedom North: Black Freedom Struggles Outside the South, 1940–1980*, edited by Jeanne F. Theoharis and Komozi Woodard, 255–86. New York: Palgrave Macmillan, 2003.

Ferriss, Susan, and Ricardo Sandoval. *The Fight in the Fields: Cesar Chavez and the Farmworkers Movement*, edited by Diana Hembree. San Diego, CA: Harcourt Brace, 1997.

Figueroa, Kenneth Juan. "Immigrants and the Civil Rights Regime: Parens Patriae Standing, Foreign Governments and Protection From Private Discrimination." *Columbia Law Review* 102, no. 2 (2002): 408–70.

Fisher, Lloyd H. "The Harvest Labor Market in California." *Quarterly Journal of Economics* 65, no. 4 (November 1951): 463–91.

Fitzgerald, Deborah. *Every Farm a Factory: The Industrial Ideal in American Agriculture*. New Haven, CT: Yale University Press, 2003.

Fox, Stephen R. *The American Conservation Movement: John Muir and His Legacy*. Madison: University of Wisconsin Press, 1981.

Galarza, Ernesto. *Strangers in Our Fields*. Washington, DC: Joint United States–Mexico Trade Union Committee, 1956.

Ganz, Marshall. *Why David Sometimes Wins: Leadership, Organization, and Strategy in the California Farm Worker Movement*. New York: Oxford University Press, 2009.

Garcia, Matthew. *From the Jaws of Victory: The Triumph and Tragedy of Cesar Chavez and the Farm Worker Movement*. Berkeley: University of California Press, 2012. Kindle edition.

Gordon, Robert. "Poisons in the Fields: The United Farm Workers, Pesticides, and Environmental Politics." *Pacific Historical Review* 68, no. 1 (February 1999): 51–77.

———. "'Shell No!': OCAW and the Labor-Environmental Alliance." *Environmental History* 3, no. 4 (October 1998): 460–77.

Gottlieb, Robert. *Forcing the Spring: The Transformation of the American Environmental Movement*. Rev. ed. Washington, DC: Island Press, 2005.

Graham, Frank, Jr., and Carl W. Buchhesiter. *The Audubon Ark: A History of the National Audubon Society*. New York: Knopf, 1990.

Green, Michael D. "The Politics of Pesticides." *The Nation* 209, no. 18 (November 24, 1969): 569–71.

Griswold del Castillo, Richard, and Richard A. Garcia. *Cesar Chavez: A Triumph of Spirit*. Norman: University of Oklahoma Press, 1997.

Guerin-Gonzales, Camille. *Mexican Workers and American Dreams: Immigration, Repatriation, and California Farm Labor, 1900–1939*. New Brunswick, NJ: Rutgers University Press, 1994.

Hahamovitch, Cindy. *Fruits of Their Labor: Atlantic Coast Farmworkers and the Making of Migrant Poverty, 1870–1945*. Chapel Hill: University of North Carolina Press, 1997.

Hall, Greg. *Harvest Wobblies: The Industrial Workers of the World and Agricultural Laborers in the American West, 1905–1930*. Corvallis: Oregon State University Press, 2001.

Hall, Melvin F. *Poor People's Social Movement Organizations: The Goal Is to Win*. Westport, CT: Praeger, 1995.

Harrison, Jill Lindsey. *Pesticide Drift and the Pursuit of Environmental Justice*. Cambridge, MA: MIT Press, 2011.

Henkin, Harmon. "DDT and the Constitution." *The Nation* 208, no. 10 (March 10, 1969): 308–10.

Hightower, Jim. *Hard Tomatoes, Hard Times: The Original Hightower Report—and Other Recent Reports—on Problems and Prospects of American Agriculture*. Cambridge, MA: Schenkman, 1973, 1978.

Hughes, Thomas P. *Networks of Power: Electrification in Western Society, 1880–1930*. Baltimore: Johns Hopkins University Press, 1983.

Hurley, Andrew. *Environmental Inequalities: Class, Race, and Industrial Pollution in Gary, Indiana, 1945–1980*. Chapel Hill: University of North Carolina Press, 1995.

"Interpreting OSHA's Preemption Clause: Farmworkers as a Case Study." *University of Pennsylvania Law Review* 128, no. 6 (June 1980): 1509–42.

Jackson, Thomas F. *From Civil Rights to Human Rights: Martin Luther King, Jr., and the Struggle for Economic Justice*. Philadelphia: University of Pennsylvania Press, 2007.

Jenkins, J. Craig. *The Politics of Insurgency: The Farm Worker Movement in the 1960s*. New York: Columbia University Press, 1985.

Jones, Jacqueline. *The Dispossessed: America's Underclasses from the Civil War to the Present*. New York: Basic Books, 1992.

Jones, Robert A. "Fratricide in the Sierra Club." *The Nation* 208, no. 18 (May 5, 1969): 567–70.

Kinkela, David. *DDT and the American Century: Global Health, Environmental Politics, and the Pesticide That Changed the World*. Chapel Hill: University of North Carolina Press, 2011.

Knox, John H. "Natural Resources Defense Council v. Environmental Protection Agency. 464 F.3d 1." *American Journal of International Law* 101, no. 2 (April 2007): 471–77.

Langston, Nancy. *Toxic Bodies: Hormone Disrupters and the Legacy of DES*. New Haven, CT: Yale University Press, 2010. Kindle edition.

Levy, Jacques E. *Cesar Chavez: Autobiography of La Causa*. New York: Norton, 1975.

Lichtenstein, Nelson. *State of the Union: A Century of American Labor*. Princeton, NJ: Princeton University Press, 2002.

Lintner, J. A. "Entomology in America in 1879." *American Entomologist* 3, no. 2 (February 1880): 16–19.

Litfin, Karen T. *Ozone Disclosures: Science and Politics in Global Environmental Cooperation*. New York: Columbia University Press, 1994.

Longhurst, James. *Citizen Environmentalists*. Lebanon, NH: Tufts University Press, 2010.

Loomis, Erik. *Out of Sight: The Long and Disturbing Story of Corporations Outsourcing Catastrophe*. New York: New Press, 2015.

Lowenthal, David. "Earth Day." *Area* 2, no. 4 (1970): 1–10.

Luckingham, Bradford. *Phoenix: The History of a Southwestern Metropolis*. Tucson: University of Arizona Press, 1989.

Lytle, Mark Hamilton. *The Gentle Subversive: Rachel Carson, Silent Spring, and the Rise of the Environmental Movement*. New York: Oxford University Press, 2007.

Makhijani, Arjun, and Kevin R. Gurney. *Mending the Ozone Hole: Science, Technology, and Policy*. Cambridge, MA: MIT Press, 1995.

Maldonado, José A. "¡Sí Se Puede! The Farm Worker Movement in Arizona 1965–1979." M.A. thesis, Arizona State University, 1995.

Markowitz, Gerald, and David Rosner. *Deceit and Denial: The Deadly Politics of Industrial Pollution.* Berkeley: University of California Press, 2002.

Martin, Hubert. *The Scientific Principles of Plant Protection.* New York: Longmans, Green, 1928.

Massey, Douglas S., Jorge Durand, and Nolan J. Malone. *Beyond Smoke and Mirrors: Mexican Immigration in an Era of Economic Integration.* New York: Russell Sage Foundation, 2002.

Massey, Douglas S., and Fernando Riosmena. "Undocumented Migration in an Era of Rising U.S. Enforcement." *Annals of the American Academy of Political and Social Science*, no. 630 (July 2010): 294–321.

Matusow, Allen J. *Farm Policies and Politics in the Truman Years.* Cambridge, MA: Harvard University Press, 1967.

Mayer, Brian. *Blue-Green Coalitions: Fighting for Safe Workplaces and Healthy Communities.* Ithaca: ILR Press of Cornell University Press, 2009.

McCloskey, J. Michael. *In the Thick of It: My Life in the Sierra Club.* Washington, DC.: Island Press, 2005.

McWilliams, Carey. *Factories in the Field: The Story of Migratory Farm Labor in California.* 1935; Berkeley: University of California Press, 2000.

McWilliams, James E. *American Pests: The Losing War on Insects from Colonial Times to DDT.* New York: Columbia University Press, 2008.

Meeks, Eric V. *Border Citizens: The Making of Indians, Mexicans, and Anglos in Arizona.* Austin: University of Texas Press.

Meiners, Roger E., and Andrew P. Morriss. "Silent Spring and Silent Villages: Pesticides and the Trampling of Property Rights." In *Government vs. Environment*, edited by Donald Leal and Roger E. Meiners, 15–27. Lanham, MD: Rowman & Littlefield, 2002.

"Methyl Bromide Ban Delayed." *Grain News*, October 21, 1998. http://www.grainnet.com/articles/methyl_bromide_ban_delayed-2408.html.

Meyer, David S. *The Politics of Protest: Social Movements in America.* New York: Oxford University Press, 2007.

Mintz, Benjamin W. *OSHA: History, Law, and Policy.* Washington, DC: Bureau of National Affairs, 1984.

Montrie, Chad. *A People's History of Environmentalism in the United States.* New York: Continuum International, 2011.

——. "Expedient Environmentalism: Opposition to Coal Surface Mining in Appalachia and the United Mine Workers of America, 1945–1975." *Environmental History* 5, no. 1 (January 2000): 75–98.

Mooney, Margarita. "Migrants' Social Capital and Investing Remittances in Mexico." In Durand and Massey, *Crossing the Border*, 45–62.

Moses, Marion. "'Viva la Causa!'" *American Journal of Nursing* 73, no. 5 (May 1973): 842–48.

Mott, Lawrie, and Karen Snyder. *Pesticide Alert: A Guide to Pesticides in Fruits and Vegetables.* San Francisco: Sierra Club Books, 1987.

Nash, Linda. *Inescapable Ecologies: A History of Environment, Disease, and Knowledge.* Berkeley: University of California Press, 2006.

————. "The Fruits of Ill-Health: Pesticides and Workers' Bodies in Post–World War II California." *Osiris* 19 (2004): 203–19.

Nelson, Gaylord, with Susan Campbell and Paul Wozniak. *Beyond Earth Day: Fulfilling the Promise*. Madison: University of Wisconsin Press, 2002.

Nye, David. *Consuming Power: A Social History of American Energies*. Cambridge, MA: MIT Press, 1998.

Olson, Andrew. "Methyl Bromide Loophole for U.S. Prolongs Ozone Hole." Pesticide Action Network. http://panna.org/print/1131.

Oreskes, Naomi, and Erik M. Conway. *Merchants of Doubt: How a Handful of Scientists Obscured the Truth on Issues from Tobacco Smoke to Global Warming*. New York: Bloomsbury Press, 2010.

Pawal, Miriam. *The Union of Their Dreams: Power, Hope, and Struggle in Cesar Chavez's Farm Worker Movement*. New York: Bloomsbury Press, 2009.

Pellow, David Naguib, and Robert J. Brulle, eds. *Power, Justice, and the Environment: A Critical Appraisal of the Environmental Justice Movement*. Cambridge, MA: MIT Press, 2005.

Peña, Devon G. *Mexican Americans and the Environment: Tierra y Vida*. Tucson: University of Arizona Press, 2005.

Perkins, John H. *Insects, Experts, and the Insecticide Crisis: The Quest for New Pest Management Strategies*. New York: Plenum Press, 1982.

————. "The Quest for Innovation in Agricultural Entomology, 1945–1975." In *Pest Control: Cultural and Environmental Aspects*, edited by David Pimentel and John H. Perkins, 23–80. Boulder, CO: Westview Press, 1980.

Pichardo, Nelson A. "The Power Elite and Elite-Driven Countermovements: The Associated Farmers of California during the 1930s." *Sociological Forum* 10, no. 1 (March 1995): 21–49.

Pincetl, Stephanie S. *Transforming California: A Political History of Land Use and Development*. Baltimore: John Hopkins University Press, 1999.

Proctor, Robert N. *Cancer Wars: How Politics Shapes What We Know and Don't Know about Cancer*. New York: Basic Books, 1995.

Pulido, Laura. *Environmentalism and Economic Justice: Two Chicano Struggles in the Southwest*. Tucson: University of Arizona Press, 1996.

Pulido, Laura, and Devon Peña. "Environmentalism and Positionality: The Early Pesticide Campaign of the United Farm Workers' Organizing Committee, 1965–1971." *Race, Gender and Class* 6, no. 1 (October 31, 1998): 33–50.

Reitze, Arnold W., Jr. *Air Pollution Control Law: Compliance and Enforcement*. Washington, DC: Environmental Law Institute, 2001.

Roberts, Leslie. "A Corrosive Fight Over California's Toxic Law." *Science*, no. 230 (January 20, 1989): 306–9.

Rodgers, William H., Jr. "The Persistent Problem of Persistent Pesticides: A Lesson in Environmental Law." *Columbia Law Review* 70, no. 4 (April 1970): 567–611.

Roe, David. "An Incentive-Conscious Approach to Toxic Chemical Controls." *Economic Development Quarterly* 3, no. 3 (August 1989): 179–87.

Rome, Adam. "The Genius of Earth Day." *Environmental History* 15, no. 2 (April 2010): 194–205.

———. *The Genius of Earth Day: How a 1970 Teach-In Unexpectedly Made the First Green Generation*. New York: Hill & Wang, 2014.

———. "Give Earth a Chance: The Environmental Movement and the Sixties." *Journal of American History* 90, no. 2 (September 2003): 525–54.

Rosales, F. Arturo. *Chicano! The History of the Mexican American Civil Rights Movement*. Houston: Arte Público Press, 1997.

Rosner, David, and Gerald Markowitz. *Deadly Dust: Silicosis and the Politics of Occupational Disease in Twentieth-Century America*. Princeton, NJ: Princeton University Press, 1993.

Russell, Edmund. *War and Nature: Fighting Humans and Insects from World War I to Silent Spring*. New York: Cambridge University Press, 2001.

Sabatier, Paul. "Social Movements and Regulatory Agencies: Toward a More Adequate— and Less Pessimistic—Theory of 'Clientele Capture.'" *Policy Sciences* 6, no. 3 (September 1975): 129–68.

Sackman, Douglas C. "'Nature's Workshop': The Work Environment and Workers' Bodies in the California Citrus Industry, 1900–1940." *Environmental History* 5, no. 1 (January 2000): 27–53.

———. *Orange Empire: California and the Fruits of Eden*. Berkeley: University of California Press, 2005.

Schaefer, Richard J. "Reconsidering Harvest of Shame: The Limitations of a Broadcast Journalism Landmark." *Journalism History* 19, no. 4 (Winter 1994): 121–32.

Schulman, Bruce J. *The Seventies: The Great Shift in American Culture, Society, and Politics*. New York: The Free Press, 2001.

Sellers, Christopher C. *Hazards of the Job: From Industrial Disease to Environmental Health Science*. Chapel Hill: University of North Carolina Press, 1997.

Setterberg, Fred, and Lonny Shavelson. *Toxic Nation: The Fight to Save Our Communities from Chemical Contamination*. New York: Wiley, 1993.

Shavelson, Jeffrey. "Bottom-Up Populism: The Lessons for Citizen and Community Empowerment." Ph.D. diss., University of Maryland, 1989.

Shaw, Randy. *Beyond the Fields: Cesar Chavez, the UFW, and the Struggle for Justice in the 21st Century*. Berkeley: University of California Press, 2008.

Stein, Judith. *Pivotal Decade: How the United States Traded Factories for Finance in the Seventies*. New Haven, CT: Yale University Press, 2010. Kindle edition.

Steingraber, Sandra. *Living Downstream: An Ecologist Looks at Cancer and the Environment*. Reading, MA: Addison-Wesley, 1997.

Stoll, Steven. *The Fruits of Natural Advantage: Making the Industrial Countryside in California*. Berkeley: University of California Press, 1998.

Tesh, Sylvia Nobel. *Uncertain Hazards: Environmental Activists and Scientific Proof*. Ithaca: Cornell University Press, 2000.

The Fight in the Fields: Chavez and the Farmworkers' Struggle. VHS. Directed by Ray Telles and Rick Tejada-Flores. Sparks, NV: Paradigm Productions, 1996.

Thomas, Sarah L. "A Call to Action: Silent Spring, Public Discourse, and the Rise of Modern Environmentalism." In Egan and Crane, *Natural Protest*, 185–203. New York: Routledge, 2009.

Thurber, Scott. "Conservation Comes of Age." *The Nation* 204, no. 9 (February 27, 1967): 272–75.

Tichenor, Daniel J. *Dividing Lines: The Politics of Immigration Control in America.* Princeton, NJ: Princeton University Press, 2002.

Tompkins, Adam. "A Different Kind of Border War: Conflicts Over Pesticides in Arizona's Agricultural/Urban Interface, 1977–1986." *Journal of the West* 50, no. 1 (Winter 2011): 59–65.

———. "Cancer Valley, California: Pesticides, Politics, and Childhood Disease in the Central Valley." In Egan and Crane, *Natural Protest*, 275–99. New York: Routledge, 2009.

Tweedy, John, Jr. "Coalition Building and the Defeat of California's Proposition 128." *Stanford Environmental Law Journal* 11 (1992): 114–50.

"The Use of Paris Green." *American Entomologist* 3, no. 9 (September 1880): 244.

Van Den Bosch, Robert. *The Pesticide Conspiracy.* 1978. Berkeley: University of California Press, 1989.

Vogeler, Ingolf. *The Myth of the Family Farm: Agribusiness Dominance of U.S. Agriculture.* Boulder, CO: Westview Press, 1981.

Vogt, Wendy. "Crossing Mexico: Structural Violence and the Commodification of Undocumented Central American Migrants." *American Ethnologist* 40, no. 4 (November 2013): 764–80.

Wade, J. S. "Leland Ossian Howard (Obituary)." *Annals of the Entomological Society of America* 43, no. 4 (December 1950): 610–12.

Wargo, John. *Our Children's Toxic Legacy: How Science and Law Fail to Protect Us from Pesticides.* New Haven, CT: Yale University Press, 1996.

Weber, Devra. *Dark Sweat, White Gold: California Farm Workers, Cotton, and the New Deal.* Berkeley: University of California Press, 1994.

Weir, David, and Mark Schapiro. *Circle of Poison: Pesticides and People in a Hungry World.* San Francisco: Institute for Food and Development Policy, 1981.

Wells, Miriam J. *Strawberry Fields: Politics, Class and Work in California Agriculture.* Ithaca: Cornell University Press, 1996.

Whitaker, Adelynne Hiller. "A History of Federal Pesticide Regulation in the United States to 1947." Ph.D. diss., Emory University, 1974.

White, Richard. "'Are You an Environmentalist or Do You Work for a Living?': Work and Nature." In *Uncommon Ground: Rethinking the Human Place in Nature*, edited by William Cronon, 171–85. New York: Norton, 1996.

Wilentz, Sean. *The Age of Reagan: A History 1974–2008.* New York: Harper Perennial, 2008.

Williams, Bruce A., and Albert R. Matheny. *Democracy, Dialogue, and Environmental Disputes: The Contested Language of Social Regulation.* New Haven, CT: Yale University Press, 1995.

Wolfle, Dael. "After Earth Day." *Science* 168, no. 3932 (May 8, 1970): 657.

Wong, Otto, M. Donald Whorton, Nancy Gordon, and Robert W. Morgan. "An Epidemiologic Investigation of the Relationship Between DBCP Contamination in

Drinking Water and Birth Rates in Fresno County, California." *American Journal of Public Health* 78, no. 1 (January 1988): 43–46.

Worster, Donald. *Rivers of Empire: Water, Aridity and the Growth of the American West.* New York: Oxford University Press, 1985.

Yvon-Lewis, Shari A., and James Butler. "The Potential Effects of Oceanic Biological Degradation on the Lifetime of Atmospheric CH3Br." *Geophysical Research Letters* 24, no. 10 (May 15, 1997): 1227–30.

INDEX